Management Practice and Creative Destruction

To my late parents, Marky and Helen Segal, whose love and wisdom created the space that allowed my brothers and me to develop our own ways of being.

Management Practice and Creative Destruction

Existential Skills for Inquiring Managers, Researchers and Educators

STEVEN SEGAL
Macquarie University, Australia

Routledge
Taylor & Francis Group

LONDON AND NEW YORK

First published 2015 by Gower Publishing

2 Park Square, Milton Park, Abingdon, Oxfordshire OX14 4RN
52 Vanderbilt Avenue, New York, NY 10017

Routledge is an imprint of the Taylor & Francis Group, an informa business

First issued in paperback 2019

British Library Cataloguing in Publication Data
A catalogue record for this book is available from the British Library.

Library of Congress Cataloging-in-Publication Data
Segal, Steven, 1959–
    Management practice and creative destruction : existential skills for inquiring managers, researchers and educators / by Steven Segal.
        pages cm
    Includes bibliographical references and index.
    ISBN 978-1-4724-2488-4 (hardback : alk. paper)—ISBN 978-1-4724-2489-1 (ebook)—ISBN 978-1-4724-2490-7 (epub)
    1. Industrial management. 2. Management--Research. I. Title.
    HD31.S4385 2015
    658—dc23

                                                        2015005299

ISBN 13: 978-1-4724-2488-4 (hbk)
ISBN 13: 978-0-367-87928-0 (pbk)

Contents

To Question is to be "in" Question: An Autobiographical Account

I came to management education precisely because I was not managing! Organizing, ordering, control and planning—the very hallmarks of managing—were very difficult for me. At school I was more often than not in trouble because my homework presentation was not neat and tidy, my books were always messy and I did not follow instructions very well. The rules just did not make sense to me. Rather than ordered, I would, through the lens of my teachers, describe myself as dis-ordered—even fragmented.

I went to a conservative school in which ordering and control of personal appearance was important. It was considered good etiquette to have one's socks pulled up and held by garters. One was well educated if one spoke in a controlled and even-tempered way. And knowing when to put one's cap on and take it off was considered part of grooming.

The first time I walked into the headmaster's office I had my cap on. In what I experienced as a fit of temper, he yelled at me to get out of his office. It took me a long time to figure out what I had done wrong. My school years were characterized by many similar instances. The main lesson I took from school was from the sports master, who used to describe me in the following terms, "Segal, you miserable specimen of a human being!"

Obviously, I was not managing at school and was eventually placed in a standard 8 leaving class. This meant that I was not considered capable of completing school. I desperately tried to get out of the standard 8 leaving class. I realized that doing Latin as a subject would give me a pathway to completing school. And so, "cap in hand" (this time), I approached the headmaster with the request to do Latin. In no uncertain terms, he told me that I did not have the aptitude for such complex thinking.

Paradoxically, however, because my way of being at school (and at home) was not well ordered, controlled and disciplined, I was challenged to think in a very existential way; in a way in which my very sense of self, my self-worth and identity were at stake in managing at school: what was it about me that could not order things properly or even present myself in an orderly way? But also, because I was continuously told to "pull my socks up," both literally and metaphorically, I began to question the significance, value and place of order, control and managing. Why were they so important—not only as means to an end but as ends in themselves (as my behavior was evaluated in terms of them)? Why should I strive to be ordered and controlled? And just because the school defined these terms in particular ways—does this mean that I needed to defer to them?

Of course most of this questioning at an early stage was experiential, that is, I lived it out rather than wrote about it. It defined the way in which I was preoccupied and involved at school—a very kind of rebellious, questioning way of being at school: lived out as defiance towards authority and order at school, smoking at smoker's corner, playing truant, going to snooker parlors, drinking alcohol, use of other forbidden substances and an expressed contempt towards the school's order of doing things.

This was in contrast to those who could take order for granted. Those whose presentations, books and personal grooming were well organized did not seem to need to think about or question ordering and organizing their work and lives. Rather than looking down to pull up their socks, they could simply get on with their school work. Rather than being confused by the work of school, they were absorbed in the flow of it. Or, at worst, so it seemed to me, they were always improving their existing ways of managing and organizing. I could not even begin to manage or organize. I was emotionally very detached, even at times disassociated, from what was occurring in the classroom.

Paradoxically, however, because I was so emotionally detached from the experience of the classroom I could begin to see, question and think about the ways of doing things in the classroom. Because managing and ordering were in question for me, I began to notice, to observe and to think about the way of being of my well-ordered fellow students.

I was conscripted into the army, as at the time military service was compulsory in South Africa. While doing my basic training in the army, I was constantly getting into trouble because I could not co-ordinate my actions very well, had difficulty putting a rifle together and was seen as counterproductive to producing team spirit. My general sense of disorder resulted in me and my platoon being in constant trouble. To say the least, I was not initially very well liked by my platoon and thought of as incapable by the sergeant in charge of the platoon.

Although no one saw it like this, I was truly not managing. Indeed, I was in a state of anxiety, fragmenting rather than being able to order my existence. In the army the anxiety was more acute than it was at school. I used to wake up in the morning with my heart palpitating. I had a generalized and free-floating anxiety coursing its way through me all day. And even at night, after a long day's exhausting series of sets of exercises, I could not fall asleep but lay in my bed with a deep feeling of emptiness and nothingness.

I was emotionally detached from the day-to-day experiences of the army. On one occasion, in the context of a platoon debriefing, the corporal in charge of our platoon once addressed the following question to me: "Segal, you think that I am an idiot?" Without even realizing it, all I could say was "yes corporal." Stunned, everyone—including the corporal—just looked at me. "How could I defy his authority?" was the thought going through everyone's mind. I did not realize how I had answered and did not notice the response from the platoon. The corporal, surprised by my response, asked the question again. And again I answered in the same way. He repeated the question a few more times with the same response from me. Eventually he slapped me on the head and laughed to the relief of my platoon. I realized what I had said … and I also realized how detached I was; how I was not "there," not present in the moment.

I later came to understand that such anxiety and detachment formed the basis of existential inquiry; that as Heidegger puts it, through anxiety the thinker is distracted from everyday ways of being and doing in order to allow the *experience* of thinking to occur.

In my late teenage years, understanding the state that I was in, my father introduced me to the writings of several existential philosophers and psychologists. They were thinkers for people consumed by anxiety and emotionally detached and disassociated. These books helped me tremendously to begin understanding the state of anxiety which had overwhelmed me. They began to help me move from the feeling that something was not quite right to an understanding of that which was not quite right. Although there are many differences between these philosophers, there is at least one point on which they all agree. This is the belief that anxiety is not simply a negative or pathological experience, but it is the very condition of becoming thoughtful and sensitive to the issue of what it means to exist. If one accepts that one has anxiety, it provides an opportunity to question, think through, observe and make sense of one's existence.

To this day, this lesson, drawn from the range of existential philosophers, has been the guiding light of my existence, my being-in-the-world. Putting it in the paradoxical form of existential philosophy, it is because I have difficulties in everyday coping that everyday coping is an issue, a question for me. It is because I have and have had difficulties in managing and organizing, that managing and organizing are explicit themes of concern for me. My anxiety has called me to inquire into, *think through* (rather than *about*) order, control, planning, leading and managing, both as concepts and as ways of being, at school, at work and even at home. I have had a desperate existential need to think through ordering, planning, controlling and administrating—the very essence of what is called "managing."

Or to put it in the language of Heidegger (which I shall later develop in more detail), it is because my way of being was in question that I began to question in an existentially (1985, p67) experiential way my way of being and the way of being that was called "managing" at school. This was not just an intellectual or cerebral questioning, but a questioning in which my way of being or existing was at stake. I could not take the performance of everyday activities for granted.

References

Benner, P. and Wrubel, J. (1989) *The Primacy of Caring: Stress and coping in health and illness*. California: Addison-Wesley Publishing Company.

Heidegger, M. (1985) *Being and Time*. Oxford: Basil Blackwell.

Lennie, I. (1999) *Beyond Management*. Newbury Park, CA: Sage Publications.

Menon, T. and Thompson, L. (2010) Envy at Work. *Harvard Business Review*. April. pp74–9.

Mintzberg, H. (2003) *Managers not MBAs: A hard look at the soft practice of managing*. San Francisco: Berrett-Koehler.

Morgan, G. (1989) *Images of Organization*. Newbury Park, CA: Sage Publications.

Smullyan, R.M. (1977) *The Tao Is Silent*. New York: HarperCollins.

Todres, L. (2007) *Embodied Inquiry*. London: Palgrave.

Watson, T. (1994) *In Search of Management: Culture, chaos and control in managerial work.* London: Routledge.

Watson, T. (2002) *Organising and Managing Work.* London: Prentice Hall.

Acknowledgments

I am grateful to the artist Alex Alemany for permitting me to use his painting "Algo Personal" on the cover of this book.

I would also like to thank Dr Ken Israelstam for his depth of insight, creating the space for me to be and live in new ways.

Introduction: Existential Anxiety and Management Inquiry

Existential Anxiety, Research and Professional Development

Although existential philosophy has had an impact on a number of disciplines, including nursing and education, one of the disciplines in which it has very little impact is in management practice and scholarship. This is strange. For, in some ways, existentialism deals with essential dimensions of management. For example, the fact that managers, as Linda Hill (2003) maintains, only *become* managers by leaping into the unknown (the "sink or swim" syndrome). The view that only through existence (experience) does a manager develop an "essence" or a set of management habits of practice. Furthermore, the belief that management and leadership are more than a set of scientific skills but a way of being and be-coming that requires risk taking is essentially existential.

Perhaps one of the reasons for the limited use of existentialism in management is the latter's claim to be a science or critical social science. In contrast to science, which deal with things that have the status of objects, existentialism deals with themes of existence. In contrast to the social and critical sciences, which deal with practices, existentialism maintains that existence underpins the notion of practice and thus deals with the existential dimensions of practice which include temporality, risk, leaping into the unknown, anxiety and uncertainty. The science of management, anchored as it has been in control, order and planning, has wanted to manage anxiety and uncertainty away. Yet uncertainty rebounds and today we see so much talk of uncertainty and anxiety in management.

In a similar way there are a group of theorists (such Henry Mintzberg, John Kotter and Linda Hill) who claim to deal with the "firsthand experience" of managers. Existentialism, however, maintains that experience is grounded in existence and in order to gain perspective on learning through experience, a theory of existence is needed. Indeed, there are existentialists such as Rollo May and historically Kierkegaard and Nietzsche, who maintain that experience is not a sufficient condition for existential education and thus for becoming a manager, or a professional in general: "Anxiety is an even better teacher than reality, for one can temporarily evade reality by avoiding the distasteful situation; but anxiety is a source of education always present because one carries it within" (1976, p43).

The fields of study that has inquired into, researched and theorized anxiety in its existential forms is existential psychology and philosophy. The discipline of existential philosophy and psychology has developed its own school and journals. Perhaps there is too much of a negative connotation associated in management with uncertainty and anxiety. For the conventions—or as Heidegger would call it, "the average everyday discourse"—of management is such that managers are "supposed" to be "strong" and assertive and not vulnerable to experiences of anxiety. Indeed, Sigmund Freud (1989) once commented that anxiety is the defining factor in what was then called the neuroses. And the Diagnostic and Statistical Manual (DSM V of Psychiatry) sees a whole cluster of "illnesses" emerging out of anxiety.

However, what if there was a form of anxiety which was not centrally focused around neuroses or medical disease, but in fact was the central phenomenon in the development of identity, of becoming and of professional development? Furthermore, what if this same form of anxiety was central to what Heidegger calls the hermeneutic circle of philosophical research; inquiry into professional and managerial practice?

The last paragraph does depict how existential philosophers see anxiety. Embracing of, rather than refusal of, anxiety is the condition of the development of professional identity, habits of being and it is the basis of reflection not so much into the self (as is psychology) but into ways of being: professional, managerial, leadership, research, teaching, medical and so on.

Furthermore, existential anxiety is the basis of a certain kind of reflection: reflection from within a practice rather than reflection from outside of a practice. It is thus not a positivistic scientific form of reflection which separates the subject and object and views things only from an objective distance, but is a form of reflection from within the activity of leading, managing and working itself.

Existential anxiety is thus the basis for reflexive forms of inquiry; for inquiry into what we are already within; whether this be the way of being of a manager, teacher, leader, researcher and professional in general. Furthermore, such reflexive inquiry, when undertaken from an existential perspective, is undertaken in a particular kind of mood: the mood of existential anxiety or a felt sense of estrangement from the profession or way of being within which one exists.

It is this mood that gives research conducted in an existential way its relevance and significance. For the mood of anxiety is one that gives an urgency and vitality to the inquiry. It makes "knowing" an "ultimate concern," as Paul Tillich (1979) will call it.

EXISTENTIAL RELEVANCE OF THEORY

Indeed, this is one of the ways in which this book will work with the crisis of the relevance of theory and the distinction between theory and practice. It will argue that theory becomes existentially relevant in those times of anxiety in which our ways of doing things, our habits of professional practice, are in question. When we are in question, we can begin to ask questions in a concerned way about our practice. Thus the book will demonstrate that existential theorizing is not just a set of empty abstractions, but is a way of being concerned with or taking care of the existence of our professional managerial or leadership practice.

THEORY AND PRACTICE AS DIMENSIONS OF EXISTENCE

Furthermore, it will also demonstrate that practice is a way of being attuned to or concerned about our world. Our practices matter to us: building a house, providing for our children, developing a career and so on are all ways in which our existence matters to us.

Thus the platform through which the relationship between theory and practice will be established is that they are both moods or concerns in which existence matters to us. Rather than—as is the case with much Western thought—beginning with the rationalist distinction between theory and practice or the separation between mind and matter, the existential perspective sees both as part of the phenomenon of existence. And, more specifically, they are both moods of concern.

EXISTENTIAL ANXIETY AND FELT SENSE

Existential anxiety does not always and only express itself in an extreme form. Eugene Gendlin (see Todres 2007) has coined the phrase *felt sense* to describe those experiences in which we find it difficult to name the experiences that we are having. It is like having something on the "tip of one's tongue" but being unable to name the thought or feeling. And the more one cannot name the feeling or thought, the more frustrated one feels. It is a feeling that things are not quite right but that which is not quite right cannot be pinpointed. It fragments our focusing; bothers us until we feel that we have "got it" or the words spring into our attention and we resonate with them. It is a process of turning what we are intuitively aware of but cannot yet articulate into something that is articulated.

Just as a scientist or artist in the process of discovery is not yet able to name what they are searching for, so in the process of focusing we have a fascination and curiosity with our own felt sense. No matter how disturbing it may be, once we are able to be curious and fascinated by the disturbance in our own felt sense, we are in the process of developing the discipline of focusing.

Felt sense may take many forms: a sense of being uncomfortable with a conclusion that has been drawn, a nagging doubt, a sense of surprise, ambivalence, emotional and cognitive dissonance, a sense of perplexity. All of these are occasions for focusing, for listening to what our body is telling us and thus are existential forms of questioning, questioning from within the context of lived experience.

EXISTENTIALISM AND CHOICE OF METHODS OF RESEARCH

Existentialism allows us to throw light on another pressing issue. As we will see throughout this book, management has assumed rather than demonstrated that positivistic science and positivistic and critical social science is the appropriate form through which to inquire into management. It has not demonstrated that science is methodologically the appropriate way to inquire into management. This is the case from its origins in Taylorism to modern-day forms of social science.

Existentialism does allow us to inquire into the appropriate methodology for the appropriate subject matter: "Back to the things themselves" is a slogan that existentialism has borrowed from Husserlian phenomenology (Heidegger 1985) and in the context of Heidegger it means allowing the thing itself to shape the methodology of inquiry. For example, if the thing has the status of an object, such as a clock on the wall, we need to study it scientifically, but if the subject matter of inquiry is a qualitative relationship, we need to study it qualitatively. As will be seen in a later chapter, there needs to be a dialogue between method and subject matter to determine the appropriate form of study.

EXISTENTIAL DISTANCE

Existential hermeneutic phenomenology is focused on the question of how we choose our methodology by going back to the thing itself. Like science, it does hold to a notion of distance, but this is not an objective distance. It is an emotional sense of detachment from work. Being existentially detached from work is a central feature of anxiety and this detachment opens up the opportunity for reflecting on the professional practice in which we are involved—whether it be management, leadership or research into or teaching of leadership and management. For it is in existential detachment that we come to be able to observe and examine our ways of doing things whilst in the midst of doing things.

EXISTENTIAL ANXIETY AS THE BASIS FOR RESEARCH QUESTIONING

Thus existential reflection—reflection from within anxiety—is a basis for managerial leadership, research and educational development. But it is more than this: as Martin Heidegger (1948) makes clear in "What is Metaphysics?" existential anxiety is the condition of existential questioning and thus is the basis for a certain kind of research: a research from within and about professional practices such as management, leadership, teaching and research: "Only when the strangeness of what-is forces itself upon us does it awaken and invite our wonder. Only because of wonder, that is to say, the revelation of Nothing, does the 'Why?' spring to our lips. Only because [of] this 'Why?' … are we fated to become inquirers" (1948, p353).

Please note the last line of the quotation: inquiry is directly linked to the strangeness of what is and this strangeness is linked to existential anxiety. Existential anxiety is not the basis for clinical psychological or psychiatric intervention, but in the Heideggerian sense is the basis for reflexive inquiry and research. Part of the aim of this work is to describe the way in which existential anxiety forms the basis for reflexive research within the broad area of management, including leadership, management, project management, strategy, research in management and teaching and education of managers.

Creative Destruction and Existentialism

At the same time, the book would also like to address the uncertainty of the market-based and sociocultural context in which management occurs, as well as a range of challenges faced by management researchers. Regarding the market-based and sociocultural context of management, it starts with an insight of Joseph Schumpeter's (1955), namely, that the free market does not tend towards equilibrium but is characterized by a dynamic uncertainty underpinned by what he called patterns of creative destruction in which new ways of doing business are destroying existing ways and even these existing ways are themselves being destroyed.

Furthermore, the lived experience of creative destruction occurs unexpectedly. Companies, industries, careers and often lives of individuals and families are destroyed at a moment's notice. The question is: how to be when a company, an industry or an individual's life is destroyed? What are the practical coping sensitivities in the context of the destruction of the old and the possibility of the new?

While Schumpeter highlighted the notion of creative destruction and the uncertainty that goes with it, he did not develop the existential anxiety or an appreciation of the lived experience of living in between the destruction of the old and the hopeful emergence of the new—for there is no guarantee that the new will emerge out of the old. He did not deal with the uncertainty of living in between, in a no man's land where the signposts of the future are not yet defined and we can no longer rely on the rules of the past. This is an essential dimension of existential anxiety. It is the uncertainty in which our traditional ways of dealing with uncertainty fail or have disrupted or broken down. This point is made by the authors of *The Clue Train Manifesto*: "This is an existential moment. It's characterized by uncertainty, the dissolving of the normal ways of settling uncertainties, the evaporation of the memory of what certainty was once like. In times like this, we all have an impulse to find something stable and cling to it, but then we'd miss the moment entirely" (Levine et al. 2011).

The first point to note is that the authors are not writing about uncertainty in general but a *specific form of uncertainty*: an uncertainty in which the normal conventions for dealing with uncertainty have fallen away. As elaborated above, existential anxiety occurs when the rules for dealing with uncertainty are themselves fragmented and we have neither a universal foundation nor an objective ground to which to turn to explain, justify and make sense of our activity. There is neither a God above, nor an objective quantitative measure, through which we can anchor our thinking and action. For the paradox of objective is that it is a subjective construct.

The theme of choosing without having a foundation is central to existentialism. Such choosing requires a leap into the unfamiliarity of the unknown. It is only through leaping into the unknown that habits of practice develop.

The felt sense of a practice cannot develop in advance of the practice but in the context of immersing oneself in the practice. In the clichés of management speak, it is the "sink or swim" phenomenon. In other words, it is only as we jump into leadership and management that we develop the feel for, the "felt sense," of leadership and management and then inhabit the practice of leading and managing.

This book will focus on developing the existential anxiety and lived experience of the uncertainty of creative destruction in the context of management, management research and education. This form of uncertainty is not a personality-based form of uncertainty but an existential form of uncertainty. It is uncertainty in which our familiar context or our ways of doing things, the habits that we have built up and the institutions and practices that we have developed, are destabilized and called into question. We are thrown into the unknown.

Pervasiveness of Existential Anxiety in Management and Leadership

There are many dimensions on which existential uncertainty is a part of everyday life in the twenty-first century. Politically, for example, we have had politicians like Condoleezza Rice speak about an existential threat to the United States of America. The State of Israel has for the last 40 years written about itself as in an existential threat, where the security of its identity is at stake. The Palestinian people feel a huge sense of being misplaced. Our traditional ways of reading the Middle East as a group of nation states is now too simple. We live in a world, as Ulrich Beck (2002) states, in which we cannot control the forms of insecurity that our ways of life are creating. Or as Dillon (1995) puts it, the very attempts to solve problems of security only add to our sense of insecurity.

This existential anxiety can be seen in the bewilderment of our political and economic leaders. An example of this is given by Alan Greenspan in his response to the global financial crisis (GFC) of 2009:

> As a perplexed Alan Greenspan confessed to Congress about his own thinking in 2008, just a few weeks after [the GFC began]: 'I have found a flaw. I don't know how significant or permanent it is. But I have been very distressed by the fact' (Ramo 2010, pp5–6).

There is no evidence that Alan Greenspan creatively destroyed his paradigm in the context of the GFC. And making this argument more broadly, there is no evidence that management schools and education in general are preparing students for living, learning and opening new possibilities in the anxiety of creative disruption.

This means that both the preparation of future leaders and managers and their professional development does little to close the gap between the realities of in-practice existential anxiety and the theoretical foundations of their leadership and management learning. The consequence of this is leaders and managers who become frozen in time—stuck in the old and familiar; unable to work with existential anxiety; and without the habits of possibilities and creative disruption—run the risk of being "run over" by changing paradigms.

Returning to the field of management: there is, if not conclusive evidence, at least support for the belief that much of the uncertainty experienced in technological change, organizational change, the changes in the conventions of doing business, the experience of cultural difference in the context of globalization and the challenging of very core beliefs is an existential form of anxiety. For all of these changes contain at least an element of going into the unknown.

Fisher (2000), for example, points out that in the context of creative destruction many American cities which were once "boomtowns" have become "bust towns." He also points out the way in which changes to the nature of industries have creatively destroyed old industries. For example, he writes of the way in which the train creatively destroyed the steam ships and the cities that grew up along the ports; of the way in which air travel destroyed the trains and the towns that had developed around stations. Today we see how the internet is creatively destroying many industries, including the printing press.

And we also see that it is not only industries and businesses, but the lives of people that are at stake in these experiences of creative destruction. Not only are businesses not built to last, but careers are no longer built to last. And the challenge is to be able to reinvent ourselves, to disclose new possibilities in the face of this anxiety of creative destruction. The alternatives are not always very exciting: suicide, drug abuse and so on.

EXISTENTIAL ANXIETY AS A CONDITION OF PROFESSIONAL DEVELOPMENT

Existential anxiety is an underestimated factor in becoming a professional. Indeed, even the act of becoming a manager or leader involves experiences of existential anxiety for it involves "leaps into the unknown." This is highlighted by the way in which managers and leaders need to immerse themselves in experiencing management and leadership before they have an embodied or felt sense of how to be in and do management and leadership. Habits develop only through being habituated. This point is shared by Aristotle and by the philosophy of existentialism: our habits of practice are developed by practicing our habits.

MANAGEMENT RESEARCH IN EXISTENTIAL CRISIS

Furthermore much of management research is in an existential crisis. This is to be found in the field of international business, for example, where there is no commonly agreed-upon meta-paradigm or rules of the game through which to conduct cross-cultural studies. Even within the broad field of organization studies and management learning there is no shared grounds for commensurate discourse. Existential anxiety is focused on how to respond to this lack of a shared ground: do we look for a new shared ground and gain security or can we embrace the uncertainty of having no secure ground on which to stand?

More generally, a question that needs to be asked is: how do we conduct research in the context of uncertainty? For if we take Joseph Schumpeter seriously, there is no stable ground in the free market and in the sociocultural context of capitalism itself. Research, at least in both its reductive and positivist forms, is based on the assumption of stability. The law of induction is based on the assumption of regularity, that tomorrow will be just like yesterday. Yet, if we assume the principle of creative destruction and indeed the philosophy of existentialism, we will also assume that irregularity is just as much part of everyday life as is regularity. How then do we conduct research when the underpinning principle of the whole edifice of positivist research is called into question? Another way of putting this is: what does existential research look like? What does research underpinned by uncertainty look like?

Tsoukas and Knudsen (2003) maintain that current trends in organizational and management research begin not from the lived experience of everyday challenges, but from abstractions from the everyday reality of managers and leaders. They argue that it is because management research is abstracted from a context of reference that its relevance and meaning is questioned. It is precisely in this context that existential research becomes important. For existential research begins with the uncertainty and particularity of the everyday. It may be in the form of pressure, stress, surprise, perplexity, confusion or bewilderment. All of these are existential conditions of uncertainty which form the basis for inquiry and reflection.

However, none of the expressions of existential uncertainty emerge as already formulated questions. From the existential perspective, uncertainty does not present itself as a question. We need to work on it to allow the question that is, as Socrates would say, pregnant within uncertainty to become manifest. And then we can begin to deal with it. But to do this, we need to listen to our uncertainties, seeing them not as a sign of weakness but as an opportunity for new possibilities.

To Question is to be in Question

In existentialism uncertainty is the driving force of questioning and thus reflexive research. Heidegger puts it this way: because our being is in question, we tend to ask questions of being. Or because our being is at stake, we tend to live in a questioning of being. Thus from the existential perspective, it is through working with uncertainty in a questioning way that we remove it from the lofty heights of abstraction and return its sense of relevance and significance. Furthermore, questioning and reflection are themselves meaningful activities in the context of working through existential uncertainty.

QUESTIONING AS A COMPETENCY OF LIVING, LEADING AND MANAGING

Questioning, especially in times of uncertainty, is a core human competency. Questioning of the assumptions in terms of which we question is a theme that lies at the heart of Socrates as a philosopher. It is central to creativity in science. For example, Einstein saw the art questioning our assumptions as central to shifting the frameworks within which problems were solved. Heidegger claims that our answers to questions emerge out of the way in which we ask questions, so concern and attention needs to be given to the way in which we ask questions. Even finance, where analysts such as Taleb (2010) note that: "My major hobby is teasing people who take themselves and the quality of their knowledge too seriously and those who don't have the courage to sometimes say: I don't know."

But as John Kotter (1999) has pointed out, we tend to be trained for a world of stability rather than for uncertainty. This needs to change. Our educational systems, pedagogies, research practices and modes of inquiry need to embrace education for uncertainty.

Heidegger's existential philosophy will also enable a number of challenges and crises within the fields of organization and management studies to be addressed.

As already stated, it will provide a framework within which to address the separation between theory and practice that has bedeviled management and organizational theorizing. Schon and Argyris (1977) have argued that theory is done under ideal and practice under real-time conditions.

THEORY, PRACTICE AND THE HERMENEUTICS OF EXISTENCE

As will be shown through the course of this book, there have been, from a Heideggerian perspective, various attempts to place theory and practice into a closer relationship to each other. However, most of these attempts have involved turning theory into a form of practice. This point is made by Sandberg and Dall'Alba (2009), who maintain that there have been a range of attempts to situate practice in terms of a "life world": for example, in developing the practice of theorizing, Etienne Wenger (1998, pp48, 286) and Schatzki (2002, pp69–70) draw on Martin Heidegger's concept of "being-in-the-world," while Robert Chia and Robin Holt (2006) use Heidegger's concept of "dwelling" to extend practice-based research on strategy. Tsoukas and Sandberg (2011), Weick (2003) and Zundel (2013), amongst others, attempt to reframe Heidegger as a theory of practice.

However, as will also be demonstrated in this book, most, if not all, of the attempts to provide a Heideggerian perspective that unifies the relationship between theory and practice have not done full justice to Heidegger's existential philosophy of the relation between theory and practice as espoused in *Being and Time*. For Heidegger, to understand practice we need to understand existence. To understand theory we need to understand existence and to understand the relationship between theory and practice we need to understand existence. Both occur within the horizon of existence.

Existence has a number of dimensions or structures to it, including temporality, thrownness, anticipatory resolve, mood, concern, anxiety, uncertainty, a heritage, projection into a future, being "always and already" in the world, an "average everyday understanding," an existential and an *existentiell* understanding and the hermeneutics of existence or being-in-the-world. These need to be taken into account in order to demonstrate that theory and practice are not simply separate from each other but form an existential hermeneutic whole of existence.

That theory and practice occur within the context of existence shows that they occur in a mood, in a mode of mattering and concern and that it is a matter of examining the mood and concerns in which theory and practice are brought together in a hermeneutic whole of existence.

As will be demonstrated during the course of the book, the basis of the unity of theory and practice will be found in Heidegger's notion of a hermeneutic circle of existence, which is the central dimension of human existence (1985, p195). Rather than the separation of mind and matter or theory and practice, what Heidegger offers us is that both theory and practice are parts of the greater hermeneutic whole of existence. Theory is not primarily a practice: just like practice, it is a way of existing; a significant one; one that is central to being at home and dealing with not being at home in the world; with working through being estranged from our familiar and habitual ways of doing things and opening new possibilities within and for being a professional

EXISTENTIALISM AND EXPERIENCE

Even those theorists who do focus on the experience of managers do not tend to explicitly focus on the existential dimensions of experience. This includes scholars such as Henry Mintzberg (2004), Linda Hill (2003) and John Kotter (1974). All of them insist that management needs to be understood in the context of "real life" experience and that managers learn best from experience, but they do not provide a theory of existence that underpins experience. Furthermore, theorizing is itself an existential experience. This leads them to make the mistake of not seeing that theorizing and practice are parts of the hermeneutic whole of existence. Experience and theorizing are dimensions of existence.

FAMILY OF EXISTENTIALISTS

An understanding of existence is to be found in that group of thinkers (philosophers, sociologists and psychologists) who have been identified as existential philosophers. Although Heidegger refuses to have himself identified as an existentialist, there is enough of a concern with existence in his writing to identify him, at certain levels, with existentialism. Indeed, in his book *Being and Time*, one of the only people to whom he acknowledges a debt is the philosopher Soren Kierkegaard, who is always recognized as an existentialist. Furthermore, in *Being and Time*, Heidegger focuses on the existence of the being of the human.

This "family" of thinkers includes those who, like so many families, are part of the same whole, even if they disagree with each other. Its founding fathers include Soren Kierkegaard, Friedrich Nietzsche, Martin Heidegger, Martin Buber and Sartre. Many have taken their thought and transformed it for their own ends. Philosophers such as Hubert Dreyfus (1993), Charles Taylor (1993) and Richard Rorty (1980) all make use of Heidegger and the work of existentialists. This list includes sociologists such as Zygmunt Bauman (1990) and psychologists such as Rollo May (1976). The range of this family will be used to develop an existential position for professional inquiry in the context of management and the study of management.

PROBLEMS TO BE WORKED THROUGH

Understanding the relationship between theory and practice in terms of the dimension of existence will immediately overcome a number of problems that have characterized management studies for several decades:

- It will enable us to understand the way in which practicing managers (rather than theorists) inquire into their practice.

- It will enable an understanding of the role of theorizing in existence of a professional practice.

- It will enable us to identify the occasions in which inquiry becomes relevant for managers.

- It will enable us to understand the relationship between rigor and relevance that has characterized the history of management and organizational studies.

- It will help us reframe management inquiry itself. Indeed, the one question that it does not take for granted is: what does it mean to actually ask a question in the context of management? And on what kinds of occasions do practicing managers' managers ask questions?

- It also enables us to ask and respond to the question concerning the conditions under which research becomes possible, valuable and significant. Indeed, what are the existential conditions under which research is undertaken? And why do research into management in the first place?

Existentialism also offers us a theory of learning, inquiry, research and education for excellence in professional practice. For as many authors have noted, this is at least one of the areas in which the separation of theory from practice is most pronounced. It manifests itself in what is known as the rigor versus relevance debate, in which many theorists believe that they need to sacrifice rigor in order to be relevant, while practitioners believe that management scholarship is so abstract that it does not speak to the practicing manager.

Structure of the Book

The book is divided into four parts, each comprising a number of chapters. Part I sets up Heidegger's philosophy of existence. Part II uses Heidegger's existential philosophy as a basis upon which to reflect on some of the recurring problems in organization studies. It will also look at the way in which Heidegger's philosophy of existence addressees research issues in the context of creative destruction. Part III looks at the implications of Heidegger's philosophy of existence for management research and Part IV looks at the significance of existential philosophy for professional development with a specific focus on managerial professional development.

References

Argyris, C. and Schon, D.A. (1977) *Theory in Practice: Increasing professional effectiveness.* San Francisco: Jossey-Bass Publishers.

Aristotle (translated by Bartlett, R.C. and Collins, S.D.) (2011) *Nicomachean Ethics.* Chicago: University of Chicago Press.

Bauman, Z. (1990) Modernity and Ambivalence. In: Featherstone, M. (ed.) *Global Culture: Nationalism, globalization and modernity.* London: Sage Publications.

Beck, U. (2002) The Silence of Words and the Political Dynamics in the World Risk Society. *Logos.* Vol 4. Fall. pp1–18.

Chia, R. and Holt, R. (2006) Strategies as Practical Coping: A Heideggerian perspective. *Organization Studies.* Vol 27, No 5. pp635–55.

Dall'Alba, G. (2009) Learning Professional Ways of Being: Ambiguities of becoming. *Educational Philosophy and Theory.* Vol 41, No 1. pp34–45.

Dillon, M. (1995) Security, Philosophy and Politics. In: Featherstone, M. et al. (eds) *Global Modernities.* London: Sage Publications.

Dreyfus, H. (1993) *Being-in-the-World: A Commentary on Heidegger's Being and Time, Division 1.* Boston: The MIT Press.

Fisher, P. (2000) *Still the New World: American literature in a culture of creative destruction.* Boston: Harvard University Press.

Freud, S. (1989) *Introductory Lectures on Psychoanalysis.* London: Penguin Books.

Heidegger, M. (1948) What Is Metaphysics? In: Brock, W. (ed.) *Existence and Being.* Indiana: Regnery/Gateway, Inc.

Heidegger, M. (1985) *Being and Time.* Oxford: Basil Blackwell.

Hill, L.A. (2003) *Becoming a Manager: How new managers master the challenges of leadership.* Boston, MA: Harvard Business School Press.

Koestenbaum, P. (1978) *The New Image of the Person: The theory and practice of clinical philosophy.* Connecticut: Greenwood Press.

Kotter, J.P. (1999) *A Force for Change: How leadership differs from management.* New York: The Free Press.

Kotter, J. (1974) What Effective General Managers Really Do. *Harvard Business Review.* March.

Levine, R., Locke, C., Searls, D. and Weinberger, D. (2011) *The Clue Train Manifesto: The end of business as usual* (10th ed.). New York: Basic Books.

May, R. (1976) *The Meaning of Anxiety.* New York: W.W. Norton and Company Inc.

Mintzberg, H. (2003) *Managers not MBAs: A hard look at the soft practice of managing.* San Francisco: Berrett-Koehler.

Ramo, J. (2010) *The Age of the Unthinkable.* New York: Back Bay Books.

Rorty, R. (1980) *Philosophy and the Mirror of Nature.* Oxford: Basil Blackwell.

Sandberg, J. and Dall'Alba, G. (2009) Returning to Practice Anew: A life-world perspective. *Organization Studies*. Vol 30, No 12. pp1349–68.

Schatzki, T.R. (2002) *The Site of the Social: A philosophical account of the constitution of social life and change.* University Park, PA: Pennsylvania State University Press.

Schumpeter, J. (1955) *Capitalism, Socialism and Democracy.* New York: Harper Tourchbooks.

Taleb, N.N. (2010) *The Black Swan: The impact of the highly improbable.* New York: Random House.

Taylor, C. (1993) Engaged Agency and Background in Heidegger. In: Guignon, C. (ed.) *The Cambridge Companion to Heidegger.* Cambridge: Cambridge University Press.

Tillich, P. (1979) *The Courage To Be.* Great Britain: Fontana Books.

Todres, L. (2007) *Embodied Enquiry: Phenomenological touchstones for research, psychotherapy and spirituality.* New York: Palgrave Macmillan.

Tsoukas, H. and Knudsen, C. (eds) (2003) *The Oxford Handbook of Organisational Theory.* New York: Oxford University Press.

Tsoukas, H. and Sandberg, J. (2011) Grasping the Logic of Practice: Theorising through practical rationality. *Academy of Management Review.* Vol 36, No 2. pp338–60.

Weick, K. (2003) Theory and Practice in the Real World. In: Tsoukas, H. and Knudsen, T. (eds) *The Oxford Handbook of Organisational Theory.* New York: Oxford University Press.

Wenger, E. (1998) *Communities of Practice: Learning, meaning, and identity.* Cambridge: Cambridge University Press.

Zundel, M. (2013) Walking to Learn: Rethinking reflection for management learning. *Management Learning.* Vol 44, No 2. pp109–26.

PART I
Existential Experiences of Creative Destruction

Chapter 1

Uncertainty in the Marketplace of Management

What has existentialism and existential anxiety got to do with management, organizations, the free market, management education and research?

There can be no doubt that the business environment has undergone several disruptions over at least the last 30 years. One of the major disruptions was the introduction of the internet. It has very much shaken the conventions in terms of which business is conducted. Indeed, the authors of *The Clue Train Manifesto* (Levine, Locke, Searls and Weinberg 2011) have explained the uncertainty generated by the introduction of the internet as an existential uncertainty: "This is an existential moment. It's characterized by uncertainty, the dissolving of the normal ways of settling uncertainties, the evaporation of the memory of what certainty was once like. In times like this, we all have an impulse to find something stable and cling to it, but then we'd miss the moment entirely."

The first point to note in the quotation above is that the authors are not writing about uncertainty in general, but a specific form of uncertainty: an uncertainty in which the normal conventions for dealing with uncertainty have fallen away. As elaborated above, existential anxiety occurs when the rules for dealing with uncertainty are themselves fragmented and we have neither a universal foundation nor an objective ground to which to turn to explain, justify and make sense of our activity. There is neither a God above, nor an objective quantitative measure through which to anchor our thinking and action.

The theme of choosing without a foundation is central to existentialism. Such choosing requires a leap into the unfamiliarity of the unknown. It is only through leaping into the unknown that habits of practice develop. The felt sense of a practice cannot develop in advance of the practice, but in the context of immersing oneself in the practice. In the clichés of management speak, it is the "sink or swim" phenomenon. Only as we jump into management and leadership do we develop the felt sense for, and thus inhabit, the practice of leading and managing.

Paradoxically, the authors of *The Clue Train Manifesto* argue that the search for security through rules, formulae and methods has generated a greater existential insecurity in which we cannot rely on rules, methods or formulae to choose for us. This is because there are so many rules and formulae that, instead of there being one universal, there are many from which we need to choose. And there is no formula for choosing how to choose between the different rules and formulae: "There isn't a list of things you can do to work the whirlwind. The desire to have such a list betrays the moment. There may not be twelve or five or twenty things you can do, but there are ten thousand. The trick is, you have to figure out what they are. They have to come from you. They have to be your words, your moves, your authentic voice" (Levine et al. 2011).

The irony of this statement is that the authors are not arguing that there are no rules, formulae or methods, but that it is we who need to choose the method or rules. It is not the method or rules that is going to choose for us. Without a method or set of rules or even objective reasons, we are going to choose the kind of reasoning, the methods and rules in terms of which we practice. Often without even explicitly realizing it, the methods that we choose are based on our interpretation.

This is reminiscent of Machiavelli's understanding of leadership:

> *Because men are seen, in affairs that lead to the end which every man has before him, namely, glory and riches, to get there by various methods; one with caution, another with haste; one by force, another by skill; one by patience, another by its opposite; and each one succeeds in reaching the goal by a different method. One can also see of two cautious men the one attain his end, the other fail; and similarly, two men by different observances are equally successful, the one being cautious, the other impetuous; all this arises from nothing else than whether or not they conform in their methods to the spirit of the times.*

It is not the method *per se*, but the way we choose in a groundless uncertainty. For both Machiavelli and the authors of *The Clue Train Manifesto*, choosing in the context of the unknown is the basis of the development of authenticity. One's authentic voice is developed through choosing in the context of action. In many ways this is central to the phenomenon of practical wisdom in leadership. Aristotle was quite clear that practical wisdom emerges in the context of action and thus the wisdom of judgment in leadership and management is not something that can be taught, but requires the willingness to embrace the anxiety of the unknown.

Choosing in the context of action does not mean no theorizing, reflection or reflexivity. On the contrary, it is a reflexivity in the context of action. As Kierkegaard once said, "Life is lived forwards and understood backwards." One of the meanings of this is that understanding occurs in the context of action. The same point is made by Aristotle, who claims that theorizing in the absence of experience is empty: it is theorizing in the context of experience that leads to first principles. In a similar way, Heidegger will say that it is only in the context of existing that we reflect on our ways of existing. And he emphasizes that existential anxiety is the basis for both disclosing our historically familiar way of existing and is the basis upon which to disclose new possibilities.

The Free Market and Existential Anxiety

Building on this, it can be said that creative destruction, a phrase developed by Joseph Schumpeter to describe the essence of the free market, is an existential phenomenon. Unexpected and unanticipated world disclosure in fact characterizes the essence of capitalism. This perspective underlies the work of the economist Joseph Schumpeter, who believed that capitalism is a system which is constantly transforming itself and in doing so transforms the habits of doing business. Writing in the 1930s, he called this process "creative destruction". Schumpeter maintained that the most dangerous and challenging form of competition comes not from existing products but from new ones. New products challenge the very existence of existing producers:

> But in capitalist reality as distinguished from its textbook picture, it is not [price] competition which counts but the competition from the new commodity, the new technology, the new source of supply, the new type of organization … competition which … strikes not at the margins of the profits and the outputs of the existing firms but at their foundations and their very lives (1955, p26).

Continuing his point, Schumpeter maintains that whole ways of life, identities, patterns of relationships, meaning and significance are transformed through the process of creative destruction: "The capitalist process not only destroys its own institutional framework but it also creates the conditions for another … things and souls are transformed" (1955, p162).

Schumpeter is introducing an existential language into our understanding of capitalism. The idea that competition strikes at the "lives" and "foundations" of producers takes us into the language of existential attunement. It creates an appreciation for the angst or anxiety that goes into business. Describing the process of creative destruction, Schumpeter sees it as a process "of industrial mutation—if I may use that biological term—that incessantly revolutionizes the economic structure from within, incessantly destroying the old one, incessantly creating a new one" (ibid). Schumpeter uses the imagery of a "gale" to describe the experience. There is no way of knowing how and that we will come out of the "gale" of the valley of destruction.

Schumpeter maintains that only a certain type of temperament is likely to succeed in the free market. It is one who can embrace the anxiety of the unknown: "To act with confidence beyond the range of familiar beacons and to overcome the resistance requires aptitudes that are present only in a small fraction of the population and defines the entrepreneurial type" (1955, p132).

Creative destruction involves giving up the familiar and entering the unfamiliar without a firm foundation. According to Schumpeter, this involved being able to embrace the anxiety of the unfamiliar. The space of creative destruction is well articulated by Clayton Christensen in his work *The Innovator's Dilemma* (2000): "Markets that do not exist cannot be analysed. … In known markets … customer needs are understood. In this environment, a planned, researched approach to evaluating, developing, and marketing innovative products is not only possible but desirable. … However, this is not relevant to disruptive technologies."

Adding to this, Schumpeter has said: "Thorough preparatory work, and special knowledge, breadth of intellectual understanding, talent for logical analysis, may under certain circumstances be sources of failure" (1955, p85).

In other words, objectivity—that which has replaced God—in secular society is itself not trustworthy; it creates uncertainty. Machiavelli understood this space well. He claimed that in the face of the winds of change methods or procedures will not work—and yet this is what both education and managerial training prepares us for. There is no theory that can prescribe in advance how we ought to engage in the space between destruction and creation. For it is only as we engage in the space that we build up the resilience to cope in the space.

Existential Anxiety in Undermining Businesses, Industries, Institutions and Ways of Life that Hold the Free Market Together

This theme has already been implied in the above. But to bring it out further, creative destruction defines much of the context in which business, organizing, careers and even culture takes place today. We are witnessing it in the destruction of print media and the rise of digital media. The creative destruction of, for example, bookstores in the name of online book ordering is not a free market anomaly, but is a very central principle of capitalism. It is the essence of the free market that it destroys the comfort zones of the familiar and the actual. For example, the creative destruction of many industries and businesses during the rise of the technology of the internet called many businesses and industries into question. Many simply went out of business. Others were challenged to reinvent themselves. Others had to question what kind of business they were in.

It is important to hold in the forefront of our attention that "creative destruction" does not refer to an object but to a context. We live within the context of creative destruction. This point is brought out by, amongst others, Philip Fisher (1999), who enables us to identify the anxiety experienced in breakdowns, not of this or that item of equipment, but of ways of being: "Boomtowns become backwaters or, even worse, ghost towns," he says. Not only do people lose their means of making a living but they lose their identities, their network of relationships and the sense of purpose and meaning in which they participated: "The airplanes that crisscross the skies in America today fly over tens of thousands of miles of rusting and little used railroad tracks. Some of the tracks themselves have been covered with asphalt to make recreational trails for bicyclists and weekend hikers" (Fisher 1999).

When people lose their sense of orientation in these kinds of ways, they are also estranged from life in such ways that suicide becomes a temptation and in some sense an actuality. There is, in the face of the free market of creative destruction, no guarantee of norm-like behavior. As Ernst Gellner once said: "Modern history is rather like a football cup in which only the first round was played as soccer, the second round is played as rugby, the third as ice-hockey, etc" (1964, p53).

Existential Anxiety in the Context of Changing Leadership Paradigms

Karl Marx once said that "circumstances change and the educator must themselves be educated." While he did not write about the anxiety of the transformation that educators need to undergo when circumstances change, there are many examples in the field of leadership which show this to be the case. For example, Mort Meyerson, former CEO of Ross Perot systems, writes quite explicitly about the anxiety he experienced when his way of being a leader was challenged by technological changes. He demonstrates that it was through embracing his anxiety that he was able to "destroy" his habitual practices of leadership and open the way for new practices:

> When I returned to Perot Systems, my first job as a leader was to create a new understanding of myself. I had to accept the shattering of my own self-confidence. I couldn't lead anymore, at least not in the way I always had. There was a time during that first year at Perot Systems when I would go home and look in the mirror and say to myself, "You don't get it. Maybe you ought to get out of this business. You're like a highly specialized trained beast that evolved during one period and now you can't adjust to the new environment" (Meyerson 1996.)

The point is that he was able to see and experience his anxiety as the basis upon which to question and open up new ways of being a leader for himself:

> I told myself I was having the same experience as a caterpillar entering a cocoon. The caterpillar doesn't know that he'll come out as a butterfly. All he knows is that he's alone, it's dark, and it's a little scary. I came out the other end of the experience with a new understanding of leadership. I don't have to know everything. I don't have to have all the customer contacts. I don't have to make all the decisions. In fact, in the new world of business, it can't be me, it shouldn't be me, and my job is to prevent it from being me (Meyerson 1996).

Although he does not use the word "anxiety", Andrew Grove speaks about the significance of what he calls "paranoia" and the "valley of death" in the face of unexpected competitors which disrupt one's habitual and conventional way of doing business. Based on his own lived experience, he maintained that it was only as he destroyed his habitual and conventional ways of leading that he moved away from being a "drill sergeant" to a leader who was able to listen to all levels within the organization. Indeed, Grove went as far as to say that in the face of anxiety, "when your business gets into serious difficulties, in spite of the best attempts of business schools and management training courses to make you a rational analyzer of data, objective analysis will take second seat to personal and emotional reactions almost every time" (Grove 1996).

Bewilderment of Leaders in the Face of Existential Anxiety

In both these cases we see acts of creative destruction occurring and these acts are the basis of an existential education: one that destroys present habits of practice and discloses new ones. There are leaders who do not adapt to change. They refuse to embrace the moment of creative destruction. An example of this is given by Alan Greenspan in his response to the global financial crisis (GFC) of 2009:

> As a perplexed Alan Greenspan confessed to Congress about his own thinking in 2008, just a few weeks after [the GFC began]: 'I have found a flaw. I don't know how significant or permanent it is. But I have been very distressed by the fact' (Ramo 2010, pp5–6).

There is no evidence that Alan Greenspan creatively destroyed his paradigm in the context of the GFC. And making this argument more broadly, there is no evidence that management schools and education in general are preparing students for living, learning and opening new possibilities in the anxiety of creative disruption.

Existential Anxiety in the Face of Globalization

And in the context of globalization there is the phenomenon of what Segal (1998) called the anxiety of strangers, which is an anxiety experienced where:

> one does not have the conventions or scripts for making sense of unfamiliar national contexts in which one may be managing or leading.
>   And one cannot rely on the conventions of one's own culture to guide one.

This is often called culture shock. In a Richard Dimbleby lecture, former President Bill Clinton remarked that globalization has broken down boundaries to trade but it has not broken down cultural boundaries. On the contrary, he remarks, people still live in the boxes of their own way of doing things: "somewhere along the way, we finally [need to] come to understand that our life is more than all these boxes we're in. And that if we can't reach beyond that, we'll never have a fuller life. And the fanatics of the world, they love their boxes and they hate yours. … And it's easy to give the right answer but it's hard to live."

Hubert Dreyfus gives a good example of this:

> *People in various cultures stand different distances from an intimate, a friend, a stranger. Furthermore, the distances vary when these people are chatting, doing business, or engaging in courtship. Each culture, including our own, embodies an incredible subtle shared pattern of social distancing. Yet no one explicitly taught this pattern to each of us. Our parents could not possibly have consciously instructed us in it since they do not know the pattern any more than we do. We do not even know we have such know-how until we go to another culture and find, for example, that in North Africa strangers seem to be oppressively close while in Scandinavia friends seem to stand too far away. This makes us uneasy, and we cannot help backing away or moving closer (1993, p234).*

In the meeting of strangers we are estranged from our own way of doing things. We cannot rely on them. But precisely because we are estranged from them, they become explicit. We are detached in an existential way from our everyday practices such that they become the focus of our attention. This moment of estrangement or existential detachment is central to theory as a journey of estrangement from the familiar. Jager maintains that "Theorising was from the beginning never a mere shadow play of concepts, of disembodied ideas used in a game of empty possibilities. It was rather from the start a commerce with the distant, a desire to reach out beyond the comforts of mundane life towards the distant, festive realm" (1983, p165).

Jager shows how for the ancient Greeks theorizing was a practice of journeying or travelling from the safety of the familiar homeland to strange and unfamiliar cultures. In the movement beyond the familiar they were estranged from their habitual ways of doing things. Such reaching out through journeying gave them insight not only into the other, but into themselves as well: "Theorising made its first appearance as an arduous journey to a place of divine manifestation. ... It required ... a leaving behind of the familiar and comforting sounds and sights of familiar life" (1983, p162).

In this sense migration, journeying to a new land, being with people of other cultures or nations involves acts of theorizing. For on all such occasions we cannot take our habitual ways of seeing things for granted, but in fact bump against them. They become explicit themes for our consideration. The experience of the stranger is thus an opportunity for a conversation with the stranger, an ecstatic conversation about the relationship between our different ways of being within the world. In such a conversation we are enriched and transformed by the otherness of the other. The sense of this ecstatic conversation is well expressed by Richard Rorty (1980) when he says that meetings with the strangeness of the way of being of the other offers us the opportunity "to reinterpret our familiar surroundings in the unfamiliar terms of [the other]. ... Discourse [with the other] is supposed to be abnormal, to take us out of our old selves by the power of strangeness, to aid us in becoming new beings."

Existential Anxiety and the Hermeneutics of Management Education

Richard Rorty puts the point about discourse with the strangeness of the other in an educational context. Substituting the word edification for the word education, he maintains that edification is rooted in the way we respond to the strangeness of the unfamiliar: "The attempt to edify (ourselves or others) may consist in ... the attempt to reinterpret our familiar surroundings in the unfamiliar terms of" our encounter with other "culture[s] or historical period[s]" (1980, p360).

This experience is not unfamiliar to leaders and managers who work across national boundaries. It is a theme that Gundling et al. (2011) write about. It is exemplified in a quotation of a manager:

> In my 8 years abroad, I saw lots of new things that I had not seen at home. You learn to see your own country and yourself from an outsider's point of view. ... But when I talk to other Asians or Europeans, people ask me about my country with questions like "Why do you do things that way?" I get thousands of questions. When you are asked, it is difficult to answer. I wasn't ready.

Gundling et al. (2011) use another quotation from a leader to demonstrate that it is not necessarily the case that leaders and managers will learn through the experience of having their conventions disrupted. They may very well become defensive:

> I saw people who were prominent leaders at home who crumbled in global roles. Those who failed were inflexible, simply followed rules, and did what they were told to drive an existing process. They couldn't get the job done and couldn't understand why; they would raise their volume 5 times louder but the others still did not understand no matter how loudly these executives yelled or stamped their feet.

In working across difference one cannot rely on one's historical conventions, but managers or leaders on international assignments, who work across national boundaries and have no prior felt sense or embodied "know how" to work in an unfamiliar set of conventions, are in need of an existential form of education.

It is in this range of experiences of creative destruction that an existential form of education is crucial. For existentialism uses moments of creative destruction as bases for reflexive inquiry and for opening new worlds. Existentially, our own pre-conceptual understanding of the world is made explicit in times of creative destruction. It is in these moments that we are confronted not with the texts of experts but with our own taken-for-granted conventions for being in the world. And as we examine and critique our own taken-for-granted assumptions, we can open up the possibility of new ones. But we need to be able to work with the anxiety of destruction in order to do this. There is as yet no evidence that management education is moving in this way. Indeed, if anything, the management of management education seems to be working in the contrary way: not education as existential questioning but education for already packaged information; a production line logic of education.

Existential Education as the Basis for Experiencing Uncertainty as the Basis for Inquiry and Opening of New Opportunities

Existential education provides an educational framework for turning uncertainty into opportunity. "There where the danger is, so the saving power grows" says the poet Holderlin (cited by Heidegger 1993). Another interesting example of this is to be found in the Chinese word for crisis and opportunity: wēijī. Here we see how opposites are part of the same phenomenon. Dealing with danger is the condition of existential education.

But the bigger question is: how do we prepare students for an existential education which deals with the anxiety generated in a world of uncertainty?

The framework in which we do this is what we call an existential hermeneutic circle. The principle behind the hermeneutic circle is that embodied habits of practice are not developed in a sequential or linear way but in a circular way. In reflecting on the lived experience through which he became an entrepreneur, Steve Jobs said that he did not know in advance of becoming an entrepreneur that he was going to become an entrepreneur. Like Kierkegaard, he said that the "dots" of one's life cannot be joined in advance;

only in retrospect can the formation or pattern of the dots be seen. This is a central principle of hermeneutic education, where it is only through living that the parts and the whole form a pattern. Until then, there is a constant forward and backward movement in which habits of practice, identities, professional or otherwise, are being formed. In the forward and backward movement there is no manual, blueprint or theory to guide one. There is only what Kierkegaard calls the "dizziness" of anxiety, that dizziness in which one does not have a felt sense of habits until one has inhabited a way of doing things. Hermeneutically and existentially habits can develop in no other way. Lyotard brings this point out well when he says that a researcher:

> is in the position of a philosopher: the text he writes, the work he produces are not in principle governed by pre-established rules, and they cannot be judged according to a determining judgement, by applying familiar categories to the text or to the work. Those rules and those categories are what the work of art itself is looking for. The artist and the writer, then, are working without rules in order to formulate the rules of what will have been done (Lyotard 1984).

The Existential Uncertainty of the Professional

But we need to clarify one further point in relation to Lyotard: it is not only the rules that are created through the act of writing or research, the way of being of the artist and the writer; their identity only comes into being through the act of writing. Heidegger claims that it is not only the work of art that comes into being through the artist, but the artist that comes into being through the artwork. A painting by the Spanish painter Alex Alemany illustrates this. In a painting called "Algo Personal" (shown on the front cover), he paints himself painting himself. What he makes visible and what we hardly see in everyday life is the hidden hand which paints us while our hands are impressing themselves on the world. Furthermore, it was his own existential self-doubt that led him to see how he emerged as an artist through his artwork:

> My work is, essentially, the result of an inner dialogue in which I question my own existence that shall not be understood without my work. My life and my vocation are in a complete endless circle. More than half of the final result is indebted to the discussion between the artwork and I, with continuous criteria changes and a lot of doubts. In those reactions, are implicit the difficulty of recognizing myself and the impossibility of defining the difference between being and pretending.

What is crucial is that Alemany recognizes that he is in an existential self-doubt and is able to reflect within the circle of his existence on his way of existence. This is central to reflexivity from within a hermeneutic circle.

Management Uncertainty

This point applies not only to artists and writers but to leaders, managers and professionals in general. In the context of management, Linda Hill makes this point: "They [managers in her study] were responsible for the lives of others, yet they had to make decisions and act before they understood what they were supposed to do" (Hill 2003, p67). Indeed, it was only as they made decisions in the context of action that they became managers. This point is central to all existential philosophers. As Sartre, for example, claims, no one is born a hero or a coward, one becomes as such through the actions one performs. And one can slip and slide from one to the other. No hermeneutic circle is ever complete but is always in formation.

Existential hermeneutic education is the lived experience of working in the dizziness of the forward and backward movement of the development of effective habits of practice; of the development of practical wisdom or the virtuoso.

We have developed the hermeneutic circle into a practice used in the development of researchers, MBA students and in in-service professional education. The classroom or the workshop space has become a kind of agora in which we learn from each other through working with, rather than against, the uncertainty and vulnerability of developing the way of being a professional through being in the lived experience of becoming but never actually being a professional, a manager, a leader, a researcher or a teacher.

Creative Destruction of Education

And how do we open management schools and universities to those forms of inquiry which can work with the uncertainty of having no rules in advance? For they themselves are being creatively destroyed. As Fernando Flores (2000) has said: "Our school and university systems funnel young people into specific professions and occupations, encouraging investment in the expectation of lifelong careers." In the face of the creative destruction of the notion of a lifelong career, he says: "This inheritance is becoming an impediment to developing fully viable forms of working life. Radical reform is imperative." Concluding his point, he says: "Government investment in workforce education is too narrowly focused on re-skilling for new careers—a shallow response to the pace, scale and depth of change we face."

And we need to ask, are we as educators and researchers coping with the anxiety of creative destruction in ways that open up possibilities, that enable us to educate ourselves and students for a world of creative destruction? Our Western universities and societies in general are, to say the least, over-regulated. Can we get beyond this need for regulation and make do with regulations?

Existential Uncertainty and Career Paths

As Fernando Flores maintains, career paths are no longer built to last. While fifty years ago a career path may have been set for a lifetime, today, not only do we not have the assurance of staying at the same organization for a lifetime, but our careers themselves are morphed in unexpected and unanticipated ways:

> *The career, as an institution, is in unavoidable decline. The emergence of knowledge-based economies means the creative destruction of many time- honoured practices, including those at the core of traditional career structures. This change implies a fundamental shift in the attainable aspirations of the working majority, but so far it is little understood (Flores 2000).*

Bill Gates (2009) has expressed the sense of anxiety in being caught between the old and not yet of the new:

> *Perhaps the most widespread and personal anxiety is: "How will I fit into the evolving economy?" People are worried that their jobs will become obsolete, that they won't be able to adapt to new ways of working, that their children will get into deadened industries that will close down, or that economic upheaval will create wholesale unemployment, especially among older workers. These are legitimate concerns. Entire professions and industries will fade. But new one's will flourish. ... We can't predict what the new job categories will be. ... It isn't easy to prepare for the next century because it's almost impossible to guess the secondary effects of even the changes we foresee, much less of those we can't.*

Adding an acute existential element to this, Grove (1996) points out that we are alone in dealing with the breakdown in our careers. There are no public institutions to protect us from this. We are, as he maintains, on our own: "Who knows what your job will look like after cataclysmic changes sweep through your industry and engulf the company you work for? Who knows if your job will even exist and, frankly who will care besides you?"

References

Christensen, C. (2000) *The Innovator's Dilemma*. New York: Harper Collins.

Dreyfus, H. (1993) *Being-in-the-World: A Commentary on Heidegger's Being and Time, Division 1*. Boston: The MIT Press.

Fisher, P. (1999) *Still the New World*. Boston: Harvard University Press.

Flores, F. (2000) *Entrepreneurship and the Wired Life: Work in the wake of the career*. London: Demos.

Gates, B. (2009) *Business @ the Speed of Thought*. London: Grand Central Publishing.

Gellner, E. (1964) *Thought and Change*. London: Weidenfeld and Nicolson.

Grove, A. (1996) *Only the Paranoid Survive*. London: Harper Collins Publishers.

Gundling, E., Hogan, T. and Cvitkovich, K. (2011) *What Is Global Leadership? 10 key behaviours that define great global leaders*. Boston: Nicholas Brealey Publishing.

Heidegger, M. (1993) *Basic Writings: Revised and expanded edition*. (ed. David Krell). San Francisco: Harper.

Hill, L.A. (2003) *Becoming a Manager: How new managers master the challenges of leadership*. Boston: Harvard Business School Press.

Jager, B. (1983) Theorizing and the Elaboration of Place: Inquiry into Galileo and Freud. In: Giorgi, A., Barton, A. and Maes, C. (eds) *Duquesne Studies in Phenomenological Psychology, Volume 4* (pp153–80). Pittsburgh: Duquesne University Press.

Levine, R., Locke, C., Searls, D. and Weinberger, D. (2011) *The Clue Train Manifesto: The end of business as usual* (10th ed.). New York: Basic Books.

Lyotard, J.F. (1984) *The Postmodern Condition: A report on knowledge*. Minneapolis: University of Minnesota.

Meyerson, M. (1996) Everything I Thought I Knew About Leadership Was Wrong. *Fast Company*. April.

Ramo, J. (2010) *The Age of the Unthinkable*. New York: Back Bay Books.

Rorty, R. (1980) *Philosophy and the Mirror of Nature*. Oxford: Basil Blackwell.

Schumpeter, J. (1955) *Capitalism, Socialism and Democracy*. New York: Harper Torchbooks.

Segal, S. (1998) The Anxiety of Strangers and the Fear of Enemies. *Studies in Philosophy and Education*. Vol 17, No 4. pp271–82.

PART II
Introduction to Martin Heidegger's
Being and Time

Chapter 2
Heidegger's Existential Hermeneutic Phenomenology in Management

How to Make Sense of Heidegger's Existential Philosophy

Why introduce the work of Heidegger into the study of management? Indeed, why introduce the work of a writer who is explicitly philosophical into the study of management which has historically been and assumed itself to be both a science and a social science?

To address this question, we need to know what Heidegger means by philosophy. However, both the activity of philosophizing and the language that Heidegger uses to describe philosophy is challenging and, to many, obscure and even meaningless (Adorno 1996, Carnap 1959). Heidegger in *Being and Time* was well aware of this (1985, p63). The obscurity of his language was in fact intentional as he wanted to disrupt the way in which language functioned so as to open the space for disclosing the world in new ways (1985, p63). For, as he later came to believe, language is the house of being (1998, p217). To be deprived of our language—for example in migrating to a cultural context of another language or even in being unfamiliar with an organizational nomenclature—is to be deprived of our way of sense-making,[1] but inhabiting a language is also the basis of disclosing a new way of seeing the world and thus a new way of being at home in the world. Thus when we acquire a new language or an organizational nomenclature, the new way of being-in-the- world opens up to us.

Furthermore, Heidegger believed that even our own language can be deprived of its felt sense. This is existential anxiety at its height and this anxiety is not an illness but a condition for the world to be disclosed in new ways. It is depicted in the painting "The Scream" and the experience is vividly described

---

1   See Helen Keller, for example, cited in Part IV, Chapter 11 of this book.

in Sartre's book *Nausea*, where the narrator constantly chokes on the words he is using because he has lost the felt sense of the meaning of words:

> *Things have broken free from their names. They are there, grotesque, stubborn, gigantic, and it seems ridiculous to call them seats or say anything at all about them: I am in the midst of Things, which cannot be given names. Alone, wordless, defenceless, they surround me, under me, behind me, above me, … Words had disappeared, and with them the meaning of things, the methods of using them, the feeble landmarks which men have traced on their surface (1976, p11).*

As Ulrich Beck remarks, the shock and continuing aftershock of 9/11 represents the fragmentation of language: "September 11, 2001, will stand for many things in the history of humanity. Among these, no less for the failure, for the silence of language before such an event: 'war', 'crime', 'enemy', 'victory' and 'terror' — the terms melt in the mouth." Continuing his point regarding the way in which 9/11 was an assault on language, he says: "The notion, of 'enemy' is misleading. It stems from an imaginary world in which armies conquer or get conquered and then sign 'cease fires' and 'peace treaties'" (Beck 2002, p1).

He concludes his point by noting that we still do not have a language to describe the post-9/11 era:

> *This silence of words must finally be broken. We can no longer afford to keep quiet about this. If we could at least succeed in naming the silence of single ideas, to name the distance between idea and reality, to presume and to prudently break the bridges of understanding to the novel reality that stems from our civilizing actions, most likely not much, but something, could be gained (2002, p2).*

In the only remark that Ludwig Wittgenstein made about Heidegger, he identifies the relationship between the lived experience of dread and bumping up against the limits of language:

> *I can readily think what Heidegger means by Being and Dread. Man has the impulse to run up against the limits of language. Think, for example, of the astonishment that anything exists. This astonishment cannot be expressed in the form of a question, and there is also no answer to it. Everything which we feel like saying can, a priori, only be nonsense. Nevertheless, we do run up against the limits of language (Finch 1995, p63).*

Yet for Heidegger, it is precisely in this experience of the nonsense that emerges in bumping up against the limits of language that existential thinking begins. It's the beginning of opening the space for a new set of terms in which to make sense of the world.

Although not always in Heideggerian terms, in the above few paragraphs the three movements which dominate Heidegger's work have already been mentioned: common sense, disruption and disclosure. For Heidegger, philosophy is the disruption of common sense and this disruption is the basis for the possibility of the disclosure of new "worlds." I say possibility because at least two responses are possible in the disruption of common sense: a defensive retreat into common sense and what Heidegger calls a "destruction" (1985) of common sense. The latter is philosophy and the former is an attempt to hold on to what has been shattered.

In *Being and Time*, Heidegger does not use the phrase "common sense" and the notion of "disclosure." In his later work he does not use the word common sense but he does use the word disclosure. In his early work he uses the phrase "average everyday intelligibility" to describe common sense and the word "authenticity" to describe the space of disclosure of new worlds and possibilities. In *Being and Time*, he does use the word disruption.

Because the phrase "average everyday intelligibility" does not make immediate sense, I want to borrow a set of terms from a writer in marketing to act as a transition to the language of Heidegger as used in *Being and Time* (1985). Jean Marie Dru writes in a very broad and sketchy way about what he calls "convention, disruption and vision" (1996). I will use Dru's language as the basis upon which to introduce the activity of philosophizing as seen by Heidegger. The first two terms of Dru will be accepted but, because of the way in which the word "vision" is overused in organizational and management discourse, I want to replace it with the words disclosure or sight; insight, foresight and hindsight. Vision is a function of sight. For to have a vision is to *see or imagine* a possibility which is not yet actual or the case.

The architecture of Heidegger's way of thinking in *Being and Time* can be organized around this set of terms. Heidegger sees philosophy as a destruction of conventions that clear the way for disclosing new possibilities. To put this in the technical language of Heidegger: "Tradition takes what has come down to us and delivers it over to self-evidence; it blocks our access to those primordial 'sources' from which the categories and concepts handed down to us have been in part quite genuinely drawn" (1985, p43).

Heidegger wants to destroy the tradition or conventions until we arrive at the primal—or what I shall call aboriginal sources—so that new possibilities of ways of being can be disclosed. It is the basis of, as he puts it, staking out "positive possibilities" (1985, p44). It is only by destroying the so familiar conventions in which we are embedded that we create the space for disclosing new worlds. However, it is not that Heidegger wants the destruction of conventions for its own sake. Rather, it is under the conditions of changing circumstances, where the traditions bog us down in the past rather than allow for the disclosing of new possibilities, ways of doing things or worlds, where the tradition becomes a set of empty rituals that are mimicked, in the state of existential anxiety where we can no longer rely on the traditions of the past that a destruction of traditions emerges as a possibility. Thus, it is in the context of range of lived experiences that destruction opens up as a possibility. On the other hand, as we shall see for Heidegger, there is often a temptation to play it safe, become defensive and not change our way of doing things, thinking and being with the way in which circumstances change. This, as we shall see, is a more dangerous option than destruction for Heidegger. For on the latter view, we become wedded to a past that has been surpassed.

While it is tempting to say that for Heidegger destruction is a method or process, it is in fact more than both of these. It expresses itself as a way of being. It is experienced as a disruption of our habitual and conventional ways of doing things. In its most extreme case this disruption is the experience of existential anxiety. In less intense cases, disruption functions like a Gestalt switch in which our way of being attuned undergoes a shift from working with equipment to examining equipment as an object. In the same way conventions and disclosures are ways of being. They are not just detached ideas but embodied scripts that are encountered in the ways in which we do things. It is impossible to fully explain how they are ways of being until the phenomenon of ways of being has been explained, but the framework for making sense of the notion of a way of being itself needs to be established first. We will circle back to the notion of way of being once we have established the basis for making sense of it. If the reader is prepared to accept this, we are already in the circle of Heidegger's thought. And so the logic of Heidegger's thought will itself be explained in terms of a hermeneutic circle in which we continuously circle back to the same thought, but hopefully at a clearer, more detailed and nuanced level.

It should therefore be noted that this chapter will be moving from what is hopefully clear and self-evident to what is more nuanced, less self-evident but very important in understanding the philosophy of Heidegger. The chapter will also be developed in the form of a re-iterative cycle in which a continuous return to the same set of concepts or ways of being will be made in, hopefully, more nuanced ways.

Dru as Laying the Groundwork for a Turn to Heidegger

Because the book is primarily intended for a professional audience and for research and education within management, I will assume that the most self-evident place to start is from within the field of management. I shall be using a text within the field of marketing to start the hermeneutic process of moving forward and returning to the thought of Heidegger. The work with which I shall begin is a book by Jean-Marie Dru called *Disruption: Overturning Conventions and Shaking up the Marketplace* (1996). It is important to note that the word "disruption" and even the way in which Dru uses the word disruption cuts across many fields within management. For example, in the context of economics, Joseph Schumpeter (1955) wrote about creative destruction which is focused on capitalism or the free market as a dynamic process that constantly destroys and creates itself. The free market constantly destroys the conventions of industries and businesses and discloses new ways of doing things—as, for example, online retail is constantly destroying the conventions of buying and selling in a store and disclosing the possibility of exchange online—or online education is destroying conventional forms of education and disclosing new possibilities.

Clayton Christensen (2000) has written on the way in which technology creatively destroys organizations and forms of economic life. Fernando Flores (2000) writes on the way in which careers are being creatively destroyed. And Nietzsche wrote on the way in which the death of God creatively destroyed forms of life in general. While Heidegger did not write about creativity *per se*, he did call his philosophical methodology destruction (1985) and he did see destruction as the basis for disclosing new worlds and possibilities. Indeed, both Nietzsche and Heidegger articulated the challenges to be faced in a world of creative destruction. And so it is not unreasonable to begin a text on Heidegger for managers with a work that deals with the way in which new possibilities emerge out of practices of disruption.

There are three moments to Dru's (1996) dynamic logic of disruption: convention, disruption and vision. He believed that it is through the disruption of existing conventions that new visions are disclosed.

According to Dru, conventions consist of the background scripts which allow us to get on with the tasks of everyday practical coping without having to think about them. Conventions allow us to do things such as drive cars, sit in lecture theatres, manage a business, go to the movies, and so on, without having to think about how to conduct ourselves in each of these contexts.

It is because we do not have to think of them while performing acts based on them that they are in the background, rather than the foreground, of our attention. In the context of management, there are conventions for managing, leading and following. They enable the managers to perform the activities of managing without having to think about managing while they are managing, leading while they are leading and following while they are following. Conventions thus allow us to cope without having to think about our conventions for coping, As Dru says: "Although conventions are everywhere, they are generally hard to see. These are things that we don't even notice because they are so familiar. ... Depending on the case, we will talk about unquestioned assumptions, good old common sense, or the current rules of the game" (1996, p56).

Conventions open and close possibilities. They allow us to see the world in certain ways and not in other ways. For example, the conventions of finance in management allow the finance manager to see things in one way and not in another way; someone who has been habituated in marketing will see the world in one but not another way; similarly, a manager with an engineering background will see the world in one but not another way. In *Reframing Organizations*, Bolman and Deal (2003) call these "frames." Our frames open up and close down possibilities. And because they exist in the background of our attention, we do not even begin to know that our way of seeing is shaped and limited by a set of frames or conventions. We assume that the way in which we see the world is the natural way in which to see the world.

Although this is not expressed by Dru, for Heidegger, it is important to say that we are embedded in conventions and frames for seeing things. We are also embedded in habits of practice and ultimately in existence itself. We are hardly ever free of being embedded in conventions, frames and habits of practice. But we are never free of being embedded in existence. How we are always embedded in the latter and not always in the former will be explained through certain kinds of disruption in Heidegger: the de-familiarization that arises through the anxiety of not being able to make sense of our world. Anxiety distances us from our familiar ways of being in the world (our conventions) such that we come face to face with existence itself.

Dru too sees disruption as central to seeing our own ways of seeing. It takes an act of disruption to see our own frame or set of conventions, to question them and to open up new possibilities. Dru sees the act of disruption in terms of the notion of de-familiarization of our familiar conventional way of seeing the world. When we are estranged from our conventions through acts such as surprise, perplexity or disbelief, we stand at an emotional distance from our beliefs such that we begin to see what we had taken for granted. Dru maintains that the "idea of viewing the familiar in a different manner" is achieved by making the "unstrange strange, the familiar unfamiliar" (1996, p69). The act of de-familiarization emotionally distances us from our familiar conventions such that we can see them and question them. We cannot do this when we are simply embedded in them. The act of questioning our conventions paves the way for seeing new possibilities or disclosing new worlds.

Although Dru does not acknowledge the philosophical ancestry of the notion of de-familiarization, it has a long history. It is expressed by, for example, Richard Rorty, who maintains that "The attempt to edify (ourselves or others) may consist in … the attempt to reinterpret our familiar surroundings in the unfamiliar terms of our encounter with other culture[s] or historical period[s]" (1980, p360). The process of de-familiarization through disruption, for Rorty, is called re-description, which takes "us out of our old selves by the power of strangeness, aids us in becoming new beings" (Rorty 1980).

A version of the same idea may be found in the work of Spinosa et al. (1997), who demonstrate how disruption of a paradigm is the basis for disclosing new worlds. They focus on our "ability to appreciate and engage in the ontological skill of disclosing new ways of being" (1997, p1). This ability, they claim, relies on becoming "sensitive to anomalies that enable us to change the style of our culture" (1997, p181).

None of the authors above make reference to the Heideggerian proposition that disruption through de-familiarization is an existential experience. It is not only a cognitive or intellectual activity, but one that is conducted with one's whole being. An author who allows us to make clear sense of this existential form of disruption is Douglas-Mullen, who in a work on Kierkegaard says: "One feature peculiar to humans is the ability to detach ourselves from our lives and see ourselves as if we were 'just one of them.' For some of us the thought of this comes more often and stays longer. This type of person is described as 'reflective,' 'self-conscious,' 'neurotic,' 'ironic,' 'pensive,' 'deep' etc." (1981, p11).

It is important to note that the form of detachment being referred to by Douglas-Mullen is not the detachment of the positivist scientist who stands at a separate, neutral and objective distance from the subject matter of the research. It is the activity of experiencing oneself as at a distance from one's own set of conventions so that we see ourselves, as Douglas-Mullen says, as "just one of them." It is the experience of watching oneself in the activity of doing things, the experience of being detached from one's own beliefs or sense-making habits. It is experienced as existential anxiety. And thus we begin to lay the grounds ffor one of the central theses of this book; namely that reflection is a form of experience; not so much experience in the form of a sensory but an existential experience. For the experience of being detached from what we are involved in is a lived experience and it is an existential experience—one that defines itself in terms of an emotional detachment as when a person is preoccupied or "not there." This being "not there" for Heidegger is not an undynamic state. It is a state of being drawn, disclosing the world in new ways. It is the space of insight, foresight and hindsight.[2]

It is also the state of being in existential questioning. For existential questioning is that kind of question which involves mood, body and cognition. It is this state of detachment that, for Heidegger, allows us to question our heritage or history. Heidegger calls this kind of questioning "destruction," which, as Samuel Ijsseling maintains, "is ultimately oriented toward trying to direct attention to the unthought [das Ungedachte] in thinking and to the unsaid in saying. … The unthought or the unsaid can be that which was never expressly thematized although it was presupposed in [philosophical] thinking and which, indeed, can be thought and said" (1982, p15).

But for Heidegger destruction applies not only to thought and saying but to habits of practice and conventions for doing as well. It is the unstated ways of doing things that is the subject matter of the form of questioning that arises in the disruption of destruction. It is interesting to note that Plato, in *The Republic*, also called philosophy an activity of destruction. However, it seems that he did not go beyond destruction as a logical operation that worked through contradiction, whereas Heidegger sees destruction as an existential act in which our very way of doing things, our conventions and habits of practice are in question.

For Heidegger, the link between questioning and disruption is crucial. Questioning occurs in experiences of disruption.

---

2   It is expressed technically by Heidegger (1968) in the following way: "What withdraws from us, draws us along by its very withdrawal, whether or not we become aware of it immediately, or not at all. Once we are drawn into the withdrawal, we are drawing toward what draws, attracts us by its withdrawal. And once we, being so attracted, are drawing towards what draws us, our essential nature already bears the stamp of 'drawing towards.' As we are drawing towards what withdraws, we ourselves are pointers pointing toward it."

Re-describing Dru in Terms of Heidegger's *Being and Time*: The Hermeneutic Circle of Understanding

Heidegger does not simply assume the notion of convention. He seeks to explain it and to locate philosophizing in relationship to it. His explanation of it is in terms of the notion of a hermeneutic circle. Convention, habit or what Heidegger calls "average everyday" (1985) ways of being take the form of a hermeneutic circle. We exist within the hermeneutic circle of conventions. They are neither outside nor inside of us but we become who we are through being a part of the conventions. We are beings in convention.

The notion of a hermeneutic circle plays a number of roles in Heidegger. In general, it can be said that the hermeneutic circle both describes what it means to be human and is also a philosophical way ("methodology") for inquiring into what it means to be human. Human existence takes the form of a hermeneutic circle. This is because understanding of existence is, if not *the* central dimension of existence, *a* central dimension of existence, that is, understanding of existence is itself part of what it means to exist and is thus not something that the human does from a position detached and independent from existence: "An entity for which, as Being-in-the-world, its Being is itself an issue, has, ontologically a circular strcuture" (1985, p195).

Not only is it from within the circle of existence that understanding occurs, but understanding is a dimension of what it means to be human. So the hermeneutic circle here is: to understand existence we need to understand that understanding existence is itself an existential dimension of what it means to exist. Furthermore, it is through staying or dwelling in the notion of this hermeneutic circle that we work through the fact that understanding existence is a central dimension of existence.

The Existential Hermeneutic Circle of Understanding

Understanding is not primarily a theoretical activity. It embraces all activity. In all activities sense-making is occurring. Thus in our everyday practical coping we are always making sense. To catch a bus, work, manage or lead are forms of sense-making. For if we did not have a sense of what these practices meant, we would not be able to perform them. Thus our everyday know-how or coping with the world presupposes a form of sense-making. Furthermore, everyday sense-making is our historically primary mode of sense-making. It is through the way in which we get involved in the world that we make sense of the world.

For example, it is by being cared for that we learn the meaning of care. It is by playing or working that we learn the meaning of work. We develop what Heidegger calls a familiarity with, an average everyday understanding, an understanding of the conventions of our society through this form of sense-making, that is, sense-making through involvement in our activities.

The next two levels of understanding are closer to what we would call objective and theoretical forms of understanding. Heidegger maintains that when something we are using breaks down or is absent, it becomes an object to which our focus is drawn. Instead of using it, we think about it. If it is something that we can repair or replace, we return to the state of being involved in the world. If, however, we cannot continue to use it, it becomes an object that we seek to make sense of in an explicit way. It is here that science and even traditional philosophical reasoning emerges. For science is a focus on the properties of things. Examining the properties of things or the casual relationships between things is a different form of understanding than the form of sense-making that occurs in using things. In the latter, we develop a felt sense of the item of equipment. In the former case, we stand at a distance and have a cognitive and representational understanding of the thing. The same point applies when we try to understand things philosophically in terms of, say, the essence of things.

The third and fourth forms of understanding are hermeneutic forms of understanding. The third form is making sense of the sense that we make of the world, that is, making sense of our conventions that allow for everyday practical coping.

This is followed by the fourth form of understanding: making sense of the fact that we are sense-makers. This is making sense of the fact of our ways of being-in-the-world, including the notion that understanding the world is part of being-in-the-world, and thus what needs to be understood when focusing on being-in-the-world. It is not just that we understand things or objects or even ourselves; but we need to understand the relation between understanding and that which is understood—this is an essential dimension of being-in-the-world.

The third form Heidegger calls a hermeneutic *existentiell* form of understanding and the fourth form is what he calls an existential understanding. The difference between the two is understanding of existence in a particular time, place, set of conventions and average everyday understanding and the existential is understanding of the conditions of human existence in general. Adding a further layer of complexity, the hermeneutic circle of convention and the hermeneutic circle of existence are not independent of each other but are nestled inside each other—or, more specifically, the hermeneutics of convention is nestled inside the hermeneutic circle of existence—like the currents of the ocean.[3]

It is the third and fourth terms that are hermeneutic. In both cases it is from within existence that existence is understood. In the third case, it is from within our conventions that we are examining our conventions. In the fourth case, it is from within being-in-the-world that we examine being-in-the-world; all circles within circles. This is in contrast to a traditional scientific and philosophical approach which is focused on understanding things from the spectator's or outsider's point of view. Hermeneutic understanding is understanding from within and not without; an on-the-court rather than in-the-stands perspective.

As the layers of the hermeneutic circle are complex, challenging and strange, it may sound offensive to the conventions in which the history of Western thought are embedded. This is why Heidegger spends much time in *Being and Time* "destroying" (1985) the history of Western thought. It is such a destruction that paves the way for the emergence of the different layers of the hermeneutics of existence. While Heidegger devotes much space in *Being and Time* to this destruction, in the next chapter I will summarize it briefly as the basis upon which to develop the hermeneutics of existence.

References

Adorno, T. (1996) *The Jargon of Authenticity*. London: Routledge and Kegan Paul.

Beck, U. (2002) The Silence of Words and the Political Dynamics in the World Risk Society. *Logos*. Vol 4. Fall. pp1–18.

Bolman, G. and Deal T.E. (2003) *Reframing Organizations: Artistry, choice, and leadership*. San Francisco: Jossey-Bass.

Carnap, R. (1959) The Elimination of Metaphysics through Logical Analysis of Language. In: Ayer, A.J. (ed.) *Logical Positivism*. New York: Free Press.

---

3   Heidegger does not like metaphors at this level and calls the relationship between the existential and *existenitell* an "ontological difference." However, for our purposes there is no point in opening up this phrase.

Christensen, C. (2000) *The Innovator's Dilemma*. New York: Harper Collins.

Douglas-Mullen, J. (1981) *Kierkegaard's Philosophy: Self-Deception and Cowardice in the Present Age*. New York: A Mentor Book.

Dru, J. (1996) *Disruption: Overturning Conventions and Shaking up the Market Place*. New York: John Wiley & Sons.

Finch, H.L. (1995) *Wittgenstein*. Dorset: Element Books.

Flores, F. (2000) *Entrepreneurship and the Wired Life: Work in the wake of the career*. London: Demos.

Grafton, A. et al. (2010) *The Classical Tradition*. Boston: Harvard University Press.

Heidegger, M. (1998) *Pathmarks*. Cambridge: Cambridge University Press.

Heidegger, M. (1985) *Being and Time*. Oxford: Basil Blackwell.

Heidegger, M. (1968) *What Is Called Thinking?* New York: Harper Torchbooks.

Ijsseling S. (1982) Heidegger and the Destruction of Ontology. *Man and World*. Vol 15. pp3–16.

Rorty, R. (1980) *Philosophy and the Mirror of Nature.* Oxford: Basil Blackwell.

Sartre, J.P. (1976) *Nausea*. Harmondsworth: Penguin Books.

Schumpeter, J. (1955) *Capitalism, Socialism and Democracy*. New York: Harper Torchbooks.

Spinosa, C., Flores, F. and Dreyfus, H. (1997) *Disclosing New Worlds: Entrepreneurship, democratic action, and the cultivation of solidarity*. Cambridge, MA: MIT Press.

Chapter 3
The Hermeneutic Circle
of Existence

The history of Western thought, according to Heidegger (1985), from Plato (1968) to positivist science, has "forgotten" that underlying a philosophy of essences or a science of objects is a network of relationships. If we want to understand the nature of our world, we need to include and not exclude the range of ways of being in relationship to the world. In other words, to understand our world, it is no good to simply study essences or objects that are supposedly independent and "out there," separate and at an objective distance in the world. We need to include in our examination the way in which we stand in relation to the "essences," "objects," network of items of equipment or the conventions that shape the way we experience the world. Placing ourselves, our relationship to the world, in the inquiry is expressed in the phrase the "hermeneutics of existence." For the hermeneutics of existence means the way in which we examine or make sense of existence is not simply by understanding things out there but by including our ways of relating as part of the ways in which we exist. One of the dimensions of hermeneutics is that we come what Heidegger calls "face to face" (1985, p233) with our own way of existing. To understand our world is to come face to face with our way of existing.

The Relational Nature of Existence

Understanding not only objects or essences that are out there but understanding the network of relationships within which we stand to objects is challenging for a Western way of thinking that is based on a logic of the distinction between observer and observed, subject and object, philosopher and essence. This is complicated by the fact that, according to Heidegger, the ways in which we stand in relationship to the world constitute entities either as items of equipment to be used or objects of observation to be analyzed. Neither objects nor items of equipment are things in themselves but are constructed through the kinds of relationships we have: for example, when we are using an entity, it is an item of equipment, and when we are observing it, it becomes an object. When we are using an item of equipment, it is not an "it" or object that we are thinking about. It becomes an "it" or thing to be observed when we stand at a distance from it such that we examine it. Observation constitutes it as an object. Platonic contemplation constitutes it as essences.

It is interesting that the quantum physics of Heisenberg came close to the Heideggerian point when, in terms of his uncertainty principle, he maintained that the observer affects and constitutes the observed. As we shift our position the object shifts its nature. We cannot get outside of being in relationship to see the thing in itself and thus the relationship between the observer and observed are in a dynamic interplay with each other.

Heisenberg does not go on to highlight this "relationship" as a central theme of study but Heidegger does. Heidegger's central contribution to the study of being or what is, is to highlight neither the observer nor the observed; neither the subject nor the object but the *context* of relationship in which they are present to each other. Whereas Descartes saw both subjects and objects, he did not focus on the context in which they are in relationship to each other. Indeed, he did not seem to see that they were situated in a context and that the separation between them is itself a form of context or relationship.

The human being is "always and already" (Heidegger 1985) in context and relationship. An interesting way of understanding this is in a distinction made by the anthropologist Hall (1976). He pointed out that, in general, Western societies tend to be what he calls "low context" rather than "high context" societies. Whereas low context societies are concerned with what can be observed or represented, high context societies are concerned with the context in which observer and observed stand in relationship to each other. The latter see entities in context.

Heidegger is a thinker who wants to return ways of making sense of being embedded in a context to Western ways of thinking. Existence is contextual and relational for Heidegger. Average everyday ways of doing things or conventions, as described above, are contextual. So too are habits of practice. Human beings are contextual. In this sense it can be argued that culture is neither a subject nor an object, but a contextual phenomenon. For culture and conventions describe the way we are embedded in a way of doing things; a relationship between being and world.

Hermeneutics as Referential Wholes

Heidegger (1985) gives the relational notion of existence two names. The first is being-in-the-world and the second is a German word, *Da-sein*, which means being-there. The human being is "always and already" in the world. It is always in and part of what Heidegger calls a "referential whole." It is always in context. Heidegger hyphenates both phrases to indicate that being and world, while not the same as each other, are not simply other to each other. They are part of the same phenomenon.[1] For example, artist and artwork are, for Heidegger, both part of the phenomenon of art (1971). Leader and follower are part of the phenomenon of "leadership." Researcher and researched are part of the phenomenon of research. And put in more metaphysical terms, subject and object are not simply separate from each other but separation is a form of being in relationship to the world; so too is what Homi Bhaba and Martin Buber call the sphere "between" "man and man" (Buber, quoted in Hodes 1998) and colonizer and colonized (Bhaba 1990). These phenomena, or ways of being-in-the-world, are all ways of existing.

This point can be generalized further to say that any practice, habit, role or profession is a way of being-there or being-in-the-world and that to understand our habits or our professional practices, we, as beings-in-the world, need to become attuned to these practices hermeneutically and as ways of existing. To understand existence hermeneutically is to understand the relationship between the whole and the parts. Heidegger's favorite example is that of art. He claims that we only become an artist through engaging in an artwork, driver through driving or a professional through engaging in the profession. The human's way of being as a driver is part of what Heidegger calls the referential whole of driving. Identities, habits, professions and ways of doing things are always given only through forming part of what he calls a "referential whole" (1985). The latter describes a relationship between entities such that they refer to each other, co-constitute each other and the whole of which they are parts.

The Experience of a Room as an Example of the Hermeneutics of Existence

Heidegger gives the following example of a referential whole which he contrasts with cognitive knowledge:

---

1   They cannot be reduced to what Descartes would call "clear and distinct" ideas.

My encounter with the room is not such that I first take in one thing after another and put together a manifold of things in order then to see a room. Rather, I primarily see a referential whole ... from which the individual pieces of furniture and what is in the room stand out. Such an environment of the nature of a closed referential whole is at the same time distinguished by a specific familiarity. The ... referential whole is grounded precisely in familiarity, and this familiarity implies that the referential whole is well-known (quoted in Dreyfus 1993, p103).

I would like to emphasize that in the above quotation Heidegger ends by saying that "the referential whole is grounded precisely in familiarity," which is another way of saying that the whole that is constitutive of a hermeneutic circle is grounded in familiarity, that is, familiarity is the basis upon which the parts are integrated into a whole. However, familiarity does not emerge directly or in one movement. Familiarity emerges out of the way in which the being of the human engages with the parts of the room—the aspects of the furniture, slowly but surely. Familiarity with the parts enables the human to develop a sense of the room as a whole and the whole allows the human to understand the place of each of the parts in the whole.

The Existential Significance of Familiarity

Because the word "familiarity" may sound theoretically nebulous, it is worth bringing out the significance of it in organizational studies. Karl Weick (1993) provides us with the example through which to do this. It is in his now very often quoted analysis of Maclean's description of the Mann Gulch fire. A group of firefighters from different regions across the state of Montana were dropped near to Mann Gulch in order to put out a fire. The fire took an unexpected turn which caught the men by surprise. In addition, what also caught them by surprise was the leader of the group's instruction. He instructed them to "throw away your tools!" (Weick 1993, p226) and burn a fire around them through which to protect themselves. In the context of the specific form of fire at Mann Gulch, none of the firefighters trusted the advice of the leader. They thought that he had "gone nuts" and so, rather than listening to him, they ran away. With the exception of the leader, who did build a fire wall around himself, all perished in the fire.

The point from a Heideggerian perspective is that although they were all technically competent at fighting fires, as a group or team, they had no familiarity with each other. Weick alludes to this point:

What holds organization in place may be more tenuous than we realize. The recipe for disorganization in Mann Gulch is not all that rare in everyday life. The recipe reads, Thrust people into unfamiliar roles, leave some key roles unfilled, make the task more ambiguous, discredit the role system, and make all of these changes in a context in which small events can combine into something monstrous. Faced with similar conditions, organizations that seem much sturdier may also come crashing down (Weick 1993, p220).

The word "unfamiliar" in Weick's quotation resonates strongly with Heidegger's notion of familiarity as the basis of a referential whole or what Weick wants to understand as an organizational structure. Without a sense of familiarity, a whole cannot be formed. Furthermore, this sense of familiarity can only be gained in action, through interacting and being involved with each other. It cannot be formed through detached and theoretical analysis.

They did not know each other and so they had no basis upon which to either trust or mistrust each other. The consequence was that they had no conviction or felt sense of the leader's instruction in the face of the surprising turn of the fire. Indeed, they slipped into a state of existential anxiety, where they experienced their very existence to be under threat: "the moment quickly turns existential. If I am no longer a firefighter, then who am I? With the fire bearing down, the only possible answer becomes, An endangered person in a world where it is every man for himself" (Weick 1993, p221).

They did not form a referential whole that could be called a team. Indeed, if we want to keep with existential language, they were more like what Sartre calls a "series" than a team. A "series" for Sartre is a group of people who have no sense of familiarity with each other. Familiarity is the glue which holds a whole together.

The problem with most of the history of philosophy and science, according to Heidegger, is that it has unknowingly abstracted objects from their familiar context and assumed them to be natural beings to be studied as objects in themselves. This was in fact the case with the firefighting team that Weick describes. Each of the firefighters was abstracted from the familiarity of their referential context (their home base) and placed in an unfamiliar context. They became decontextualized individual firefighters who had no established familiar relationship with each other and were nothing more than instruments to be deployed to fight fires. The underlying assumption being that familiarity in context is not an important dimension. Heidegger again wants to argue that familiarity is of ultimate importance. It is the basis of developing a felt sense of the world; the basis of inhabiting a world. It is the basis of knowing one's way about, recognizing and trusting others. As Zygmunt Bauman, a hermeneutic sociologist, has observed, familiarity is the basis for making sense of the world. Take away familiarity and the basis for sense-making is disrupted, creating a hermeneutic or sense-making crisis (Bauman 1990).

It is only when we abstract beings from their referential whole, or workshop context, that they become objects to be examined, observed, analyzed, represented. It is here that people become "human resources" and in fact that the environment itself becomes a resource. In these latter cases our attunement or concern becomes that of the objective and calculating form of the rational[2] scientist rather than the involved artisan. It is only as an abstraction from within the context of the whole that a driver can be torn apart from the act of driving. It is again only as an abstraction from the context of being a professional that a professional can be torn apart from engagement in the profession. This is what occurs, for example, in psychometric tests which want to evaluate the personality of a professional. Here the social scientist becomes an observer and tester and the person becomes an object to be examined, analyzed and written up in a report. Heidegger is not concerned with the (internal) world of the professional or the objective rules of the profession, but with the habit or way of being of a professional practice in which both the rules and internal world are situated.

Heidegger's concern is not with the "object" abstracted, but with getting to the context or referential whole through which the parts are integrated into a whole and in which the whole defines the relationship between the parts. Heidegger uses the notion of a "referential whole" (1985) to explain the notion of hermeneutics. A referential whole is a relationship between the parts and the whole in which the parts and the whole co-constitute each other. The parts are parts only in relationship to each other. And the network of relationship between the parts forms the whole. The whole in turn situates the parts in relationship to each other.

This idea is not new to Heidegger but is part of the history of hermeneutics (Palmer 1969). What Heidegger adds is that hermeneutics defines the nature of existence. For Heidegger hermeneutics not only applies to texts, but human existence takes the form of a hermeneutic circle. As we shall soon see,

---

2   Please note that I am not maintaining that all rationality is calculative. Following Pendlebury (1990), there is a distinction between calculative and constitutive rationality.

Heidegger uses the notion of a workshop as a form of a hermeneutic circle of existence. But all contextual understanding, as I will argue, takes the form of a hermeneutic circle. A context is a referential whole; so too is a network of relationships. And thus Heidegger adds that because the human being is a being that is "always and already" in relationship, its existence takes the form of a hermeneutic circle.

There are several dimensions to understanding being-in-in-the-world as a hermeneutic circle or referential whole. I shall begin with an understanding of convention or "average everyday" being as a hermeneutic circle, then open the space of inquiring into the hermeneutic circle of existence and then develop an understanding of the hermeneutic circle as a form of understanding of both the hermeneutics of convention and the hermeneutics of existence.

Workshops as Hermeneutic Contexts

Heidegger maintains that the world is not made up primarily of either objects or items of equipment but contexts of relationships. We are never not in relationship: if we are managing we are always in the context of a relationship. Leading occurs in the context of a relationship. Philosophy, science and research in general occurs in the context of a relationship—even separation is a form of relationship.

The primary context of relationship in which the human being exists and makes sense of its world is in the context of what Heidegger calls a "workshop" (1985). Heidegger understands a "workshop" as what he calls a "referential whole." The parts in a workshop are only parts in relationship to each other and the way in which the parts stand in relationship to each other form the referential whole, called a workshop. Thus for Heidegger a hammer is a hammer only in relation to nails, which are as such only for joining things together in, say, the form of a chair or table, which is as such only as something to be eaten or worked upon. All of these are as such only in relation to the human being who is conducting these activities. Together, this network of relationships constitutes both the whole and the parts of the workshop. Thus the parts are constituted through the whole and the whole is constituted through the parts.

It is important to note that the human being is itself part of the referential whole and does not stand outside of it. For it becomes who it is through the way in which it is involved in the workshop. It always is only in relation to the workshop or context of activities within which it is involved. Thus the very idea of eating on a table is a convention that is formed through the referential whole.

Furthermore, the human being inhabits this convention without even knowing that it is inhabiting it. For example, as a child in the "Western" world, we learn to eat by sitting on a chair at a table. In other parts of the world, we learn to eat by sitting down and eating with our hands.

As already indicated, the phenomenon of art, of driving and of professional are all names for referential wholes. The artist and artwork are part of the referential whole called "art." Each is established in relationship to the other. The driver and car driven are parts of the referential whole called driving. The professional and the work of a professional are part of the referential whole called "profession." In a similar way a "habit" or context is always a network of relationships called a referential whole. The identity of a person is always a part of a referential whole. There is no identity outside of a referential whole. Indeed, there is no person outside of a referential whole for a person is always being-in-context (hyphens indicating the insuperability of being and context)

The Hermeneutics of Conceptual and Pre-conceptual Understanding

For Heidegger our primary understanding of the referential whole is not given through explicit deliberation about the workshop but by dwelling in the workshop. For example, we learn what a home is by dwelling in the home. We learn what a school is by being at school. More generally, we learn about our and other cultures by being in the culture. Heidegger insists that the understanding that emerges out of our way of being in context is not a cognitive understanding but an embodied understanding based on a sense of familiarity through involvement in the context. The notion of familiarity is significant for Heidegger. For it is as we become familiar with a referential whole that we develop an inhabited and embodied understanding of it.

Heidegger calls this pre-cognitive understanding gained through the familiarity of involvement a pre-thematic or pre-conceptual understanding. He adds that this non-cognitive inhabited and embodied understanding cannot be reduced to or explained in terms of a cognitive understanding. On the contrary, cognitive understanding takes place from within the contextual understanding of the referential whole. We do not, for example, learn caring through thinking about it but by being involved in it. We only begin to examine or think about the meaning of caring much later. Our primary understanding of it emerges out of being cared for. Similarly, our sense of home emerges through being at home; only later will we think about the notion of home.

Thus our conceptual understanding is formed through our pre-conceptual understanding. For example, we learn the conventions for managing, organizing, order, controlling and leading in the context of, say, school without even being aware that we are learning them. They form part of the background or hidden curriculum, part of our pre-conceptual understanding. This pre-conceptual understanding will form the basis of our conceptual understanding at a later date. For example, when at a later stage in life, we become curious about the notion of managing and look it up in a dictionary, textbook or even do a study of managing, our explicit understanding of it will be guided by this implicit pre-conceptual understanding that emerged out of our way of being involved at school. Often without even knowing it, our conceptual understanding is shaped by our pre-conceptual understanding.

Understanding our pre-conceptual understanding is itself a hermeneutic circle. This is because we are circling back to the pre-conceptual understanding that shapes our understanding. Many would understand this as a vicious circle, but Heidegger sees understanding as operating in this way: understanding our way of understanding. It is reminiscent of a Platonic notion of re-collecting or re-connecting to the pre-conceptual understanding with the proviso that for Heidegger there is no metaphysical understanding that shapes our understanding. Understanding is always historical.

However, not only is our pre-conceptual understanding shaped by our involvements so too is our behavior and the way in which we relate to people. It is the basis of our practical coping, as Dreyfus calls it. Practical coping refers to knowing our way around a workshop, context or referential whole without having to think about our way around the workshop. We can move from one to another activity in our world without having to think about the activity of moving about.

The Hermeneutics of Convention

Thus our conventions for doing things are shaped by our pre-conceptual understanding. Furthermore, these conventions take on the form of a referential whole. We do not stand outside of the referential whole but are part of the referential whole of a network of conventions. For the most part, we do not realize we are part of a network of conventions or referential wholes because these are in the background of our attention. We get on with the tasks of everyday living without thinking about our way of getting on with these tasks. If we were to think about our way of getting on with the tasks of everyday living, we would not be able to get on with the tasks of everyday living. Just like driving a car, they are embodied and inhabited. And this is what enables and allows us to perform these activities.

For Heidegger a workshop or the items in the workshop are not primarily physical objects but items of use that are defined in relationship to other items of use. It is the way in which things are used that shapes the form of these things. And it is the network of relationships of use that form themselves into a whole that is called a workshop or set of conventions. The physical building that houses a workshop is constituted through the network of the relationship between parts and whole.

Unfortunately, the history of Western thought has taken the physical appearance or the representational idea of a thing in itself to be real, or that which is to be destroyed, and not soon that the physical appearance or the object emerges out of its place in a referential whole.

Being-in-the-world does not mean physical being of one thing in another. It means being in a referential whole or being in a context.

Authentic and Inauthentic Ways of Responding to Disturbance

It seems that, for Heidegger, the human being can respond in two ways when coming face to face with its average everydayness. In the horror of anxiety[3] it can either attempt to lose itself in average everydayness by clinging to the now explicit principles or beliefs which characterize its way of being-in-the-world, or it can "resolutely" deconstruct or destroy its average everydayness by questioning the taken-for-grantedness of this way of being: "Anxiety both motivates falling into in authenticity—a cover up of Da-sein's true structure—and undermines this cover-up, thus making authenticity possible" (Dreyfus 1993, p313). Expanding on this, Dreyfus says: "fleeing is inauthentic

---

3 The horror of anxiety can be seen in the claim that people would rather involve themselves in the confrontations with war than experience the terror of anxiety. Here is an example: "One soldier, describing his first panic attack in 1944 almost forty years later, could still recall the time of day and location of the attack, what he was doing at the moment, and who he was with. Five months before, he had participated in one of the first troop waves to land on the Normandy beaches on D-Day. He said the anxiety he felt landing on the beaches was mild compared to the sheer terror of one of his bad panic attacks. Given the choice between the two, he would gladly again volunteer to land in Normandy" (Sheehan 1983, pp41–2). Putting this in analytical terms, Tillich has said: "Anxiety strives to become fear, because fear can be met by courage" (Tillich 1979, p47).

Da-sein's response to its sense of its unsettled way of being. … But this same … anxiety that reveals it could equally well reveal Da-sein and its world as an exciting manifestation of Da-sein's finitude" (1993, p317).

It must be emphasized that anxiety does nothing more than bring the human being face to face with everydayness as something which has never been seen before. As Heidegger says, "Anxiety merely brings one into the mood for a possible resolution" (1985, pp231, 394, 344). This seeing of something that has not been seen before does not of itself lead to an interrogation of everydayness. It can lead to a blind love of everydayness (as I hope to show is the case with respect to nationalism or anything that defines itself in terms of the idea of a "love of one's own"). Something more is needed to interrogate everydayness. Heidegger calls this "resoluteness." This is a standing firm in the numbness, paralyses and powerlessness of anxiety. Resoluteness is a letting oneself be rather than a resisting of anxiety. Its archetype, for Heidegger, is the figure of Socrates, who "All through his life and right into his death … did nothing else than place himself into this draft, this current, and maintain himself in it. This is why he is the purest thinker of the West. This is why he wrote nothing" (Heidegger 1968, p17).

The opposite of resoluteness is an attempting to hold on to what has been lost in anxiety; it is the will to hold on to everydayness which must be distinguished from being absorbed in everydayness. Being absorbed in everydayness, the human being has no explicit attunement to everydayness. For such a person there is, as we have already indicated, only an involvement with equipment ready-to-hand. For someone willing themselves into everydayness, everydayness is an explicit theme of concern. As Heidegger puts it, in anxiety "falling, as fleeing … does not flee in the face of entities within-the-world; these are precisely what it flees towards—as entities alongside which our concern, lost in the 'they', can dwell in tranquillized familiarity" (1985, pp233–4).

This latter quotation calls for a distinction between fleeing from entities within the world and fleeing towards that sort of world which is characterized by possibilities such as flight from entities. To flee towards entities in the world (that is, to flee towards that sort of world in which flight from entities is possible) is to flee towards being absorbed in the world. When, in anxiety, the human being responds by fleeing, he is attempting to will back the world in which he, prior to anxiety, had been existentially absorbed. As Heidegger suggests, such a person wishes that he could be absorbed in the world in the same way that he was prior to anxiety. Such a person is willing himself to be involved in his everyday involvements (even to the extent of having the very fears that those already involved within the world run from). They have made involvement in everydayness an explicit aim or goal (that is, involvement) (1985, p234).

An example of this can be extracted from Tolstoy's autobiography. Faced with a crisis of anxiety, Tolstoy felt all of his everyday involvements to be meaningless. As much as he willed himself to find these involvements meaningful, he could not lose or absorb himself in these involvements. He "willed" himself to find meaning in "family values" and in writing, but he experienced only emptiness: "The two drops of honey that have longest turned my eyes away from the cruel truth, the love of family and the love of authorship … are no longer sweet to me" (Tolstoy 1987, p54).

Tolstoy could not will his own will to experience things as meaningful. John Stuart Mill, in a similar crisis, talks of the desire to will himself to feel part of the world and of his anguish at being unable to do so, noting that "All feeling was for ever exhausted in him [Mill]." Ruth Borchard, his biographer, comments: "He strained his will to the utmost—but how can one will to feel?" (1957, p30).

Willing *of* everydayness can be distinguished from willing *within* everydayness by the fact that the latter is a concern with equipment and objects within the world , whilst the former is a willing of, or involvement with, not the equipment or objects *per se* but of the concern with the objects and items of equipment. It is a concern with a concern; what Heidegger in his works on Nietzsche will call a willing of the will itself. What I am suggesting is that in the context of *Being and Time* the willing of the will takes the form of fleeing (1985, p234) in the face of anxiety, a fleeing which endeavors to recreate its forms of being involved in the world, to recreate, that is, an involvement in an everyday form of involvement.

Here we are confronted with an existential tautology. This can be made more transparent by the following example given by Dreyfus. In anxiety we may flee in the following way: "I try to become so involved in what I am doing that I cannot stand back and ask myself why I am doing it" (1993, p182). I may, for example, try to enjoy my work (try to become absorbed in the tensions of the work—the very thing that those absorbed in work are wishing to escape from!) or try to be preoccupied with loving of my lover.[4] In Heideggerian terms

---

4   Here I am attuned not to the beloved but to the feeling of love between myself and the beloved. I am in love with being in love. Or many people who are alone and lonely desperately want to experience love. They too are in love with love, absorbed with a particular form of involvement.

"trying" is a form of involvement. To try to become involved is thus to involve myself in my involvements; not in the objects of my involvements (for when I am involved with things as such I am not trying to be involved in things) but in my way of being involved—in the mood or absorption of involvement. I am therefore involved in my involvements or attuned to my attunement.

Leslie Farber (1965) explores the impossibility of being successful in willing the will. Giving admiration as an example, he says, "I could no more will to admire him [an other] than I could will him to admire me. If I try to will my admiration of another, all I can grasp is the visage or posture of admiration." Admiration is not an object of will but arises in response to an engagement with an other. Similarly, I cannot will myself to be in love with another. Besides the fact that such a form of willing is an involvement with myself rather than another, the way I care for the other arises in response to my being-with the other and is not something that I can impose on my relationship to this other. As Rollo May says: "Affect is not something you strive for in itself but the by-product of the way you give yourself to a life situation" (1969, p15). Using anxiety as another example, Farber says: "I could not will anxiety in myself, only the mannerisms of anxiety would be accessible to me and these not only would fool no one but would defeat our joint pedagogical and therapeutic goal" (1965, p15).

Furthermore, as the examples of Tolstoy and Mill indicate, the will cannot succeed in its endeavors to will itself. It cannot succeed in willing itself back into its average everydayness. It cannot manipulate or circumspectively produce an involvement in average everydayness. As Heidegger says: "[The environment] is itself inaccessible to circumspection, so far as circumspection is always directed towards entities" (1985, p105). That is, it is only within the world that the human being can will in the way characterized by the term circumspection: manipulate, produce, manufacture, act on, extract, transform, and so on. It cannot do these same kinds of things to its "average everydayness." It cannot manipulate itself back into average everydayness; it cannot reproduce this relationship to the world.

That it cannot be successful in reproducing average everydayness does not mean that the human being cannot engage in the activity of trying to reproduce it. Engaging in the Sisyphusian task of willing the will manifests itself in activities such as willing to be in love, willing to sleep, willing to be creative and spontaneous—that is, willing different ways of being involved in the world rather than being involved in the world in these ways. Today, as Rollo May points out, we endeavor to will the very form of our own will:

"People go to therapists to find substitutes for their lost will: to learn how to get their unconscious to direct their lives, or to learn the latest conditioning technique to enable them to behave, or to use new drugs to release some motive for living" (1969, p15). In all of these cases we see therapy as a place for people to attempt to manipulate or transform their wills.

The difference between resoluteness and holding on to average everydayness is the difference between two kinds of responses to anxiety. Resoluteness is an acceptance of impotence in the face of anxiety; willing of everydayness is a refusal to accept the nullity and insignificance of human being. In the context of fleeing, anxiety is "experienced as something terribly wrong with (the human being)." Here the insignificance of being that is experienced in anxiety "shows up as a constant threat to (the human being's) security—a threat that it cannot face." If, however, as Dreyfus remarks: "Dasein accepted its nullity, the same structure that seemed to threaten all its secure projects and its very identity would be seen to be challenging and liberating. Anxiety then would not be paralysing like fear but would make Dasein clear-sighted and fearless" (1993, p317).

The details of the two types of responses to anxiety can be brought out by looking at them in terms of Victor Frankl's (1967) notion of "paradoxical intention." In the context of anxiety, this principle would state that the more we try to escape anxiety by willing ourselves to be free of it, the greater the anxiety becomes. For we are willing ourselves to do kinds of things for which the will is inappropriate. Just as we cannot will ourselves to sleep or to stop being embarrassed, we cannot will ourselves to feel or stop feeling anxious or nervous. An example given by Frankl refers to the notion of pleasure: "The more a man aims at pleasure by way of a direct intention, the more he misses his aim" (1967, p17).

It is worth noticing that this is a belief that John Stuart Mill came to hold. Initially, he postulated that a search for or the will to happiness underpinned all of humankind's efforts. Later, he came to maintain that happiness cannot be willed or intended:

> But I now thought that [happiness] was only to be attained by not
> making it the direct end. Those only are happy (I thought) who have
> their minds fixed on some object other than their own happiness; on the
> happiness of others; on the improvement of mankind. ... Aiming thus
> at something else, they find happiness by the way. The enjoyments of
> life (such was now my theory) are sufficient to make it a pleasant thing,

when they are taken en passant, without being made a principal object
(1989, p117).

For Frankl, we do not overcome anxiety by intending or willing its overcoming, but it is by letting ourselves be overwhelmed by the anxiety that we are experiencing that we are able to surpass it. By accepting rather than resisting it, we are able, as he maintains, to take the wind out of its sails (1967, p224). It loses its power to dominate us. Speaking, as he does, in the context of neurotic illnesses, he says: "If we succeed in bringing the patient to the point where he ceases to flee from or to fight his symptoms, but, on the contrary, even exaggerates them, then we may observe that the symptoms diminish and that the patient is no longer haunted by them" (1967, p224).

Translating this into the language of the Heideggerian perspective, it is by accepting, rather than fleeing or willing to overcome, the anxiety of nothingness that the human being begins to inquire into the nature of being-in-the-world itself. The more the human being accepts anxiety, the more it "deconstructs" its average everydayness and the more it "deconstructs" average everydayness the closer it comes to an attunement to being-in-the-world itself. As Dreyfus says: "The ultimate choice … is no choice at all. It is the experience of transformation that comes from Dasein's accepting its powerlessness" (1993, p319). Accepting such powerlessness is the basis of becoming clear sighted.

The process underpinning the notion of resoluteness is not unique to Heidegger but can be found in the writing of Kierkegaard. In his book *The Concept of Anxiety* he sees the resolute affirmation of anxiety as the basis of Socratic education. For Kierkegaard, the resolute person:

> *does not shrink back, and still less does he attempt to hold [anxiety]*
> *off with noise and confusion; but he bids it welcome, greets it festively,*
> *and like Socrates who raised the poisoned cup, he shuts himself up with*
> *it and says as a patient would say to the surgeon when the painful*
> *operation is about to begin: Now I am ready. Then anxiety enters his*
> *soul and searches out everything and anxiously torments everything*
> *finite and petty out of him, and then it leads him where he wants to go*
> *(1980, p159).*

Socrates, represented in an existential and hermeneutic way, was resolute because, rather than fleeing in the face of not knowing, he accepted that he did not know anything. This acceptance was not only an intellectual or cognitive one but permeated his entire being. He was a stranger to himself and saw in himself the possibilities of being many "dark" and sinister beings. For example, as Frankl maintains, he saw in himself the possibility of being a criminal (1969, p20). Rather than denying this possibility in himself, he saw it as a basis upon which to inquire into himself; to ask himself the question, "who am I such that I can be a criminal?" On the Heideggerian and Franklian logic, it was precisely by accepting that he could be a criminal that he was ready to inquire into his being.

Heidegger uses the word "destroy" to characterize the activity of deconstruction. The activity of "destroying" takes place in the context of being freed from tradition, for, as Heidegger puts it:

> Tradition ... blocks our access to those primordial 'sources' from which
> the categories and concepts handed down to us have been in part quite
> genuinely drawn. Indeed it makes us forget that they have had such an
> origin, and makes us suppose that the necessity of going back to these
> sources is something which we need not even understand (1985, p43).

"Primordial sources," from a Heideggerian perspective, does not mean temporally prior or historically first. It means that dimension in which the human being is concerned with the realization of the finitude of human being given in anxiety. It is the dimensions in which we come to experience the being of being human in a world. It is this dimension that is covered over by tradition and average everyday intelligibility (1985, pp210–28).

Destruction is the endeavor to uncover what has been covered up through tradition and average everyday intelligibility. This it does through an anxiety-instigated questioning of tradition and average everydayness: "The question of Being does not achieve its true concreteness until we have carried through the process of destroying the ontological tradition" (Heidegger 1985, p49). Destruction, or deconstruction, can be thought of in Frankl's terms as an existential distancing or detachment. Putting this explicitly in the language of Victor Frankl, "when paradoxical intention is used, the purpose is to enable the patient to develop a sense of detachment toward his neurosis" (1969, p225), thereby allowing this person to explicitly see it rather than be overwhelmed by feeling lost within it. From Frankl's perspective, such detachment occurs by accepting rather than resisting the anxiety, by letting the anxiety be.

Of course the Heideggerian and Franklian contexts are different; Heidegger's is not the language of neurosis but of the anxiety of nothingness. The anxiety of nothingness can be seen to perform the Franklian activity of existential detachment; it detaches the human being from its everyday involvement in the world. By accepting, rather than resisting, such anxiety we are able to focus explicitly on the involvements from which we have been detached. From the Heideggerian perspective, this means to have an explicit focus on the taken-for-granted traditions which guide us in our everyday interactions within the world.

For Heidegger such destruction takes place in the name of phenomenology. Phenomenology is the activity of seeing through "letting being be," which is a form of resoluteness that follows an affirmation, rather than a fleeing, in the face of anxiety (fleeing is a refusal to let being be). Phenomenology is thus the activity of learning to see one's involvements by letting oneself be overwhelmed by anxiety and thereby "letting [oneself] be summoned out of [one's] lostness in the one" (Heidegger 1985, pp299, 345).

In summary, it can be said that Heidegger makes it possible to think of two responses to anxiety: one of holding on to that which is ruptured and one which resolutely affirms the letting go of that which is ruptured. As we shall see in the discussion of nationalism in Part III, the one is a valuing of one's values, the other is the condition for a re-evaluation of one's values; the one is a preoccupation with the desire for security, the other is a "letting go" or "letting be" in the face of insecurity.

References

Bauman, Z. (1990) Modernity and Ambivalence. In: Featherstone, M. (ed.) *Global Culture: Nationalism, globalization and modernity.* London: Sage Publications.

Bhaba, H. (1990) *The Location of Culture.* London: Routledge.

Borchard, R. (1957) *John Stuart Mill: The Man.* London: C.A. Watts and Co., Ltd.

Dreyfus, H. (1993) *Being-in-the-World: A Commentary on Heidegger's Being and Time, Division 1.* Boston: The MIT Press.

Farber, L. (1965) *Will and Anxiety.* Humanitas.

Frankl, V. (1967) *Psychotherapy and Existentialism: Selected papers on logotherapy.* London: Penguin Books.

Hall, E.T. (1976) *Beyond Culture.* Garden City, NY: Anchor Books.

Heidegger, M. (1968) *What Is Called Thinking?* New York: Harper Torchbooks.

Heidegger, M. (1971) The Origin of the Work of Art. In: *Poetry, Language and Thought.* New York: Harper and Row Publishers.

Heidegger, M. (1985) *Being and Time.* Oxford: Basil Blackwell.

Hill, L.A. (2003) *Becoming a Manager: How new managers master the challenges of leadership.* Boston: Harvard Business School Press.

Hodes, A. (1998) *Encounter with Martin Buber.* London: Penguin Books.

Kierkegaard, S. (1980) *The Concept of Anxiety.* Princeton: Princeton University Press.

May, R. (1969) *Love and Will.* London: Collins.

Mill, J.S. (1989) *Autobiography.* London: Penguin Books.

Palmer, R. (1969) *Hermeneutics.* Evanston, IL: Northwestern University Press.

Pendlebury, S. (1990) Practical Arguments and Situational Appreciation in Teaching. *Educational Theory.* Vol 40, No 2. pp171–9.

Sheehan, D. (1983) *The Anxiety Disease.* New York: Charles Scribner's Sons.

Tillich, P. (1979) *The Courage To Be.* London: Fontana Books.

Tolstoy, L. (1987) My Confession. In: Hanflig, O. (ed.) *Life and Meaning.* Oxford: Basil Blackwell.

Plato. (1968) *The Republic* (translated by Lee, D.). London: Penguin Books.

Weick, K.E. (1993) The Collapse of Sensemaking in Organizations: The Mann Gulch Disaster. *Administrative Science Quarterly.* Vol 38. pp628–52.

Chapter 4
Being-in-the-World

Introductory Description of Being-in-the-World

Conventions, habits or average everyday ways of doing things are only one dimension of existence; so too are moods of mattering, understanding, temporality, being in question, throwness, resolve and care. Together they form the phenomenon called existence, or being-in-the-world. The latter are phrases that Heidegger uses to articulate his understanding of the nature or essence of what it means to be human. He critiques most previous attempts to understand the nature or essence of the human being as not getting to the essence of the human being as a being that is "always and already" in relationship to the world. Thus all those views of the human being that are based on the idea that the human being is primarily a subject against a world of objects are seen by Heidegger as abstractions from the essence of being human, which means to be in relationship. For example, to understand the human being primarily as a mind, self, psyche or personality are abstractions for the concreteness of being already there in the world. So too are the theories and debates that underpin these views of the human being seen as abstractions. For example, the debate between nature and nurture, and freedom and determinism miss the point from a Heideggerian perspective. For example, for Heidegger, it is not the case that the human being is determined by its environment. Its environment is already part of what it is as a human being; so too is its nature. For to be a human being is to be "always and already" "there" (*Da-sein*) in an environment, or a context or the world. Part of being "there" in the world means that its environment or, more broadly speaking, its history is part of what it already is. One way in which this is so is that we do not pre-exist the conventions that we have. We exist through our conventions. We find ourselves "always and already" within a set of conventions. We are beings in conventions; in context; in existence. Similarly, we find ourselves always and already in a way of making sense of the world. Just as there is no separation between ourselves and our conventions, there is no separation between being a person and the way in which we make sense of the world. And we find ourselves already and always in a way of making sense of the world.

To see the human being as a self, an individual, a subject, a personality is to have already abstracted it from the concreteness of its existence or context. The latter is what Heidegger does not want to do. He wants to understand the human being in the concreteness of its existence. And to do this is to understand that being and world are not separate from each other. They form a relational whole; a referential whole. Heidegger uses hyphenated phrases to express these referential wholes. Thus being and world are bound together as being-in-the-world or being-there (in German, *Da-sein*).

Being-in-the-world as a referential whole[1] is made up of several parts, each of which imply or co-constitute each other and are held in relation to each other by the whole, called being in the world. Thus inhabiting the world, being in time, being in question, being in a mood, a state of understanding, an average everyday set of conventions and care are all parts of the referential whole called existence, being-in-the-world or being-there.

Before elaborating on each of these dimensions, it is important to understand, again, what Heidegger means by "being in" in all of the phrases above. To "be in" is to say that all of the above dimensions are part of the essence of the existence of being human. For example, it is not that the human being cares; it is that care is part of what it means to be human. It is not that the human being has moods. It is that the human being is always and already in a mood. It is not that the human being asks questions; the human being is by its very essence in question.

Rather than a logical switch, Heidegger is calling his readers to make a Gestalt switch in his understanding of the human being. Again, it is not that time is something outside of, or at a distance from, the human being. It is also not that time is inside the human being. The human being is in itself a being-in-time, a temporal being. Many psychologists like to say this by the idea that we are always developing and philosophers like to say that we are always becoming. These both suggest that time is neither inside nor outside of us but that time is part of who we are; for developing and becoming imply a temporal dimension. But what Heidegger argues is that both psychologists of development and philosophers of becoming do not access or make explicit being-in-time itself.

---

1   At this point Heidegger changes his language and instead of speaking about referential wholes, he writes about what is translated into English as "equiprimordial wholes" and "ontological differences." However, for the sake of ease and consistency, I will continue with the phrase "referential whole."

It is also important to note why the phrase being-in-time needs to be hyphenated. For it could easily be confused with being in time for this or that occasion. And Heidegger wants to make a distinction between being-in-time as part of the essence of the existence of the human being and being in time for a party or lecture or any other event. So to understand the human being is to understand the way it is being-in-a-mood; being-in-question; being-in-understanding and ultimately being-in-the-world. We are not beings in the world as though there is first a world and then a being in it. We are always and already within the world. The inseparability[2] of being and world is called being-in-the-world.

Thus it should be clear by now that being-in-the-world does not refer to the physical proximity of one thing to another as, say, tea may be in a tea cup, or a person may be in a house, or water may be in a jug. Rather being-in-the-world is of a qualitative rather than a quantitative nature. It is, as we shall see, a way of being-in a set of concerns; being familiar with and making sense or meaning in the world—and also breakdowns in sense- or meaning-making, for sense-making cannot be taken for granted. Sense-making means being-in-time. Being-in-space does not even mean being in a physical space but in a referential whole. It also means being in a set of habits or inhabiting the world. Being-in-question rather than simply having a question to ask.

Within the scope of this work, it is impossible to detail all of these dimensions and so I will give an overview of some of the referential wholes called being-in-the-world. I will focus on those aspects which have to do with being a professional—whether it be a manager, a researcher, a leader, teacher, engineer or doctor. It is my contention that, for the most part, the existential dimensions of being a professional are not considered in the education, teaching, research, training and personal reflections on inhabiting a profession. For the most part, it is the theories and techniques that form the subject matter of education of professionals and so the concreteness of being a professional or the existential experience of being a professional are not touched upon. Part of the aim of this work is to explore this unspoken, but all-important, dimension of the existential experience of being and becoming a professional.

---

2   This is called an "ontological difference" in Heidegger: a relationship consists of two terms that are not reducible to each other but are not simply other to each other.

Being-in-Question

Heidegger opens his study of being-in-the-world by pointing to the way in which the human being is a being-in-question: "The very asking of this question [the question of its being] is an entity's mode of Being" (1985, p27). In another place he says that "existence gets sorted out through existing" (1985, p33). Kierkegaard says this in a simpler way when he says that "life is lived forward and understood backward" (1996, p161). Steve Jobs (2005), in his Stanford address describing his becoming an entrepreneur, says this in an even simpler way when he says that he did not know in advance that he was going to become an entrepreneur. Only in retrospect could he define himself as an entrepreneur. And so he maintained that we cannot join the dots of our life going forward; only in retrospect can we see the formation of the dots of our life. Note here that the imagery of joining the dots is a hermeneutic circle or referential whole. It is neither a sequential nor linear process.

This is a theme that is central to all existential philosophers and to the philosophy of Aristotle. It is only as we act that we become. Thus Sartre will say that it is only through our choice-in-action (not rational or deliberate choice in advance of action) that we become a "hero" or "coward" (1948). Buber uses the notion of an existential test to describe how our identities emerge out of the actions that we perform. Aristotle will say that the virtue of practical wisdom and theoretical knowledge emerges in the context of action. And although not an existentialist, Edger Schein (1999) claims that culture emerges as we act and interact within our environment. Part of Schein's definition of culture is that it is a "pattern of shared basic assumptions that a group has learned as it solved its problems." Two points are worthy of note: culture emerges as we are immersed in existence and the second point is that it is more than a set of assumptions but, as already established, a background set of "average everyday" conventions for doing things.

Returning to Heidegger, it can thus be said that we make sense of existence through existing. Putting it more colloquially, our theories or philosophies of existence do not develop by armchair speculation but emerge out of our way of existing.

Because being-in-question plays a central role in this work, I devote a separate chapter (Chapter 5) to it, so I will now move on from it.

Being-in as Inhabiting the World

As already stated, "being-in" is not to be understood in terms of the physical positioning or proximity of one entity in relationship to another. Rather, it is to be understood in terms of the notion of inhabiting the world. To be in the world is to inhabit the world. And, as has already been outlined, we inhabit the world through becoming familiar with the world. Familiarity is itself built up in terms of our ways of being involved or immersed in the world and for Heidegger we are always and already involved in the world. We are never not involved in the world. Even taking a break or taking time out is a way of being involved in the world. Furthermore, as Heideggerian commentator Baren Jager points out, inhabiting the world is closely linked to the phenomenon of developing habits of practice. As he puts it, "being-in is the trusted familiarity of the habitual" (1983, p154). Inhabiting the world is the basis of the identification of physical space and place. It is in the familiarity of inhabiting the world that a physical place comes into view. For example, the boundaries of countries are not primarily the physical mountains or rivers but the meanings that are attributed to these through dwelling in the world: "All positions and locations refer us back to a fundamental manner of being-in-the-world" (1983, p154).

We find ourselves already in a way of inhabiting the world through the patterns of familiarity established through being involved in the world. The lived experience of the familiarity of inhabiting is also linked to the issue of power, for the familiar is a place in which we "know-how" to get around. As David Jardine (1994) has said, the familiar is "the world wherein one felt at home and able (playing as this does with the wonderful etymological link between *habilite* and ability)." Unlike in unfamiliar situations where we may need to rely on others, the familiar is a place in which we are enabled and thus empowered. To lose the familiar is thus to lose the horizon which allows us to be powerful. And to lose power is to be helpless.

This, as we shall soon see, is what happens in existential anxiety or in the strangeness of the unfamiliar—we lose our sense of familiarity and thus the power of our know-how or habits of practice.

Inhabiting as Practical Coping

Another way in which Dreyfus reads Heidegger's notion of inhabiting the world through being involved in the world is in terms of the notion of practical coping. It is as we are involved in the world that we develop ways of coping practically with the world. And as we develop our ways of practical coping, our habits of practice and thus our way of inhabiting the world develops. Although Dreyfus does not say this practical coping is not a linear activity but it is itself developed in a hermeneutic way, that is, it is by the forward and backward movement through the parts of the referential whole that the dots are joined such that a way of inhabiting the world is developed. And thus inhabiting is itself a referential whole.

Again, in our everyday world, Heidegger privileges the embodied knowing that comes out of practical coping: we know our way around our referential wholes without having to think about them and they form the basis of our thinking.

Context of Significance, Meaning or Sense-making

As already implied, the human being lives in a context of sense-making. Familiarity, conventions, habits of doing things are always making sense of the world. Furthermore, it is not that sense-making is "in" or "outside" of the human being. Sense-making is a constitutive dimension of being-in-the-world. As already indicated, even the physical dimension of place and space are defined in terms of sense-making. Sense-making, it will also be clear, is not just a cognitive or intellectual matter but is a fully embodied practice. Thus making sense of another city, country or even company is not just an intellectual activity but a fully embodied activity. We have already made sense of eating, going to the bathroom, work, school, in order to attend to them effectively. We are not even attentive to our ways of sense-making in order to act in terms of this way of sense-making. It constitutes the background of our attentiveness and makes practical coping possible.

Being in sense-making, meaning or significance is itself a referential whole made of three dimensions. They are context of concern, content of interpretation and context of convention.

CONTEXT OF CONCERN

Dreyfus (1993) unpacks the context of concern by contrasting the being of the human with that of the computer. While both may be able to calculate, neither its location nor the way it inhabits the world matter to the computer. In fact, things neither matter nor don't matter to the computer. In contrast to this, while the concerns that the human being may have may vary, the being of the human is always in a state of concern. Things always matter to it. Again it is crucial to make a distinction between things that matter and the human being a being-in-concern. The human being is always and already a being-in-concern. We cannot take a break from being concerned. We wake up and go to sleep being concerned. We go away being concerned. Even when we attempt to numb ourselves through various means, we are still in a state of concern.

Another way of saying this is that the human being always has what Gendlin (quoted in Todres 2007) calls a felt sense of its world, whereas a computer has no felt sense at all. It is through its felt sense of the world that it makes sense of the world. Furthermore, the human being does not have only one concern at a time but exists in a network of concerns. It is through its concerns that the world is disclosed to it. It sees the world, activities in the world or even things in the world because its context of concerns disclose them in a particular way. For example, it is its concerns that disclose the computer as a computer.

Concerns for Heidegger are made up of moods and feelings. As Dreyfus notes, it is important to note that moods and feelings are not in us. We are always in a mood or feeling (1993, p171). We are "always and already" in a mood. We wake up and go to sleep in a mood. Moods are the background in terms of which things make sense. We are affected by situations in terms of the moods that we are in.

The German word *sorge*, as Bass Leverung (1993) informs us, has a double meaning: it is both care and worry, and it is because we care and worry that we notice things, that we become situationally attuned. The difference between people and computers is that while both may be able to calculate, only the human can worry. If we rely only on technological devices and techniques, we deprive ourselves of our situational appreciation. This point is made by Benner and Wrubel (1989, p87) in the context of parenting and nursing: "Parenting techniques do not work unless a basic level of attachment and caring exists. In fact, parenting techniques are not even useful or possible unless the parent is already engaged in the parenting situation through caring."

They go on to maintain that if we do not care we do not even begin to notice situations of danger (which a computer cannot do): "A common place example is a mother's awareness that her baby is crying. It is an everyday occurrence for someone other than the mother, to comment, 'Is the baby crying? I didn't hear anything'" (Benner and Wrubel 1989, p87). While the above examples are drawn from parenting, Benner and Wrubel situate it in the context of medicine and management. A doctor who simply applies techniques often does not see the seriousness of a problem suffered by patients … often not until it is too late.

Similarly, managers who operate only in terms of routines and procedures are often very late in spotting danger and very bad at developing their people. Andrew Grove (1998), founder and CEO of Intel, made this point in relation to organizations. He said that organizations are too reliant on forms of communicating information on paper and in ways that do not allow the recipient to understand the mood or context of the situation. What is more important is to be able to understand the worry that emerges concretely only in relationships between people. He saw his chief weapon in developing his leadership style as the ability to develop a disciplined sense of worry and thus of observation. In his book *The Prince*, Machiavelli (1908) makes the same point, where he says that the function of a ruler is to be on guard and prepare for the possibility of war.

CONTEXT OF UNDERSTANDING

While understanding is different from mood, both are parts of being concerned. Understanding, for Heidegger, reveals itself through the activity of interpretation. Interpretation is not just an intellectual activity. It is something we are doing all the time. To go to the movies, for example, is to be able to interpret a movie as a movie. To go to school, to observe the practices of being at school, or managing is to be always and already in an act of interpreting. Interpretation has the structure of seeing things as the particular kinds of things they are. For example, an entity is used as a hammer for hammering. The entity called a bus is seen as a way of transport. As said above, a movie is seen as a movie in order to attend it.

Heidegger distinguishes a hermeneutic from what he calls an apophantic form of interpretation. The hermeneutic form of interpretation refers to the way in which parts of a phenomenon are constituted as such through their relationship to each other in a referential whole. Thus in a workshop a hammer is constituted as such in terms of its relation to a nail, a table, a screw and screwdriver and so on. They are seen as the phenomenon that they are through the referential whole. "As" is thus always a relational phenomenon. It is only when we abstract it from its context that it becomes an object or appearance that looks like a thing in itself.

Apophantic interpretation, in contrast, is a secondary or derived form of interpretation in which something that is already constituted by a referential whole is seen or used as something else. As Dominiek Heil claims, "when someone says 'I am using the fork as a screwdriver', this 'as' is not a hermeneutic 'as', since it does not articulate an always already interpretation" (2011, p72).

It is extracted from an already existing referential whole—that of eating—and used as an instrument in another referential whole. All metaphors are dimensions of this apophantic form of interpretation. They are ways of seeing something that belongs already in one referential whole and placing it in another referential whole. For example, when an organization is seen as an "elephant." Or a house is seen as a container.

RETURN TO CONTEXT OF CONVENTIONS

Through interpretation we have returned to the "average everydayness" of conventions. For it is through conventions that referential wholes are formed. We see things in the way we do because we find ourselves always and already in a set of conventions of referential wholes which enable us to see and do things in the particular ways that we do. But at this stage Heidegger "complexifies" his understanding of conventions or average everydayness. It is not just an inert event that occurs to us. There is a kind of agency to the set of conventions in which we find ourselves. In German he calls the set of conventions of everydayness *das man*, which has been translated into English as the "they." Dreyfus has given a clear exposition of these terms: "the roles and goals available to Dasein are not first experienced as yours or mine, rather, as public possibilities provided by the culture; they make no essential reference to me, but are available to anyone. For this reason Heidegger refers to the public as 'das man,' or the 'Anyone.' The public, whatever its activity, is certainly not a sort of self-conscious subject" (1993, p123).

There is a specific reason for calling the network of roles in which we are involved the "they." The "they" is part of who we are. It is a condition of our being human. Our roles are not just an abstracted or disembodied concept of functions but human beings are always embodied in a set of roles or way of doing things. A role or network of roles is a way of inhabiting the world. For Heidegger, the public is defined as the "they": "We take pleasure and enjoy ourselves as THEY take pleasure; we read, see, and judge about literature and art as THEY see and judge; likewise we shrink back from the 'great mass' as THEY shrink back; we find 'shocking' what THEY find shocking" (1985, p164).

Heidegger does not necessarily see the "They" in a negative light. "They" define the conventions that make everyday living and practical coping possible. However, because the they governs us without us even knowing, we become functions of the they without even knowing it. We are constituted through the they and have fallen into the they. We do not see that we are shaped in a particular way or the world is disclosed to us in a particular way or that our possibilities are circumscribed by the they. The "they" defines the spectrum of possibilities that are available in a public world. They constitute the network of practices that are available to us. However, because they are in the background, we tend to think that the way of the they is *the* way of doing things. We do not see that they are a particular way in which everyday living is possible. We do not see that the "they" we inhabit is one set amongst other sets of possibilities.

Every "they," every network of conventions of average everydayness opens one way of being and doing in the world and closes down other ways of being, seeing and doing in the world. Disclosing new possibilities or new worlds means going beyond the they, and thus the way in which it defines a particular world. This occurs through the experience of existential anxiety.

Referential Context of Being with Others

An essential structure of human being is what Heidegger calls "being-with." This refers to the human being's relationship to other human beings. To be human is always to be referenced in some relation to another human being; isolation or a hermetic existence is a form of being in relationship to others: "Even being-alone is Being-with" (1985, p156). Even the being of the self is possible only in relation to the other, for the notion of a self does not make sense unless there is an other than self. Heidegger also stresses that being-with is not primarily a constitution of the other as an object of attention or observation, but is a way of being familiar with or in relationship to the other (1985, p156). For example, I do not come to know my child by first thinking about it but in the way in which I care or stand in relationship to it. The human being thus develops its understanding of the other not by thinking about it but through the familiarity or felt sense of being with the other. Furthermore, it develops its understanding of itself in the way it is with others (1985, p161). It comes across itself through the other.

Heidegger distinguishes between two kinds of ways of being with others: an inauthentic and an authentic way. The inauthentic way he defines in terms of the notion of "leaping in" and the authentic way he defines as "leaping ahead" (1985, p158). The latter form is one in which one human being enables another human being to become transparent to themselves and to free them for their possibilities (1985, p159). It is not to be confused with empathy but is the condition of possibility of empathy.

Although Heidegger does not say this, it is the creation of what Winnicott (1971) calls a "holding space" which allows the other to become. Leaping-in, on the other hand, is a form of dominating the other, takes control and takes over the concerns and cares of the other, thus enhancing their sense of dependency (Heidegger 1985, p158). It is to be found in the frightened immigrant or even authoritarian parents.

Thus what we see is that being-in-the-world is a referential or hermeneutic whole which includes a context of conventions, being with others, being in meaning or sense-making. It is through being-involved in the world that we develop our ways of practical coping with the world and it is through our involvements in the world that we embody the sense-making of the world.

There is a paradox in Heidegger that we have not yet accounted for: we make sense by being involved in the world but we are also thrown into a particular context of sense-making. To say that we are thrown is to say that we find ourselves always and already in a way of sense-making. We do not choose this, but all our choices, actions and deliberations emerge out of this sense-making. Thus, even though our sense-making is inhabited through our involvements, we do not know that we are inhabiting them. They are what Heidegger calls pre-thematic. An example of this is the hidden curriculum of schools: the way we inhabit patterns and practices of organizing, discipline, order, freedom without even knowing that we are inhabiting them.

Being-in-Time (in Contrast to Being in Time)

The starkest of these is being-towards-death. Death is the essential dimension of the being of the human. It means that being human is a passing through being. We cannot stop the lived experience of passing through. An image of Freud's used to describe the experience of free association may be helpful here. He says: "Act as though, for instance, you were a traveller sitting next to the window of a railway carriage and describing to someone inside the carriage the changing views which you see outside" (1913, p135).

Sitting at the window, when the train is going at a speed, means that one can never fix one's attention on anything for more than a passing moment. As the object in the environment comes into view, it recedes into the background. From a Heideggerian perspective, this is the essence of time and of the human being as a being that is forever passing through. Just as we cannot focus on the object for more than a fleeting moment, so we are always passing through time. We can never arrest it; never hold on to a moment—for example, no matter how much we are enjoying an experience, it is already beginning to pass by.

But not only are experiences passing by. We ourselves are a passing-by or a passing-through. Heraclitus, the pre-Socratic Greek philosopher, once said that we cannot step in the same river twice. For once we have stepped in it, the water is already passing us by. Heidegger takes this point one step further. It is not only the river that is a passing-by. The being of the human is itself a passing-by or passing-through. This cannot be arrested. We have no control over our temporality—only in clock time do we have the appearance of control of time. We draw up diaries, schedule appointments as though we are in control of time, but as Mintzberg (2004) has noted, it is not long before a leader or manager's diary is turned upside down.

Thus we are not only always and already in time but the essence of our being is time bound or temporal. We cannot get outside of time. As can be expected, for Heidegger, there are different dimensions of time. There is originary or primordial time, familiar time and abstract or clock time. His critique is that Western thought has taken the third form of time, clock time, to be the fundamental form of time, whereas in fact it is an abstraction from originary and familiar time and that in order to understand lived experience we need to situate time in originary and familiar time.

What follows is a brief description of his three dimensions of time. But before reflecting on the different dimensions of time, it is worth bringing up the issue as to how time, in Heidegger's sense of the word, becomes an explicit theme of thought. For when we are absorbed with everyday practical coping, we do not tend to think about time. It is only when our way of being in time breaks down that it becomes a subject matter of thought. This point is brought out well by Bodil Jonsson in reflecting on the relationship between her grandmother's sense of time and a "modern" sense of time. She makes the claim that time was never an issue for her grandmother. Although life was difficult for her, Jonsson says, "she never seemed to run out of time." Indeed, continuing her point, Jonsson says that her grandmother "simply did not think of life in terms of time" (Jonsson and Nunally 2001, p3). It was not a category in terms of which life or ways of being were ordered.

Jonsson and Nunnally go on to maintain that it is only when time becomes a problem that we begin to think of it. They say that we moderns have become a society "whose members all feel time deprived" (Jonsson and Nunnally 2001, p11). They trace this to the Industrial Revolution, which required order, standardization and clockwork precision and which left people "less able to control their time" (2001, p12).

So it is under the breakdown of our way of being in time that time becomes an explicit theme of concern. A more academic example of this is Cohen and Taylor's work *Escape Attempts* (1992), which was a study of prisoners and their experience of time. A central theme of the work was that it was under conditions of being oppressed by the boredom of having too much time on their hands that time became an explicit theme of concern to them. They brooded over time. They were preoccupied with time; they were confronted by time. If they were busy, time would not have manifested itself as a concern.

As already stated, primordial or originary time is much more like a blur which managers dwell in. It is like sitting on a moving train, looking out the window but without being able to fix one's gaze on anything in particular. For just as one looks at it, it recedes into the background and another "thing" appears only to recede into the background. Neither the past nor the present nor the future are static. They blur into one. We cannot seize hold of the current moment or even the future or past. They are not "things" or objects within our control. In the context of management, Mintzberg quotes a manager as saying "the work of managing is one damn thing after another" (2004, p18), in which we cannot control the speed at which events whizz by us.

Originary time manifests itself in an exquisite sense of timing. The CEO of Honda compares it to telling the punchline of a joke: "Joking is very difficult. You have to grasp the atmosphere of the occasion and the opportunity. It exists only for that particular moment, and not anywhere else. The joke is in the timing and it doesn't work at any other moment. ... To joke is to understand human emotion" (Helgesen 2008, p5).

Originary time is thus the call of judgment to seize the moment. Later it will be demonstrated that this is the sense of timing of a master or virtuoso.

Familiar time is derived from originary time. It is an embodied form of time and expresses itself in "dinner time" or "lunch time" or time for sleep. It's a form of time that is defined by habit rather than, say, by a diary. It is the familiar sense of time that one gets, say, for completing a job or piece of work, for travelling from one place to another. Just as one may know one's way from place to place, so one develops an embodied or familiar sense of movement from time to time. John Kotter describes this well in the context of management:

> *Time-management experts still tell managers to compose lists of priorities and to limit the number of people they see. However, the successful ones I watched rarely did so. They "wasted" time walking*

down corridors, engaging in seemingly random chats with seemingly
random people, all the while promoting their agendas and building
their networks with far less effort than if they'd scheduled meetings
along a formal chain of command (1999, p159).

This so-called waste of time was a way of developing and building up familiar time; habits and practices of time such that they knew their way about the time of their day just like they knew their way about the space of their office or teams or departments.

Originary and familiar time is contrasted by Heidegger with what he calls clock time. Clock time is defined by Heidegger in terms of a discrete series of "nows." It is time that can be numbered and counted: a minute, an hour, a day. It is an abstraction from and a representation of originary time. Clock time is turning time into an arithmetic representation and affords us a sense of the illusion of control over the uncertainty of the never-ending flow of time. It is best expressed as diary time—as though we can reduce time to a static series of hours—and all that we need to do is then follow the blueprint of our diaries.

Clock time becomes important in a world in which familiar time is constantly disrupted. It is under conditions of disruption that we are called upon to map out our time in terms of a diary. Paradoxically it is when our time becomes disembodied that we need to regulate it rather than allow it to be woven through us.

Being-in Care

But Heidegger is quite careful not to exclude the possibility of not feeling at home in the world; of not being able to experience the sense or the meaning of being-in-the-world. He has a special word for this and it is connected to the phenomenon that the being of the human being is one that is in question. Being not at home in the world, Heidegger calls "anxiety." Anxiety is the experience of being disconnected or even disassociated from the lived experience of inhabiting or being at home in the world. It is the loss of the sense of the familiar. The loss of the sense of the familiar is an earth-shattering experience for the human being. It loses all its bearing in the world. The familiar ways of being that it inhabited no longer make sense to it. It loses all felt sense of purpose, direction and order of being. Indeed, it is in a state of dis-order (which needs to be distinguished from being clinically disordered).

The state of anxiety is both frightening and exciting. It is frightening because it fragments the familiar and so the being of the human loses all its bearing, but it is also exciting because it is the basis for going beyond the blinkers of the familiar and is thus the ground for opening up new possibilities of existence. In the previous section this was exemplified by Steve Jobs, who, in turning his back on what he was "supposed to do," that is, go to college, he resolutely embraced the unknown in such a way that he was dwelling within possibility until this concretized itself in its various forms: the Mac, Pixar, Apple and the "iWorld" in general. He was a master at being able to move between actuality and possibility—whereas most of our corporate, business, political and organizational leaders are stuck within the world of actuality. They have not embraced the anxiety of possibility. Yet today more than at any time in the last two centuries, we need leaders who are able to embrace the anxiety of possibility, who are able to dwell in the paradox of actuality and possibility.

Thus, for Heidegger, central to existence is this tension between inhabiting or being at home in the world and the anxiety of estrangement from the world. It is quite clear what path he took in his own life. He shunned the anxiety of estrangement and with it the possibility of disclosing new worlds. Rather, he withdrew into a narrow-minded xenophobic nationalism and, as demonstrated in the "Black Notebooks," a preoccupation with anti-Semitism that was obsessive and, even in his own terms, was a set of "average everyday" opinions that he failed to destroy. Although this is not the place for it, it would be good to do an existential psychoanalytic destruction of the relationship between Heidegger's philosophy and his politics rather than only historical studies of this relationship.

As could be expected, sense-making or meaning is not just a free-floating term in the work of Heidegger, but has its own structure. There are a number of ways in which Heidegger unpacks the structure of meaning. One is specific to the human being and one is more general to the historical dimension of being human. The second emerges out of the first and so I will begin with the first.

According to Heidegger, meaning or sense-making is centered in care. As Hubert Dreyfus has argued and pointed out, what distinguishes a human being from, say, a calculating computer is that care is an improper category to be applied to computers. While computers are not the kinds of entities that care, human beings are always and already in a mood of caring. The being of the human cannot help but care. Unlike computers, things matter to the human being and the human being is always concerned about something or other. It is never not concerned. Care is neither "negative" nor "positive." It can be directed at noble ends and it can be directed at base ends. Both kinds of ends are states of caring. Even indifference, numbing oneself through alcohol or other means, is being in a state of care.

Care defines the being of the human. It is that which situates the human as being always and already in relationship to the world. The word used to describe care in German also brings it into line with Heidegger's understanding of the being of the human as a being who is in question. For *sorge* means both concern and worry and worry is linked to questioning in Heidegger. For to worry is to hold something or to be in a state of questioning. In anxiety we question because our being is in question.

References

Benner, P. and Wrubel, J. (1989) *The Primacy of Caring: Stress and coping in health and illness.* Menlo Park, CA: Addison-Wesley Publishing Company.

Cohen, S. and Taylor, L. (1992) *Escape Attempts: The theory and practice of resistance to everyday life.* London: Routledge.

Dreyfus, H. (1993) *Being-in-the-World: A commentary on Heidegger's Being and Time, Division 1.* Boston: The MIT Press.

Finch, H.L. (1995) *Wittgenstein.* Dorset: Element.

Freud, S. (1913) On Beginning the Treatment (Further Recommendations on the Technique of Psychoanalysis I). *Standard Edition.* Vol 12. pp121–44.

Grove, A. (1998) *Only the Paranoid Survive.* London: Harper Collins Publishers.

Heidegger, M. (1985) *Being and Time.* Oxford: Basil Blackwell.

Heil, D. (2011) *Ontological Fundamentals for Ethical Management: Heidegger and the corporate world.* London: Springer.

Helgesen, S. (2008) The Practical Wisdom of Ikujiro Nonaka. *Strategy + Business.* Vol 53, No 3. pp1–10.

Jager, B. (1983) Theorizing and the Elaboration of Place: Inquiry into Galileo and Freud. In: Giorgi, A., Barton, A. and Maes, C. (eds) *Duquesne Studies in Phenomenological Psychology*, Volume 4 (pp153–80). Pittsburgh: Duquesne University Press.

Jardine, D. (1994) Student-Teaching, Interpretation and the Monstrous Child. *Journal of Philosophy of Education.* Vol 28, No 1. pp17–24.

Jobs, S. (2005) *You've Got to Find What You Love.* Available at: http://news. stanford.edu/news/2005/june15/jobs-061505.html.

Jonsson, B. and Nunnally, T. (2001) *Unwinding the Clock: Ten thoughts on our relationship to time.* Orlando, FL: Harcourt.

Kierkegaard, S. (1996) *Papers and Journals: A selection* (translated by Alastair Hannay). London: Penguin Books.

Kotter, J. (1999) What Effective General Managers Really Do. *Harvard Business Review.* March.

Leverung, B. (1993) "Hoeveel 'Heimat' heeft enn mens nodig? Een poging to beantwoording naar aanleiding van 'Nieuwe geborgenheid' van O.F. Bollnow." in *Tijdschrift voor Vredesopvoeding.*

Machiavelli, N. (1908) *The Prince* (translated by W.K. Marriott). New York: E.P. Dutton.

Mintzberg, H. (2004) *Managers Not MBAs – A hard look at the soft practice of managing and management development.* San Francisco: Barrett-Koehler Publishers.

Sartre, J.P. (1948) *Existentialism and Humanism.* London: Methuen.

Schein, E.H. (1999) *The Corporate Culture Survival Guide.* London: John Wiley & Sons.

Todres, L. (2007) *Embodied Enquiry: Phenomenological touchstones for research, psychotherapy and spirituality.* New York: Palgrave Macmillan.

Winnicott, D. (1971) *Playing and Reality.* London: Tavistock.

Chapter 5

Disruption as the Existential Basis of Being-in-Question

Different Kinds of Disruption

For Heidegger there are different forms of disruption of conventions. Furthermore, there are different kinds of sight or disclosure emerging out of these different forms of disruptions. Using the language that has already been established, I want to show that for Heidegger there are disruptions *within* conventions and disruptions *to* or *of* conventions. Disruptions within conventions are disruption to what Heidegger calls our way of using equipment. When, for example, a hammer that we are using breaks down, our way of being attuned to the hammer shifts. Instead of having a relationship of use to the hammer, on the occasion of its breakdown we are distanced from the hammer and enter a relationship of thought to the hammer. The hammer becomes an "object" to be thought about and observed. In part following Dreyfus and Heidegger, I want to call the kind of sight or disclosure that emerges out of this disruption a focus on the "means," a "scientific" and "rational" sight. For there are different levels of disruption within convention: in temporary forms of disruption, we can either repair or replace an item of equipment. We see the item of equipment as a means to be worked on, that is repaired or we find a new means. In more permanent forms of disruption, the item of equipment becomes an object about which we develop a curiosity such that we will want to examine its properties or the way it interacts with other objects in the network of objects. In repairing something, we can speak of an instrumental relationship. And in examining the object and its relation to other objects, we have a more scientific form of relationship.

The second form of disruption, disruption of convention, can be split into two dimensions of disruptions of sense-making and conventions underpinning ways of coping in the world. While they overlap, they are not necessarily the same. Easily accessible examples of the way in which they overlap can be found in managers who go on international assignments to unfamiliar cultures where they do not have the embodied "know-how" through which to navigate and make sense of the way in which the people of the unfamiliar culture do things. They do not have a felt sense of their conventions for doing things. They are neither able to cope practically nor are they able to make meaning or sense in the unfamiliar situation.

However, there are breakdowns in sense-making in which people can continue with their everyday ways of practical coping but do it mechanically and without an inhabited sense of meaning. Leo Tolstoy (1987) and John Stuart Mill (1989) report examples of being able to continue with their work while being overwhelmed by a sense of meaninglessness and a sense of being disconnected from their work. There are people who struggle with coping with the tasks of everyday living but who do not experience a breakdown or disruption in meaning. The novice, for example, has not yet developed the practices for everyday coping in terms of the set of conventions of a culture but does not necessarily experience a sense of meaninglessness. On the contrary, they may experience a sense of excitement and the journey of learning that lies ahead of them (sight). Or when someone is "stressed" or "burnt out," it is not that there is primarily a breakdown in items of equipment but in their way of practical coping. As psychologists might say, they need to develop more effective resources for coping.

The breakdown in meaning will be called existential hermeneutic philosophy and the breakdown, or the lived experience, of not yet being able to cope in terms of the conventions—the position of a novice or of not being able to "manage"—will be called a breakdown in practical coping as such. It is important to note that, for Heidegger, all of these breakdowns lead to qualitatively different way of being in relationship to the world. It is not that there is a change in either the external or internal world but in our very way of standing in relationship to the world. Thus when equipment breaks down, when we cannot cope with the tasks of everyday living and when there is a breakdown in meaning, our way of standing in relationship to the world shifts.

For Heidegger, in contrast to much of the history of Western philosophy, we are not primarily objective spectators of the world. We are engaged players within the world. It is only when there is a breakdown in the equipment or even when the equipment is absent that we are shifted from being engaged players to objective spectators and only when meaning is disturbed do we become attuned to the question of the meaning of existence or the conventions in terms of which we make sense of the world. Similarly, when there is a breakdown or disruption in our practical coping, our practical coping becomes an issue for us.

Each of these forms of breakdown or disruption in living lead to different ways of questioning. Questioning has several dimensions in Heidegger's understanding of existence. This is the case on five levels. Firstly, as will be seen more clearly, the human being is in question in its everyday practical coping. It does not know who or what it is in advance and cannot take its way of being for granted at any moment. Existence gets sorted out by existing, as Heidegger says (1985). Thus, just simply in becoming or inhabiting the world we are in question.

Secondly, it is in the context of the breakdown *within* everyday practical coping that questioning moves from being "lived out" in our everyday lives to becoming explicit. It is here that our way of relating to the world changes. It changes from one of "use" to one of "thought or thinking about." In this transition our attention shifts to thinking about the world in terms of objects or concepts. Heidegger uses this moment to highlight the fact that beings only occur as objects when there is a breakdown in items of use and explicit rational and scientific occur at the same time.

Thirdly, when there is a breakdown in our way of practical coping, we move from simply doing things to thinking about our way of doing things. This is not a breakdown in items of use but those kinds of experience in which we find difficulty in managing our world. In this instance our ways of practically coping are disclosed to us. We become preoccupied with our ways of coping in the world.

Fourthly, when there is a breakdown in sense-making, our way of making sense of the world is disclosed to us.

Finally, breakdown of meaning also leads to disclosing of the structure of existence itself.

There are some generic process points that apply to all forms of questioning:

Firstly, existential questions do not announce themselves to us as already formed in language. We need to find the language in which to articulate the question. At best we may have a felt sense of the question, a vague sense or nagging doubt of something troubling us, being on the "tip of our tongue" but not yet quite expressed.

Secondly, we need to learn how to inhabit the way of being of questioning. We need, as Rilke will say in the next chapter, to be willing to live into the question. Heidegger calls this willingness to live into the question "resolve" (1985, p343).

Point three is that questioning is a discipline, one that needs to be developed and cultivated. We should not assume that we simply know how to question and respond. In an essay called *What Is Metaphysics?* Heidegger points out that each academic discipline has its own form of discipline and we should not reduce disciplined questioning to scientific questioning.

Fourth, theoretical questioning is a way of taking care of our being-in-the-world. For when we are absorbed in the world, we do not tend to think of the effect that we are having on the world and the way in which we are being transformed by the world. Existential theoretical questioning allows us to become sensitized to the effect that we are having on the world and the world is having on us, of how we are both transformed and transforming our way of being-in-the-world.

The fifth dimension is that when we question, we are always questioning from within a framework, or what Heidegger calls a pre-conceptual or pre-thematic understanding, that is passed down through the tradition or cultural context out of which we emerge. We find ourselves "always and already" within a certain way of understanding the world. Yet we are not simply explicitly aware of it. It is in the background rather than the foreground of our understanding. This background understanding defines the way in which we will ask questions. Thus, it is important to understand the effect of our pre-conceptual understanding on the way in which we ask questions. Indeed, sometimes we need to go beyond our pre-conceptual understanding to open up a new horizon through which to ask and respond to the question. Einstein understood this well when he said that a question is not answered within the framework in which it is asked but discloses a new way of seeing things: "We cannot solve today's problems using the mindset that created them."

In questioning the pre-conceptual understanding in terms of which we question, we are in what Heidegger calls a hermeneutic rather than a vicious circle, a circle which through questioning the assumptions of our questions allows us to open up new possibilities. But to do this, we need to simultaneously be in and estranged from our own pre-conceptual understanding.

Point six is that being-in-question forms the basis of education, inquiry and research. This may sound obvious, but when it is situated in so many of the practices of both undergraduate and postgraduate education, it is not: for it is often the case that the curriculum is structured in such a way that it assumes what the students need to know. It does not tap in to the way they are asking questions or the way their being is in question. This is often the case even at a PhD level, where very little explicit attention is devoted to exploring the felt sense of the question being asked.

Heidegger believes that being-in-question is an essential feature of the human being that manifests itself in all the activities of the human being. Thus the human being's being is never not in question. The human being cannot take a break from living or being. Its living or its being is always in question. However, as we shall see through the book, there are different ways in which we are in question and thus different ways that we question. There are, as we shall see, different ways of attempting to avoid being-in-question.

Thus this chapter is divided into the primary ways in which the being of the human is in question: everyday practical coping as a way of being-in-question, instrumental rational and scientific inquiry as ways of being-in-question, hermeneutic attunement as making explicit the question of being-in-question and the "gaze of the other" as a specific form of hermeneutic inquiry.

Everyday Practical Coping as Being-in-Question

Even in its everyday practical coping the human being is in question. For it cannot simply be assumed that the human being is going to be able to cope in its everyday world. Ian Lennie (1999) makes this point in terms of the notion of managing, which, just like practical coping, is "part of the fabric of everyday life." He goes on to say that "we may manage or fail to manage our family, our finances, our career." Managing is not a given but an accomplishment. It is, as he claims, a competence in everyday living. It is the basis of "organizing ourselves in daily life."

For Heidegger, while practical coping is about "organizing ourselves in daily life," it is more than this. It is about dwelling in the world, developing a sense of home in the world. As already discussed, being at home in the world is not primarily a physical occupancy of a building called a home. It is a way of knowing one's way about the world. It is an inhabiting and a development of a familiarity with and felt sense of our world such that we do not need to think about what we are doing while we are doing it. We can get on with the task without thinking about how we get on with the task. This applies to any and everyday activity—whether it be driving a car or leading an organization.

Practical coping or managing is thus the development of effective habits of existence.

However, for both Heidegger and Lennie, there are various ways in which we may not manage. One of the ways, as Lennie points out, is in the context of what he calls a "nervous breakdown." In such experiences, he argues, people are not able to take care of their everyday concerns. Existentially, a "novice" is someone who is not yet quite able to manage. Because they are at the beginning, they have not yet inhabited the practices for managing and practical coping. So too is a migrant in an unfamiliar cultural context. There are practices that we might not ever be able to manage or inhabit.

Furthermore, for Heidegger, as for all existentialists, we do not know in advance whether we are going to manage and develop effective habits of practice. As Kierkegaard says, "life is lived forward and understood backwards" (1996, p161). And Steve Jobs says we cannot join the dots of our lives, professions and habits in advance, but only in retrospect. We thus not only do we not know that we are going to manage, but we do not have the "how" of managing in advance of leaping into the situation. Furthermore, our identity emerges only as we respond to situations. Who we are is never given in advance of living. As Sartre (1968) says, "Man's existence precedes his essence."

This for Heidegger is an essential way in which our being is in question. Without even knowing it explicitly, we are in question in the way we go about developing a sense of being at home in the world. Furthermore, some of us will more often than others experience a felt sense of not being at home in the world, a sense of not inhabiting the world as thus a way of being constantly in question. The next chapter will be devoted to various ways of practical coping as a way of being-in-question.

Heideggerian Conditions of Inquiry

What are the conditions, then, under which we become inquirers in the explicit sense of the word?

It is here that we need to be careful. For Heidegger distinguishes between three modes of inquiry: firstly, he writes of what I will call an instrumental deliberation; secondly, a scientific and rational form of inquiry; and, thirdly, he writes of a hermeneutic form of inquiry. All three involve forms of deliberation, but *different* forms of deliberation. In the first form, through disruption, the world is transformed from a place of practical coping to one in which we come to think about, improve or change the means we choose for particular ends. Thus instead of only using entities as items of equipment, we come to think about, fix or find new entities or even ways to achieve our ends. Thus it is a breakdown in means and not ends.

In the second or scientific form of deliberation, we come to think about things as objects, or what Heidegger calls entities present-at-hand. We come to think about their properties and even the relationship between their properties.

In the third or hermeneutic form of inquiry, we become attuned to the phenomenon of our habitual or average everyday way of being-in-the-world. For Heidegger, although we are "always and already" being-in-the world, we do not explicitly become aware of ourselves as being-in-the-world until there is a breakdown in our sense-making. Once there is a breakdown in our sense-making, we come to make our own ways of making sense explicit. In doing this, we open up the possibility of transforming our way of seeing, framing and thus being and doing in the world.

Another way of making the latter point is to say that although the human being is always and already part of a hermeneutic circle or network of parts and wholes, it is only in breakdowns in sense-making that it comes to see the hermeneutic circle of which it is a part.

A final way of putting this point is that while during its practical coping with the world the human being develops a felt sense of its world, this felt sense remains implicit and in the background. It is only when there is a breakdown in felt sense that the human being comes to see the felt sense through which it is formed and transformed.

As will also be shown, coming to see the hermeneutic circle and felt sense of which it is a part is also the condition for transformation of its way of being-in-the-world. It is the basis for what Spinosa et al. (1997) call disclosing new worlds, or what Heidegger calls *"eigentlichkeit,"* (1985, p231), that is, becoming the authors of our way of being-in-the-world rather than just passively taking over a way of being-in-the-world.

Instrumental Deliberation

When an item of equipment breaks down or is absent, our relation to the entity changes such that it becomes an object to be thought about. Putting the conditions under which things become explicit in a more general way, Heidegger says: "When its unusability is thus discovered, equipment becomes conspicuous … (W)hat cannot be used just lies there; it shows itself as an equipmental Thing which looks so and so" (1985, p103).

Thus we move into a mode of "looking at" or observing the item of equipment as a thing. This occurs, for example, when a hammer, because it is broken or defective, can no longer be used for hammering. Heidegger believes that the inability to use the item of equipment for its designated purpose transforms *Dasein*'s relationship to it in that it causes *Dasein* to stand back from its involvement in the thing as an item of equipment and comes to see the thing that it is involved in; that is, the defective hammer is now an object seen or examined in its own right, whereas while it was being used it was not an object to be gazed at.

However, it is also in such breakdowns that the possibility of being a scientific observer or a rational analyst of objects occurs. For in the disturbance of using or manipulating equipment, we stand at an objective distance from things. In this case, we become concerned with the properties of objects or the causal relationship between objects or the way we represent them as concepts.

Heidegger is quick to point out different degrees of disruption or interruption in the use of equipment. Some interruptions are temporary. We are either able to fix the equipment or replace it with new items of equipment of the same sort. In this case there has been some standing back and deliberation, but it has been temporary. As Dreyfus points out, there are also temporary breakdowns in items of equipment. In such cases, we are called upon to think about other means to achieve our ends: "Normally, we do not notice that things are accessible; we just transparently use them, or notice the difficulty of access to them, but go on anyway. But if there is an obstacle I may have to stop and think about how to reach my goal" (Dreyfus 1993, p138).

Based on the writing of Heidegger, I would like to call this "instrumental reasoning." For it involves deliberation regarding how to refine the means appropriate for a particular task at hand. It is about fixing, replacing or finding new instruments that we can then use in the context of practical coping. It is reasoning about the best means to achieve ends, but it is not reasoning about the ends themselves. As Dreyfus says, when equipment is disrupted, "we try to fix or improve it and get going again" (1993, p84). This involves what Dreyfus calls "deliberate action" (1993, p76) to get things working again and in which "we act deliberately paying attention to what we are doing" (1993, p72). Dreyfus maintains that in deliberation "one stops and considers what is going on and plans what to do" (1993, p72). Then of course one implements or applies it.

Again, just to re-emphasize, it is a question of the means and not the ends or even the relation between the means and ends that have become explicit themes of concern here.

Scientific Deliberation

However, some interruptions are more permanent in such a way that we cannot simply return to the work. As Dreyfus puts it, "Once our work is permanently interrupted, we can either stare helplessly at the remaining objects or take a new detached theoretical stance towards things and try to explain their underlying causal properties. Only when absorbed, ongoing activity is interrupted is there such theoretical reflection" (1993, p79).

This occurs, for example, when a hammer, because it is permanently absent, broken or defective, can no longer be used for hammering. Heidegger believes that the inability to use the item of equipment for its designated purpose transforms the human's relationship to it. The rupture establishes a separation between the human being and the equipment with which it is involved. This separation is the condition in terms of which an entity is constituted as an "object" to be observed and thought about. For example, the permanently defective hammer is now an object seen or examined in its own right, whereas while it was being used it was not an object to be gazed at.

It is under such conditions of permanent disturbance that an entity becomes an object, as Heidegger says, "for knowing the 'world' theoretically" through a "bare perceptual cognition" (1985, p95). As Dreyfus remarks, it is under such conditions that detached, objectifying scientific analysis becomes possible.

Dreyfus's reading of Heidegger allows us to see that the Heideggerian logic of science applies not only to objects in the environment but to the environment itself, to culture, to history, to society at large. In fact, it applies to all of those forms of study that have been called either the sciences or the social sciences. They tend to turn networks of relationships into things or substances to be studied.

Dreyfus writes of the way we see "any discipline from physics to factual history" in terms of a "detached, objectifying thematization" (1993, p83).

In this sense he points to the need for an acute sensitivity in which we view our context from within or from without. Because of the detached attitude of science, we have forgotten the discipline of seeing things from within. We are habituated into seeing things from without. More about this will be said once we have dealt with the existential forms of disruption.

It can be said that, for Heidegger, we have at least two kinds of relationship to beings: one in which we are absorbed or involved in them and one in which they become explicit themes of concern—engagement in and thinking about things. The difference between the two modes in which beings are revealed are termed by Heidegger "ready-to-hand" (items of equipment) and "presence-at-hand" (objects of explicit concern). Beings are ready to hand when we are involved with them as items of equipment that are usable. Under such conditions, they are literally ready for our hands, ready for our use. When items of equipment cannot be used, they become present to us. They become objects at which we can gaze. They are present-at-hand.

For Heidegger, the terms "ready-to-hand" and "presence-at-hand" designate different modes of being involved or concerned with the world. To be concerned with things "present-at-hand" is to be detached from the world. It is to look at, observe and analyze the world. The world becomes an object for our concern. We come to know the world by thinking about it rather than through our familiarity with it. Such a mode of relationship functions in terms of the distinction and distance between subject and object and thus implies all the debates that go with this distinction, such as the desire for greater objectivity and neutrality, freedom from irrationality and emotionality, the distinction between mind and matter, the need for a criterion of truth. The form of knowledge appropriate to it is a representational knowledge that can be articulated in the form of statements. It is also a form of knowledge based on arithmetical and mathematical measurement.

Heidegger is very quick to point out that scientific and detached theoretical observation is dependent upon and arises out of the sense of familiarity that emerges out of being involved in the world through play and using items of equipment: "the ready-to-hand ... provides the basis on which entities can for the first time be discovered as they are 'substantially' 'in themselves'" (1985, p122).

Heidegger makes this point even more generally. Rather than cognitive and theoretical knowledge being independent of the understanding developed out of our pre-conceptual interpretation or sense of familiarity arising out of our way of being involved in the world, Heidegger maintains that it is the other way around: all our explicit knowledge is grounded in the understanding developed out of our being involved in the everyday world of the ready-to-hand. Thus our sense of "caring," for example, is first developed in the context of the sense of being cared for. Our primary understanding of order, authority, structure, managing, and so on, are all developed on the basis of our familiar sense of them. Only much later will we come to think about, examine and be critical of them. But at first, they emerge out of a felt sense. If we do not have the felt sense of them, we do not have the most primordial understanding in terms of which to make sense of them. They cannot even begin to be critiqued.

More than this, all the roles that we play or will play in society are shaped by the familiar sense we develop through involvement. Taking this one step further, the conventions and scripts which make it possible for us to know our way about our society or culture are developed on the basis of the familiar sense developed out of involvement. We need to have the felt sense of being a father, a plumber, a doctor, and so on, before we can develop an explicit sense of these roles or ways of being.

Heidegger uses various types of language to describe the understanding based on familiar sense. He calls it a pre-conceptual understanding, a pre-thematic understanding or an "average everyday" understanding. They are "pre-" understandings because they are for the most part not explicit. They guide us without us knowing that we are even guided by them. We take them to be natural rather than shaped by our ways of being involved in the world. It is not until we experience a breakdown in sense-making that we begin to see that they are conventions for being and doing rather than the natural way of doing.

Hermeneutic Attunement for Reframing of the Relation between the Whole and the Parts

The third form of disruption Heidegger calls existential anxiety. Existential anxiety may be defined as a breakdown in the familiar felt sense of meaning that makes everyday living possible. It is, as already stated, the experience of the absurdity or uncanniness of being; the experience in which we have no felt sense of the scripts or conventions which guide and give everyday living its sense of purpose and structure.

This does not refer to breakdowns within practical coping but breakdowns of practical coping itself, that is, it is not to breakdowns in items of equipment but to breakdowns of sense-making itself. Examples of this have already been seen in the phenomenology of creative destruction in which the entrepreneur leaves the familiar of the old, is able to withstand the uncertainty of the familiar as the basis upon which to create new way ways of doing things. It is also fundamental to the experience of Kuhn's (1970) notion of paradigm crises in which anomalies call the conventions of a paradigm into question such that scientists are left in the uncertainty of having no ground upon which to stand. It is also to be seen in travelling to a new land where one does not have the common sense with which to cope in the unfamiliar environment. It is a breakdown in taken for granted patterns of familiarity or conventions for doing things.

At its extreme, hermeneutic uncertainty expresses itself in existential anxiety. In existential anxiety the human being's "taken-for-granted cultural ground drops away" (Dreyfus 1993, p304). In anxiety, as Heidegger says, "The threatening does not come from what is ready-to-hand or present-at-hand, but rather from the fact that neither of these 'says' anything any longer. Environmental entities no longer have any involvement. The world in which I exist has sunk into insignificance" (1985, p393).

Leo Tolstoy, in his autobiography *My Confession*, describes how such an experience interfered with his life to such an extent that he was unable to get on with the task of fulfilling his everyday obligations:

> *Five years ago something very strange began to happen with me: I was overcome by minutes of perplexity and then of an arrest of life, as though I did not know how to live or what to do, and I lost myself and was dejected. ... These arrests of life found their expression in ever the same questions: "Why? Well, and then?' ... So long as I did not know why, I could not do anything. Amidst my thoughts of farming, which interested me very much during that time, there would suddenly pass through my head a question like this: 'All right, you are going to have six hundred desyatinas of land in the government of Samara, and three hundred horses—and then?' And I completely lost my senses and did not know what to think farther. ... I felt that what I was standing on had given way ... My life came to a standstill (1987, p10).*

Although it may be argued that such experiences are simply pathological experiences of madness, from a Heideggerian perspective they are seen as experiences in which the human being comes to develop an attunement, not to any particular facet of life, but to the issue of life as a whole. In these experiences the human being is deprived of its everyday preoccupations in such a way that it is not concerned with this or that aspect of life (marriage, work, family), this or that branch of thought (biology, physics, psychology, sociology), but with life itself. It has made a Gestalt switch from its involvement with things to life as the context within which such involvements take place. As Dreyfus says: "Rather than revealing some part of the workshop world from the inside, it reveals the whole world as if from outside" (1993, p179).

In fact, what Heidegger can be seen to be arguing is that this kind of disturbance is the departure point for the beginning of the *experience* of the activity of philosophy. From this perspective, it is when, through anxiety, the human being is detached from the immediacy of its everyday concerns that it can begin to experience wonder at not this or that facet of life but at the being of life itself: "Only when the strangeness of what-is forces itself upon us does it awaken and invite our wonder. Only because of wonder, that is to say, the revelation of Nothing, does the 'Why?' spring to our lips" (Heidegger 1948, p353).

This is again indicated in the case of Tolstoy. Rather than moping in despair, his experience of the meaninglessness of all things became the existential basis upon which he began to question his taken-for-granted beliefs about pleasure, science, rationality and religion. The more he began to question in this way, the more fascinated he became not with this or that aspect of living but with life itself.

It is important to note that the form of questioning our way of being in anxiety is not a scientific or objectivist study of something outside of and at a distance from us. It is a form of questioning of that which we are already within. We are questioning our way of being from the inside out and not from the outside. We are questioning our ground while it is shaking beneath our feet.

For in anxiety the human being does not stand in a detached and disengaged relationship to the world as does a scientist. Rather it is simultaneously in and observing the world that it is in.

To think in a hermeneutic phenomenological way from within one's practice means to reflect from a position, as Eger (1993) says, of "being in" that which one is interpreting. Eger, in his writing on Heidegger, makes this point clear: "Far from being a mystical experience, what is described here is simultaneously a state of detachment and attachment" (1993, p28), driven by a sense of wonder. Existential reflexivity is that form of being attuned to what we are already in. It is an emotional distancing from what we are already in. Making this point in a general way, Douglas-Mullen has said: "One feature peculiar to humans is the ability to detach ourselves from our lives and see ourselves as if we were 'just one of them.' For some of us the thought of this comes more often and stays longer. This type of person is described as 'reflective,' 'self-conscious,' 'neurotic,' 'ironic,' 'pensive,' 'deep' etc." (1981, p11).

Putting this in explicitly Heideggerian language, in the ecstatic state of anxiety *Dasein* comes face to face with itself as being-in-the-world and with its own mode of being-in-the-world. This coming face to face with itself as being-in-the-world is not in the mode of a subject examining an object from a position of detachment. It is an existential, hermeneutic and phenomenological phenomenon in which the human being comes to experience the world that it is always and already within.

It is at this point that hermeneutic phenomenology is important for Heidegger. For hermeneutic phenomenology is the art of allowing the phenomenon to show, reveal and disclose itself from within. The word "phenomenon" from a Heideggerian perspective means "that which shows itself in itself" (1985, p51). It is the discipline of making manifest or appearing; of allowing "the entities of which one is talking [to] be taken out of their hiddenness" (1985, p56). In contrast the appearing of phenomenology is "covering up" (1985, p57). Adding to this, Heidegger says that phenomenology is the art of "letting something be seen in its togetherness with something" (1985, p56). In the context of being human, for Heidegger this means showing itself in relation to the world it inhabits. Heidegger is quite clear that phenomenology has nothing to do with "objects," these being the subject matter of specific disciplines like science and theology (1985, p59). It is ontology, our being-in-the-world and being-within-the world that is the subject matter of phenomenology (1985, pp59–60).

Furthermore, phenomenology is possible only existentially for Heidegger, that is, when there is a breakdown in meaning, the concreteness of our way of being-in and being-within the world becomes manifest (1985, p61). He is very concerned that Being, being-in-the-world and being-within-the-world become manifest in a concrete way (1985, p63) and critiques the history of philosophy for reducing Being to detached and disengaged "material for reworking."

Rather being-in-the-world is manifested concretely in experiences of anxiety (1985, p233).

Phenomenology is hermeneutic in the sense that it is concerned with interpretation (1985, p61). Interpretation is the art of being able to see the relationship between the parts and the whole of a phenomenon such as being-in-the-world, which is what Heidegger calls an "equiprimordial" whole, meaning that the parts are different from each other but simultaneously belong to each other such that they appear through each other. Hermeneutics is thus the activity of allowing the parts to be seen in relation to the whole, and seeing the whole allows for the parts to be situated in relationship to each other. The novelty in Heidegger's use of hermeneutics is that he saw it as a practice not only for interpreting texts but for making sense of being-in-the-world as a text. Furthermore, it needs to be said that hermeneutics in Heidegger is an existential activity. It is from within experiences of the breakdown of meaning that we become hermeneutic, that is, it is not primarily a research methodology but a way of being attuned to being that emerges in anxiety.

It is in anxiety that questions of "metaphysics" become existentially meaningful issues. M.A. Screech's reading of Plato's notion of philosophy is similar to the later Heideggerian articulation:

> Since wisdom is a good, men might conclude that insanity (mania) is bad, but Socrates denied this was so. Plain insanity attributable to illness is, of course bad. But lovers are insane too, so are philosophers, prophets, poets. They are insane in that their souls are all striving to leave their bodies. In the case of lovers their souls yearn to merge with the beloved; in the case of philosophers their souls yearn to soar aloft towards divine Truth and Beauty. ... These notions are not simply metaphorical (Screech 1991, p31).

It is in the disturbance named anxiety that the human being develops an explicit concern with life as a whole. This point is made by Dreyfus, who maintains that "anxiety reveals Dasein as dependent upon a public system of significances that it did not produce" (1993, p177).

In Heideggerian terms this can mean one of two things: a concern with the tradition in terms of which life makes sense and a concern with being-in-the-world itself. Because they are not identical structures, I will treat each of these two separately, beginning with the former (the latter shall be the theme of the next prism): what does it mean, in Heideggerian terms, to become explicitly attuned to traditions themselves?

Heidegger's notion of tradition can partially be depicted through the notion of a paradigm. Like paradigms, these traditions supply the conditions in terms of which things are intelligible, the horizon of intelligibility, criteria by which things are and are not significant, conditions of "proof" and ways of reasoning. We justify our actions with reference to these traditions. They supply our self-understanding and our understanding of others. Furthermore, like paradigms, we think in terms of them but we hardly ever think about them. They shape our understanding without ever becoming explicit objects of understanding themselves. They themselves are, for the most part, implicit intuitions which guide our understanding of our experience. They set models and norms for us.

Although I have framed the idea of tradition and culture in terms of the Kuhnian idea of a paradigm, Heidegger develops a vocabulary of his own to pinpoint the nuances of what he means by these terms. From the Heideggerian perspective, whereas paradigms are characterized by models for doing things, traditions are characterized by what Heidegger calls an "average everyday" way of doing things. The idea of "average everydayness" refers to the commonly accepted ways of doing things within a society. It is the web of "know-how" that is needed to survive in a particular society. Each society has "average everyday" ways of maintaining distance from friends, strangers and lovers. From the Heideggerian perspective, we have an "average everyday" way of doing most things: of eating, drinking, sleeping, engaging in sexual relationships. We do these things in a certain common way without having established these ways of doing things for ourselves. They are models that are handed down from and have the authority of the past. They are ways that have worked.

Heidegger uses a number of other terms to characterize average everydayness. It is characterized by what he calls "publicness," which in turn is characterized as "*das man*," "theyness" or "the Anyone." Dreyfus has given a clear exposition of these terms:

> *the roles and goals available to Dasein are not first experienced as yours or mine, rather, as public possibilities provided by the culture; they make no essential reference to me, but are available to anyone. For this reason Heidegger refers to the public as "das man," or the "Anyone." The public, whatever its activity, is certainly not a sort of self-conscious subject (1993, p123).*

It is only in times of existential anxiety—just as it is in the case of paradigms—that we come to develop an explicit attunement to our "average everyday" forms of intelligibility themselves. To become attuned to average everydayness is to develop an attunement to the tradition or culture to which a human being belongs. Here we start to see our network or patterns of standing in relationship to the world. We see our forms of intelligibility, our forms of interpreting and thinking and the values in terms of which we aspire and act. As I have already detailed, it is in a crisis called the "anxiety of nothingness" that the human being comes face to face with its average everydayness. As Dreyfus comments: "Anxiety reveals Dasein as dependent upon a public system of significances that it did not produce" (1993, p177).

In existential anxiety, the human being has the possibility of one or two responses: either to fall back on its average everyday way of being in the world or to question the way of being that has been made explicit to it through anxiety. Heidegger calls the former possibility a state of fallenness and a state of inauthenticity. It is an attempt to hold onto a past that has been surpassed. The second possibility is to "resolutely" question the average everyday way of being of which it has been a part. For it developed its felt sense or pre-conceptual understanding of being not by examination or questioning but through being immersed and involved in the world. It was on the latter basis that it formed a familiarity with the world. What is disclosed in the experience of anxiety is the possibility of questioning and going beyond the pre-conceptual understanding that it has inhabited without even knowing that it has inhabited it.

In anxiety it discovers its potentiality for being. Its potentiality for being is not something within itself but is something to which "Being-in-the-world has been delivered over" (1985, p233). It discovers that it is more than its history, its culture or its average everyday way of doing things. It is on this basis that it begins to be able, as Spinosa et al. (1997) put it, to discover new worlds, and thus anxiety is the basis for transformation.

There is a paradox at the heart of existential anxiety. In its average everyday absorption in the world, the question of meaning is a meaningless question. It is only when existence is experienced as meaningless that the question of meaning becomes an urgent and existentially significant question. We have seen this in the example of Tolstoy: the question of meaninglessness would not let him go. He is not alone in this. John Stuart Mill (1989) is another example. And as Screech (1991) has maintained, the history of Western thought is replete with such examples.

It can also be said that in anxiety the circular nature of existence and the way of being attuned to existence becomes explicit. This circle is a hermeneutic rather than a vicious circle. The parts and the whole are co-constitutive of each other. It is in moments of anxiety in which *Dasein* comes "face to face" (1985, p232) with itself. Putting it in what sounds like a tautology, being-in-the-world *experiences* itself as being-in-the-world. For example, if one takes climate change seriously, its logic has a circular nature: our way of being-in-the-world is destroying our way of being-in-the-world. If this is the case, there is nowhere to turn; no place to hide. Yet, for the most part, this is still dealt with as a technical rather than a hermeneutic issue. We try to respond to it with the very way of being that generated it in the first place.

With existential anxiety we return to the start of this chapter. For it is in existential anxiety that existence is called into question. Koestenbaum says that anxiety is the lived experience of reflexive awareness itself (1978, p222).

Hermeneutic Attunement and the Gaze of the Stranger

Not only anxiety but the experience of the stranger enables us to see our way of doing things in ways that call them into question and open up the possibility of seeing in new ways. This is especially important in a world of globalization and creative destruction. Bauman has given us a framework within which to understand how our ways of practical coping break down in the face of the anxiety of the stranger. Bauman calls the collapse of the familiar a hermeneutic problem. He says that "hermeneutic problems ... arise when the meaning is not unreflectively evident. ... Unresolved hermeneutical problems mean uncertainty as to how the situation ought to be read and what response is likely to bring the desired results. At best, uncertainty is felt as discomforting. At worst, it carries a sense of danger" (1995, p146).

It is important to note that breakdowns in sense-making do not arise because anything ready to hand breaks down but because our ways of practical coping do not make sense in new, strange and unfamiliar circumstances.

Many people of industrialized nations see the home as a physical space in which they are materially comfortable and secure. This point is made by, amongst others, Theodore Adorno, who writes about "modern functional habitations" that are "factory sites that have strayed into the consumption sphere, devoid of all relation to the occupant" (1992, p17).

Jager, in his reading of Heidegger, cautions against this view when he says that "a house or a city is [not just] a kind of material framework or container that indifferently holds its human cargo" (1983, p153). Rather, based on a reading of Heidegger's *Being and Time*, he points out that the home, which he sees as being rooted in the notion of inhabiting, is a place of familiarity. To be at home means to be familiar with, which in turn means to know one's way about. An example of the power of the familiar is given in the following extract from Kenneth Grahame, quoted by David Miller:

> *"And beyond the Wild Wood again?" [asked the Mole]. "Where it's all blue and dim, and one sees what may be hills or perhaps they mayn't, and something like the smoke of towns, or is only cloud drift?" "Beyond the Wild Wood comes the Wide World," [said the Rat]. "And that's something that doesn't matter, either to you or me. I've never been there, and I'm never going, nor you either, if you've got any sense at all. Don't ever refer to it again, please" (1993, p2).*

Here it can be seen that the familiarity of the home is contrasted with the unfamiliarity of a strange world. The experience of the migrant today is the exemplar of the relationship between the familiar and the strange, for in leaving the familiar environment of the home, the migrant enters an unfamiliar and strange environment in which the entire issue of identity, "know-how," cultural paradigm and sense of place has to be renegotiated. Interesting work in this regard is being done by Key Ganguly (1992), who writes of the way in which "the security of [the migrant's] taken-for-granted subject positions is disrupted in the immigrant context." Not only do migrants often find themselves without the support systems that, as Ganguly says, "they were brought up to believe in and on which they counted to provide emotional and psychic sustenance," but they do not have the cultural capital or socialization to read or interpret the unfamiliar situation in which they find themselves. In the new context they tend to be inappropriate without even knowing where and when they are inappropriate. Commenting on his experiences observing people caught between the traditional world and the modern world, van Niekerk has said: "It dawned on me that between the modern world and the traditional world there was yet another world, a half-baked world of confusion and maladjustment in all areas of people's daily existence" (1993, p103).

The experience of the migrant is one in which the world can seem strange and even absurd. As Albert Camus says, "in a universe suddenly divested of illusions and lights, man feels an alien, a stranger" (1955, p13). Ganguly speaks of the alienation from the ways of the dominant society experienced by the migrants that she studied.

A similar distinction is to be found in Heidegger's *Being and Time*. In the context of a discussion of anxiety, Heidegger distinguishes between, on the one hand, the "unheimlisch," the uncanny or the not-at-home and the familiarity of being at home in the world: "In anxiety one feels '*uncanny*.' … But here 'uncanniness' also means 'not-being-at-home'" (1985, p233). Being not-at-home expresses itself as a collapse of the familiar. Collapse of the familiar is experienced as being unable to read and make sense of situations and of self — as, for example, a migrant journeying from a rural to an urban area.

As Heidegger makes clear, the home, the familiar and the experience of ontological insecurity are linked to each other. In the work of Heidegger this is indicated by the link between anxiety and being not at home, and in Bauman's work the inability to read a situation creates a situation of uncertainty. It should also be pointed out that the experience of the familiarity of home is also linked to the issue of power, for the familiar is a place in which we "know how" to get around. As David Jardine (1994) has said, the familiar is "the world wherein one felt at home and able (playing as this does with the wonderful etymological link between *habilite* and ability)." Unlike in unfamiliar situations where we may need to rely on others, the familiar is a place in which we are enabled and thus empowered. To lose the familiar is thus to lose the horizon which allows us to be powerful. And to lose power is to be helpless.

For Heidegger, the link between the familiarity of home and the anxiety of the disruption of home is also the source of existential questioning. For it is when our way of being at home in the world is threatened and no longer can be taken for granted that *Dasein* finds itself thrown into questioning; not just intellectual or cognitive questioning as takes place in most university contexts, but into existential questioning, questioning as a way of being attuned to the world. This is a kind of questioning in which we are deprived of the sense of meaning. We do not know how to go on living.

References

Adorno, T. (1992) Refuge for the Homeless. *New Formations*. Vol 17. Summer.

Bauman, Z. (1995) Modernity and Ambivalence. In: Featherstone, M. (ed.) *Global Culture: Nationalism, globalization and modernity*. London: Sage Publications.

Camus, A. (1955) *The Myth of Sisyphus*. Harmondsworth: Penguin Books.

Dreyfus, H. (1993) *Being-in-the-World: A commentary on Heidegger's Being and Time, Division 1*. Boston: The MIT Press.

Douglas-Mullen, J. (1981) *Kierkegaard's Philosophy: Self-deception and cowardice in the present age*. New York: A Mentor Book.

Eger, M. (1993) Hermeneutics as an Approach to Science. *Science and Education*. Vol 2, No 1. pp303–28.

Ganguly, K. (1992) Migrant Identities: Personal Memory and the Construction of Selfhood. *Cultural Studies*. Vol 6, No 1. pp27–50.

Heidegger, M. (1948) What Is Metaphysics? In: Brock, W. (ed.) *Existence and Being*. Indiana: Regnery/Gateway, Inc.

Heidegger, M. (1985) *Being and Time*. Oxford: Basil Blackwell.

Jager, B. (1983) Theorizing and the Elaboration of Place: Inquiry into Galileo and Freud. In: Giorgi, A., Barton, A. and Maes, C. (eds), *Duquesne Studies in Phenomenological Psychology*, Volume 4 (pp153–80). Pittsburgh: Duquesne University Press.

Jardine, D. (1994) Student-Teaching, Interpretation and the Monstrous Child. *Journal of Philosophy of Education*. Vol 28, No 1. pp17–24.

Kierkegaard, S. (1996) *Papers and Journals: A selection* (translated by Alastair Hannay). London: Penguin Books.

Koestenbaum, P. (1978) *The New Image of the Person: The theory and practice of clinical philosophy*. Connecticut: Greenwood Press.

Kuhn, T. (1970) *The Structure of Scientific Revolutions*. Chicago: The University of Chicago Press.

Lennie, I. (1999) *Beyond Management*. London: SAGE Publications.

Mill, J.S. (1989) *Autobiography*. London: Penguin Books.

Miller, D. (1993) In Defence of Nationality. *Journal of Applied Philosophy*. Vol 10, No 1. pp3–16.

Sartre, J.P. (1968) *Search for a Method*. New York: Vintage Books.

Screech, M.A. (1991) *Montaigne and Melancholy: The wisdom of the essays*. London: Penguin Books.

Shaw, R. (2012) An Opening in Management for Martin Heidegger. Available at: http://shaw.org.nz/Heidegger_management.doc.

Spinosa, C., Flores, F. and Dreyfus, H. (1997) *Disclosing New Worlds: Entrepreneurship, democratic action, and the cultivation of solidarity*. Cambridge, MA: MIT Press.

Tolstoy, L. (1987) My Confession. In: Hanflig, O. (ed.) *Life and Meaning*. Oxford: Basil Blackwell.

van Niekerk, A. (1993) *One Destiny: Our common future in Africa*. Cape Town: Tafelberg.

Weick, K. (1993) *The Collapse of Sensemaking in Organizations*: The Mann Gulch Disaster. *Administrative Science Quarterly*. Vol 38. pp628–52.

Chapter 6
The Existential Experience of Disclosing New Worlds

Existence and Becoming

For Heidegger to say that the human being exists is to say that its being is an issue for it. To exist means to be in question and at stake in one's very way of being. As Heidegger says, "The question of existence never gets straightened out except through existing itself" (1985, p33). And elsewhere he says that the human being is "that entity which in its Being has this very Being as an *issue*" (1985, p67).

What being-in-question means concretely will be explored in this chapter. But before outlining the concrete meaning of being-in-question, it needs to be said that being-in-question applies just as much to our professional lives as it does to our private lives. Whether we are managers or leaders, educators and/or researchers, our very being is in question. Our way of being as a manager, leader, researcher or educator develops as we respond to the professional and personal situations in which we are immersed. As Martin Buber once said, responding in the context of the contingencies of life is the "naval string of creation" (quoted in Hodes 1998). As we respond to the contingencies of leading, managing, researching or educating, so our identities and way of being, our habits of practice emerge. Putting it formally, our habits emerge not in advance of being in situations but only as we inhabit situations.

A central question is: what kind of thinking goes into embracing being-in-question? It cannot be a kind of armchair thinking, a thinking in advance of action. It needs to be a kind of thinking in action. What then does it mean from a Heideggerian existential perspective to think in the context of action?

Rather than elaborating Heidegger's thinking in a formal logical way (which for Heidegger would be a kind of thinking outside of action), following the methodology of Heidegger, I will develop this in what he calls a "phenomenological" way. This means focusing on the lived experience of being-in-question.

This chapter will thus make use of real-life experiences to bring out what it means to be in question and at stake. The first exemplar that will be used is that of a poet identified by Heidegger as one whom illustrates his perspective. This is the poet Rainer Maria Rilke. In the context of entrepreneurship I will show how the way in which Steve Jobs describes his life as a journey exemplifies Heidegger's point of being in question. In the context of organizational leadership, I will show how the way in which Andrew Grove describes Intel's way of responding to a threat to what he calls its very existence exemplifies Heidegger's perspective. In the next chapter I will show how this being-in-question is exemplified in the context of research in management.

Rainer Maria Rilke

The particular text of Rainer Maria Rilke (1993) that I will focus on is a series of letters between Rilke and a person in the midst of a career transition. The person in question is a disillusioned army officer who wants to become a poet. He sends some of his poetry to Rilke with a specific question in mind: not simply does he have the talent to be a poet, but is he good enough to be a poet?

In their series of interchanges, Rilke responds by saying that nobody other than the aspirant poet can answer this. In his letters to the aspirant poet, Rilke notes that the person has asked the same question of others. He has even had his poems published, but none of this has been enough to make him feel that he is a poet. Furthermore, Rilke points out that he cannot answer this question through advanced calculation, thought or speculation. Only as he experiments through writing poetry will he be able to tell if poetry is for him; only as he immerses himself in writing will he know whether it resonates with him; and only as he experiments will his way of writing poetry develop:

> ask yourself in the most silent hour of your night: must I write? Dig into yourself for a deep answer. And if this answer rings out in assent, if you meet this solemn question with a strong, simple "I must," then build your life in accordance with this necessity; your while life, even into its humblest and most indifferent hour, must become a sign and witness to this impulse (1993).

Perhaps he shall find, as Rilke maintains, that poetry is not for him. No one else can answer the question or way of being a poet for him. Only he can answer this question. He is thus alone in the way in which he responds to the question of being a poet. There is no one but himself that can respond to his way of being-in-question:But after this descent into yourself and into your solitude, perhaps you will have to renounce becoming a poet (if, as I have said, one feels one could live without writing, then one shouldn't write at all). Nevertheless, even then, this self-searching will not have been for nothing. Your life will still find its own paths from there, and that they may be good, rich, and wide is what I wish for you, more than I can say (1993).

To be sure, he can seek guidance on the way. Rilke offers him the opportunity of entering into a correspondence with him in which they explore the possibility of his becoming a poet, but it is the army officer who will make the final decision, saying yes or no. The way in which he responds on the quest to the question of being a poet can emerge as he responds to experimenting with poetry.

Crucial to Rilke is the way in which the potential poet responds to the quest of being alone in responding to the question of being a poet: is he able to embrace the lived experience of exploring this question for himself? Or is the loneliness of being-in-question too frightening for him. In Heideggerian terms, this is a distinction between finding yourself (authenticity) and falling into the "they," the secure and pre-scripted roles of society (in authenticity). For it is when existentially alone that we have the opportunity to find ourselves, but equally, we have the opportunity the shrink back into the comfort of habitual and conventional ways of doing things.

On a number of occasions Rilke does suggest that the poet is frightened by the quest of being-in-question as a potential poet. He suggests that one of the reasons that the poet is writing to him is that he, the potential poet, does not want to make the decision for himself. Rather, he wants objective or outside confirmation that his poetry is good enough for him to be a poet. Rilke sees this as a flight from developing his own answer to the question:

You ask whether your verses are any good. You ask me. You have asked others before this. You send them to magazines. You compare them with other poems. … No one can advise or help you—no one. There is only one thing you should do. Go into yourself. Find out the reason that commands you to write; see whether it has spread its roots into the very depths of your heart; confess to yourself whether you would have to die

> *if you were forbidden to write. This most of all: ask yourself in the most*
> *silent hour of your night: must I write? (1993).*

He needs to answer for himself because only as he answers for himself will his poetic attunement, habits of practice, resonance with poetry develop. Thus he needs to be able to withstand the aloneness of responding to the question from himself. Once again, it can be said that this question cannot be addressed by pure thought or formal logic, but only as the aspirant poet throws himself into the activity of writing will he be able to discover his being and develop his habits of practice (way of being) as a poet. Only through experience will he be able to say that poetry is not for him.

Although Rilke does not say this directly, it can also be said that the kind of experience and experimentation that Rilke is referring to is not the positivist or scientific notion; that is, he is not conducting experiments from an outsider's perspective. He is the experiment himself and his life is worked through in such experimenting. He is not detached, neutral and uninvolved with his search and re-searching of his quest to be a poet. There is indeed no way of responding to the question objectively, through empirical reasoning or as a product of logic: "But let me make this request right away: Read as little as possible of literary criticism—such things are either partisan opinions, which have become petrified and meaningless, hardened and empty of life, or else they are just clever word-games, in which one view wins today, and tomorrow the opposite view" (1993).

On the contrary, he is the experiment himself. It is not an object outside of himself that is observing, but with his own being that he is experimenting. Furthermore, rather than being simply detached, it is only as he is immersed, involved, engaged and committed to experiencing the activity of writing that he will learn to write and learn whether he will want to write.

He himself is the question. If the kind of questioning is neither simply logical nor scientific in the common-sense understanding of positivism (that is, of being detached, neutral and objective), what kind of questioning is it?

Although Rilke does not use these words, I would like to suggest that this form of questioning is an existential form of questioning. Referring back to the earlier statements of Heidegger, where existential questioning and responding occur when our being and our way of being a poet are in question, we are the question. When we are the question—this is existential questioning.

What, then, is existential questioning? Returning to Rilke's response to the poet, existential questioning is questioning from within the experience. For Rilke this kind of questioning has several dimensions. This includes "loving" the question itself. It is being fascinated and in a state of wonder regarding the question of being a poet, rather than being frightened by the question.

One of the ways in which we demonstrate being frightened by the question is to seek answers to the question. Rilke recommends that the aspirant poet learn to "live into" the question; not simply answer the question but actually question the question; allow the question to question him: what is actually being asked in the question? What does it mean to have to ask a question or being in a state of questioning? Thus Rilke says:

> *You are so young, so much before all beginning, and I would like to beg you, dear Sir, as well as I can, to have patience with everything unresolved in your heart and to try to love the questions themselves as if they were locked rooms or books written in a very foreign language. Don't search for the answers, which could not be given to you now, because you would not be able to live them. And the point is, to live everything. Live the questions now (1993).*

This is against common sense today. For it is more often than not assumed that once we have a question, we simply go about answering it. In contrast to this, as Heidegger says, the very way in which we ask a question will determine the spectrum of solutions that are available to us. And so we need to take care to address the presuppositions in terms of which the question is asked: where are we asking the question from? What is at stake in our being in this question? Where is the questioning coming from in us?

Thus the poet needs to be able to allow himself to be in question and he needs to allow his way of being to emerge out of the question, that is, rather than trying to give a statement-like answer to the question. The response to the question will come in the form of his way of being within the world.

Furthermore, not only does he need to live into the question but the response to the question is not an answer that can be stated in abstract, logical terms, rather it is a way of being; it is the fact that he does or does not become a poet. If he does become a poet, it is expressed in the habits of practice that develop through responding to his being-in-question: "Don't search for the answers, which could not be given to you now, because you would not be able to live them. And the point is, to live everything. Live the questions now.

Perhaps then, someday far in the future, you will gradually, without even noticing it, live your way into the answer."

Only once the response is embedded in the habits of practice will he be able (if he so desires) to say or express in language what his habits of practice are. Thus the representation in language of his way of being as a poe, develops only after it has been developed. To repeat the quotation from Kierkegaard, "Life is lived forward but understood backward" (1987).

The Case of Steve Jobs

Some may wonder what this has to do with organizational and managerial practice and inquiry. As a clue, I will examine the life and death of Steve Jobs. It exemplifies how the Heideggerian attunement to existence and "passing through" or being-towards death is the basis for the disclosure of new worlds. It demonstrates how Jobs accounts in an existential-like way for the creation of the "iWorld" in which we live and through which we make sense of the world.

Jobs has not just created iPhones and iPads. He has created an iWorld, a world which is redefining who we are, how we relate to each other and how we do business with each other, not only in our local but in global contexts. He has opened possibilities for those of us ready to embrace this iWorld and created fear for those who see their businesses still grounded in the pre-iWorld.

In his now well-known Stanford speech (Jobs 2005), called "You've Got to Find What You Love" (all quotations and this section are based on the Stanford speech), Jobs identifies a constant attunement to death as the condition which not only kept him open to new possibilities but freed him from the constraints of following the "herd," that is, doing things because they were "supposed to be done." Anticipating his own mortality, he says, is: "the most important tool I've ever encountered to help me make the big choices in life."[1] Explaining himself, he says: "almost everything—all external expectations, all pride, all fear of embarrassment or failure—these things just fall away in the face of death, leaving only what is truly important."

A Heideggerian way of reframing the above statement is that, in the face of the anticipation of death, we are removed from being glued to the world of actuality and become open to the world of possibility.

---

1   http://www.youtube.com/watch?v=D1R-jKKp3NA.

One of the things that the attunement to death freed him from was the obligation to conform to conventions; to do things because he was supposed to do them. For example, he speaks about dropping out of university because what he was doing did not feel right to him. He was studying not what he wanted to study but what he was supposed to study: "Your time is limited, so don't waste it living someone else's life. Don't be trapped by dogma—which is living with the results of other people's thinking. Don't let the noise of others' opinions drown out your own inner voice."

His whole being rebelled against the latter. Although he does not say this, we could well imagine that while he was at college doing what he was supposed to do but not what he wanted to do, he felt a sense of emptiness and a sense of not "being-there," not being present in the courses that he was doing. "After six months, I couldn't see the value in it. I had no idea what I wanted to do with my life and no idea how college was going to help me figure it out."

Indeed, he does say that when he dropped out of university, he could "drop in" to the courses that interested him and about which he was passionate. One of the courses that he dropped into was a course in calligraphy, which became the basis of the typeface of the Macintosh. But he does say that the course had no practical value and he did it knowing full well that he had no well-developed sense of what he was going to do with it. He acknowledges a kind of existential anxiety, an anxiety of the unknown: "Of course it was impossible to connect the dots looking forward when I was in college."

Jobs is not naive enough to idealize death, but he does highlight the need to deal with his own fear of death: "No one wants to die. Even people who want to go to heaven don't want to die to get there. And yet death is the destination we all share."

He also highlights the creative potential that comes out of dealing with the fear of death. It allowed his imagination freedom to discover new possibilities. Speaking about the course in calligraphy, he says: "It was beautiful, historical, artistically subtle in a way that science can't capture, and I found it fascinating."

Overcoming the fear of death as a source of opening the world of possibility is not new to philosophers. It can be found, for example, in the philosophy of George Hegel, who speaks about the slave achieving freedom when they conquer or overcome their fear of death.

Nelson Mandela is also a perfect example of this. In his 1961 defence of himself at the Rivonia treason trial, he speaks about democracy as an event for which he was prepared to die. Because he and his people did not fear death, they were already liberated. Similarly, we can look at the Arab Spring in this light; going beyond the fear of death, the people of a range of Arab nations have begun to open up new possibilities for themselves.

And so it is with Steve Jobs: being constantly attuned to death and going beyond the fear of death was the basis of his constantly being able to open new possibilities, from the development of the Mac, through the development of Pixar and the range of iPods, iPhones and iPads. He was always ready to let go of the old, familiar routines in order to embrace the newness of possibility.

The philosopher Søren Kierkegaard (1987) has said:

> *If I were to wish for anything, I should not wish for wealth and power, but for the passionate sense of the possible, for the eye which, ever young and ardent, sees the possible ... what wine is so sparkling, so fragrant, so intoxicating, as possibility!*

It is because Jobs experienced the intoxication of possibility that, to use Kierkegaard's words, he could see things that no one else could see. He was liberated from what Kierkegaard would call being stuck in the finite or the actual, the common-sense way of seeing things.

Some people believe that it is by going overseas on journeys to strange and unfamiliar places that a person can be liberated from their everyday actual and common-sense ways of doing things. While not disagreeing with this, Kierkegaard says that if you can accept the possibility of your own death, common and everyday things become small and insignificant, and when the everyday becomes small and insignificant, it frees you to create and open the world beyond your immediate horizons. It is often said that one of the reasons that Israel as a nation is so innovative is because it constantly experiences itself as facing its own death. Consequently, everyday concerns become insignificant and as a result its people are not tied and wedded to one way of doing things.

When, as both Jobs and Kierkegaard have demonstrated, we are free from mundane concerns, we can play and experiment, virtues so central to innovation. As Jobs says: "Remembering that you are going to die is the best way I know to avoid the trap of thinking you have something to lose. You are already naked. There is no reason not to follow your heart."

We also hear Jobs saying, on countless occasions, that the resolute acceptance of the possibility of one's own death is the grounds for developing one's own voice; for becoming the author of one's own existence:

> *Your work is going to fill a large part of your life, and the only way to be truly satisfied is to do what you believe is great work. And the only way to do great work is to love what you do. If you haven't found it yet, keep looking. Don't settle. As with all matters of the heart, you'll know when you find it. And, like any great relationship, it just gets better and better as the years roll on.*

Kierkegaard calls for a healthy balance between the worlds of possibility and the everyday world of actuality. On the one hand, too much possibility detaches a person from the world in a way that can make them delusional. It is like living only in a dream. On the other hand, living only in the world of everyday actuality does not allow one to see beyond one's horizons and so leaves one unprepared for changes that are beyond one's immediate awareness.

There is also a strong hermeneutic element in Jobs description of his own career development. On two occasions in his Stanford speech, he says that the "dots" of life cannot be joined going forward but only in retrospect: "Of course it was impossible to connect the dots [of my career] looking forward when I was in college. But it was very, very clear looking backwards 10 years later."

In hermeneutics the parts are the basis of the formation of the whole and the whole situates the parts in relationship to each other. In Steve Jobs terms, this was expressed as "joining the dots." In both cases, the dots cannot be joined in advance. It is through immersing oneself in a practice, through the choices-in-action, that the whole begins to emerge out of the parts and the parts form a pattern that can be called a whole.

This also means that from a hermeneutic perspective, a person does not know how they will be shaped by their choices-in-action in advance. Becoming presupposes the resolve to leap into the unknown. Writers on Kierkegaard have often called this a "leap into faith." However, Kierkegaard did not use the notion of a leap into faith. To be more true to him is to say that he spoke about choosing as an act of leaping. It would also be more precise to say that, in the context of choice-in-action, he wrote of the need to have a faith in leaping. For in the choices-in-action, there is nothing, no one or no convention upon which to hold. There is no map of the road in advance. The map only comes afterwards, as the parts form a whole which then situates the parts in relationship to each other.

Furthermore, from an existential perspective, we are part of the relationship between the whole and parts. It is not that the whole and parts are a text that is external to us—this was the case for traditional hermeneutics. Our identities are formed through the way in which we engage. We are part of the text of life. Our lives are texts. They are texts that are not yet written and will only be written through the choices-in-action. Thus it was through the way in which "Steve Jobs" made choices-in-action that the relationship between the parts and the whole formed the identity and text that is called the life of "Steve Jobs." He did not set out to be an entrepreneur or create Apple. It was only as he leapt into it that his identity emerged and a way of being was created.

Putting this in explicitly existential terms, our way of being is formed through the way in which we make choices-in-action. We cannot pre-plan our way of being. Our habits of practice, the way in which we cope with the world is formed through the way in which we cope with the world. Again this sounds like a tautology or vicious circle, but it is part of the hermeneutic circle: only as we engage with life is our way of being formed. Furthermore, our way of being is not subjective but transcends the subject/object split. It does this through the fact that the choices in action always involve a relationship to the world. Who we are emerges not through armchair speculation but out of the way in which we relate to the world. We are part of the world and the world is part of us.

Heidegger uses the expression being-in-the-world to articulate the being and hermeneutic circle of human existence. It means that a person is "always and already" situated within a world and that whatever we do is always already within a world. The terms "being" and "world" in the phrase being-in-the-world are neither the same as nor identical with each other. They form a hermeneutic whole. So too do our lives form a hermeneutic whole—or more specifically, life is a hermeneutic whole made up of a number of parts. The parts and whole are not automatically and inevitably joined together.

Thus we see that in the case of Jobs, the encounter with the experience of existence was the basis of entering the realm of possibility through which the iWorld came into being.

There is one more theme worth making explicit: Jobs' being was always in question. It was a rollercoaster ride in which he lost his business and had to go through a period of despair before he could even begin to re-invent himself. He speaks about this most clearly when he was fired from his own company and "didn't know what to do for a few months," feeling like he had "let the previous generation of entrepreneurs down."

Return to Heidegger

In the above some of the central themes of existential hermeneutic phenomenology have been introduced in the context of the narrative of the lived experience of Steve Jobs. I would now like to take this narrative introduction as a clue through which to introduce some of the Heideggerian logic formally. Again, I would like to note that this writing will not take place in a linear way, from premise to conclusion, but in a circular way of "peeling an onion." However, in this case I would like to peel the onion from the inside out and then move back again from the outside to the inside. I would like to start with Heidegger's understanding of existence as being-in-the-world.

We have already been introduced to the hyphenated phrase being-in-the-world. I would briefly like to restate the rationale and significance for this phrase. It will be recalled that the critique that Heidegger levels against the history of Western thought, from Plato to positivist science, is that it assumes the distinction between the researcher and researched; inquirer and that which is inquired about. From Plato to positivist research, the world is set up as an object to be researched. We, for example, look at the essence of things in Plato or the object of thought in rational and scientific research. In all of the above cases, what we omit to take into account is the fact of the way in which we relate to the world as part of the world that we are seeking to understand. Especially, but not only, ancient philosophers wanted to understand the world as a whole but failed to include an essential dimension of the whole: our way of inquiring and researching the world. Yet for Heidegger "inquiry" and "research" are ways of being-in-the-world and thus, if we wish to understand being-in-the world as a whole, we need to include the lived experience of inquiring and researching in our inquiry.

Already we will detect a hermeneutic circle in relation: it is through inquiry that the lived experience of inquiring is understood; research needs to understand the activity of researching as a human concern or way of being attuned to the world. Heidegger believes that the question of questioning has not been properly considered in the history of thought. Far from being a vicious circle, he sees it as a hermeneutic circle, in which through inquiring into inquiry we are able to make explicit the lived experience of what it means to inquire.

To think that this is just semantics or an abstract question misses the point entirely. For Heidegger believes that we have forgotten how to inquire. Universities have become sites in which questioning has been reduced to a set of rituals and ceremonies. Neither students nor lecturers tend to question in a way that demonstrates their whole being is at stake.

Andrew Grove of Intel and Heidegger

In order to unpack the phenomenology of inquiry in Heidegger, we need to understand the conditions under which inquiry arises and the various forms of inquiry. Let me give a corporate example. The example is described by Andrew Grove in his book *Only the Paranoid Survive* (1996). In this book he writes about the way that he and Intel as a whole were bewildered by competition from an unexpected and unfamiliar other: competition from Japanese companies who bewildered Grove and Intel at every turn. This crisis of bewilderment is not, in Heideggerian terms, a breakdown precipitated by the inability to use items of equipment, but is a breakdown in sense-making. Indeed, throughout his book, Grove does not speak only about breakdown in equipment or even in their research practices. He writes about the fact that even though they assumed that they had the best production facilities and research department, Japanese competitors were always able to outsmart them. They could not make sense of the power of the Japanese competitors and they lost their own sense of direction and purpose in what they were doing. In other words, they lost their own sense of meaning.

The central event in Grove's paradigm switch was a crisis at Intel generated by a threat from Japanese competitors. This crisis occurred in the early 1980s when Intel dominated the microchip market. It had taken years for Intel to build itself up to be the dominant player in the market. It was proud of itself, having put much effort into building itself up. As Grove says: "We worked day and night to design the chip. … We worked as if our life depended on it, as in a way it did."

The emotional nature of Grove's language should be noted. Through the intense effort and commitment of employees at Intel, a way of doing things—the "Intel" form of practical coping—emerged. Intel was proud of its problem-solving practices and of its practices of dialogue in which ferocious arguing while remaining friends developed. It was proud of its excellence in research practices. It also developed a strong identity and culture. In this form of practical coping, "Intel stood for memories; conversely, memories meant (usually) Intel" (1996, p85). So deeply rooted were the practices of Intel that they had the character of what Grove calls "religious dogmas" (1996, p90). They were imprinted in the very being of Intel. They gave Intel a sense of confidence and certainty in the world of microchips. Intel just knew what it was doing. Its convictions allowed it to go from strength to strength, enabling it to focus on becoming more efficient and taking its culture for granted: "People were pleading with us for more parts. … We were scrambling to build more capacity" (1996, p88).

This was an exciting period for Intel. They were extremely goal-focused—until it came to the Japanese, who were able to produce better quality microchips in larger volumes and at less cost. This sent shockwaves of fear through Intel. But in the early stages Intel dealt with the threat as a challenge to develop its own efficiencies. And so it attempted to deal with the competition on the basis of its cultural strengths. It relied on its practices of problem-solving, research and dialogue to become more efficient in its production of microchips. However, the more efficient it became, so the more efficient the Japanese competitors became. Every time Intel improved, its competitors improved.

Not only did this frustrate Intel, but it caused widespread panic. For Intel tried everything that it knew to deal with the threat, yet each effort resulted in failure: "We fought hard. We improved our quality and brought costs down but the Japanese producers fought back" (1996, p87).

Senior management at Intel realized that they did not have the know-how to fight off their Japanese competitors. In fact, they were quite stunned by the way in which Japanese know-how surpassed theirs. As Grove says, the "quality levels attributed to Japanese memories were beyond what we thought were possible" (1996, p85). They saw that the Japanese were, to use the words of Grove, "taking over the world semiconductor market" and they saw this happening "in front of [their] eyes."

They had lost their way because they could no longer rely on their way of practical coping. They could not rely on this form of coping because they had seen in the Japanese a more effective way of doing things, one which they lacked both the know-how and resources to match. They felt overwhelmed by the power of Japanese competition: "All this was very scary from the point of view of what we still thought of as a little company in Santa Clara, California" (1996, p85).

Although they felt overwhelmed by the efficiencies of the Japanese, this did not stop them trying to compete with the Japanese. Indeed, their primary response to the threat was to work harder. However, hard work was also no solution. For hard work in the absence of a clear direction is self-defeating. Even though Intel could see that it did not have the means to compete with the Japanese, it would not give up "trying." Even in the face of failure they continued to try. But none of their trying helped them escape the threat to their existence: "During this time we worked hard without a clear notion of how things were ever going to get better. We had lost our bearings. We were wandering in the valley of death" (1996, p89). No matter how defiant Intel was or how intensively it believed in itself, it had lost its way. It was confused: "We had meetings and more meetings, bickering and arguments, resulting in nothing but conflicting proposals" (1996, p88).

Thus it lost its sense of existential security in its form of practical coping. In the midst of its bickering and disillusionment, Intel continued to be caught in the contradictory position of both experiencing itself going downhill yet believing in its ability to take on the threat of the Japanese. It developed all sorts of fantastic alternatives to try and outmaneuver the Japanese: "There were those who proposed what they called a 'go for it' strategy: 'Let's build a gigantic factory dedicated to producing memories and nothing but memories, and let's take on the Japanese.' … Others proposed that we should get really clever and use an avant-garde technology" (1996, p89). Yet at the same time they knew that they were not getting anywhere: "Meanwhile, as the debates raged, we just went on losing more and more money" (1996, p88)

It was precisely when he gave up "trying" to find a direction for Intel that a new way of being for Intel opened up. There came a point in Grove's struggle that he realized that he could not struggle any more, that struggling was futile. He contemplated both his own end at Intel and the death of Intel. Yet at that very moment he entered into a qualitatively different mindset. He moved away from a mindset of "trying" or "willing" to one of "resigned reflection." In this mindset he began to ask different kinds of questions about himself and Intel: "I remember a time in the middle of 1985, after this aimless wandering had been going on for almost a year. I was in my office with Intel's chairman and CEO, Gordon Moore, and we were discussing our quandary. Our mood was downbeat. I looked out the window at the ferris wheel of the Great America amusement park revolving in the distance, then I turned back to Gordon and I asked, 'If we got kicked out and the board brought in a new CEO, what do you think he would do?' Gordon answered without hesitation, 'He would get us out of memories.' I stared at him, numb, then said, 'why shouldn't you and I walk out the door, come back and do it ourselves?'" (1996, p89).

As this quote indicates, Grove and Moore were no longer trying to fight off their aimlessness. They had given up "trying." They accepted their lostness. Grove accepted the possibility of his own end at Intel. However, the moment they gave up a trying mentality, they entered a different mode of attunement; a reflexive mode of attunement; one in which they stood outside of a dogmatic commitment to the habitual way of doing things at Intel. Their minds were now free to roam; to question their current way of doing things and be responsive to other possibilities. Here Grove could pose a speculative "what if" question to himself and Gordon More about Intel, that is, he asks Moore and himself to answer the question: what if they were replaced by another CEO?

As indicated in the quote, the way in which Moore answered this question renewed both Moore's and Grove's sense of hope. It opened up new sets of possibilities for them; ones that they could not imagine while in a "trying" mentality. They moved very quickly from a sense of resignation and despair to one of excitement. Of course, the excitement was mixed with much uncertainty. For they did not have a well-developed sense of the new journey that they were about to embark on. But, in the face of the unknown, they had openness to a new direction that they did not previously have. The combination of excitement and uncertainty was more hopeful than despair and resignation.

As part of their new attitude towards Intel, they began to see that Intel had already been moving in a new direction, but because of their preoccupation with a "trying" mentality they had been blind to this new direction. At a grass-roots level a shift had already begun to take place. Middle management, Grove notes, had for a long time been shifting production from microchips to microprocessors: "By the time [senior management] made the decision to exit the memory business, only one out of eight silicon fabrication plants was producing memories. … Bit by bit [middle managers had been allocating] … our silicon wafer production capacities to those lines which were more profitable, like microprocessors" (1996, p97).

Thus the stranger disrupts our way of doing things in a way that an item of equipment cannot. Rather than an instrumental crisis, it was the very meaning of Intel, its existence, that was under threat and the transformation was both in Grove's way of making sense of himself as a leader and in the culture of Intel. Thus as a Dolan, writer for *Forbes Magazine*, says: "Grove was employee number one at Intel. In 1984 he and Intel cofounder Gordon Moore decided to abandon the memory chip business that gave the company its start for what became a dizzyingly successful string of microprocessors. He also morphed personally—from a drill sergeant and manager to industry visionary" (2008).

It was Grove and More's way of questioning Intel's way of doing things from within the crisis at Intel that disclosed a new way of being for Intel.

Conclusion

In all three cases we can see that each person raised questions because their very being was at stake and in question. In each case new possibilities were disclosed to them by being able to stay with the way in which their practice was in question. Furthermore, in these cases they did not seek detached representational solutions, but in each one of them, a new world was disclosed and created. In conclusion, we also see that living into the question rising in disruption, each of the three figures discussed allowed themselves to be open to their vulnerabilities in such ways that new possibilities were opened to them. To repeat the Heideggerian mantra of this work: we question because our being is in question.

References

Dolan, G. (2008) Andy Grove's Last Stand. Available at: http://www.forbes. com/forbes/2008/0128/070.html.

Grove, A. (1996) *Only the Paranoid Survive*. London: Harper Collins Publishers.

Heidegger, M. (1985) *Being and Time*. Oxford: Basil Blackwell.

Hegel, F. (1977) *Phenomenology of Spirit* (translated by A.V. Miller with analysis of the text and foreword by J.N. Findlay). Oxford: Clarendon Press.

Hodes, A. (1998) *Encounter with Martin Buber*. Harmondsworth: Penguin Books.

Jobs, S. (2005) *You've Got to Find What You Love*. Available at: http://news. stanford.edu/news/2005/june15/jobs-061505.html.

Kierkegaard, S. (1987) *Either/Or*. Princeton, NJ: Princeton University Press.

Rilke, R.M. and Kappus, F.X. (1993) *Letters to a Young Poet* (in an edition by M.D. Herter Norton, translator). New York: W.W. Norton & Co.

PART III
Existential Crisis of Management
Research, Education and Development

Chapter 7

Existential Reading of the Paradigm Crises in Management Scholarship

Incommensurability and Existential Crisis in Management Research, Education and Development

The irony is that management studies and organizational learning are in an existential crisis. Yet, it does not see the existential crisis as a basis upon which to question its own practice. A hermeneutic and existentially reflexive form of questioning occurs when our practices are in question in such a way that we come to question our practices. Through the way in which our practices are in question we question our ways of being in practice. In this chapter I will demonstrate that organizational theory and management studies are existentially in question. In Chapter 8 I shall demonstrate that they do not use their way of being in question as a basis upon which to question their practices. Instead they attempt to superimpose new ways of thinking onto existing existential crises. As I shall demonstrate, this prevents the crises from being dealt with. For only as researchers respond to the way in which research is in question, can researchers begin to move beyond the crisis by asking the questions the crises are calling them to ask.

It happens to be the case that, according to Tsoukas and Knudsen, management as a social science is very much in a "paradigm crisis" (2003, p3), maintaining that there "is no conceptual common ground upon which we may stand to make paradigm comparisons" (2003, p6). As, for example, Scherer has said: "Organization theory scholars are aware of ... the fragmentation of their field and addressed issues like 'paradigms', 'theory pluralism', and 'incommensurability'" (1998, pp147–8). Scherer goes on to say that, "In the 1960s there was a more coherent and widely accepted set of premises, assumptions, instruments, and techniques that were well known as the business policy framework" (1998, p178). However, he continues, "Over the last three decades, through waves of criticism, a variety of alternative concepts, approaches, and schools have emerged." So desperate is the situation that "a plea for a unifying paradigm almost 20 years ago, the field actually has become more and more fragmented" (1998, p179).

According to Burrell and Morgan (1979, pp1–4), differences in ontology, epistemology and methodology create insurmountable barriers between different paradigmatic perspectives, therefore they cannot be related to each other in a meaningful way. Tsoukas and Knudsen, for example, acknowledge a series of crises in organizational theory, all of which give rise to a "crisis in self confidence" (2003, p5) that is current in organizational theory. They point to a number of dimensions of the crisis, including a sense of fragmentation of the field, an incommensurability of paradigms that obstructs communication, a perennial anxiety regarding the relevance of the field, all of which lead to a kind of self-doubt (2003, p5), and, as Weick maintains, a kind of narcissistic reflexivity (2003).

It is in the context of such self-doubt, when the very ways in which we have attempted to solve problems become part of the problem, that we are in what Kuhn (1970) calls a paradigm crisis. This is a crisis in which the fundamental assumptions of our discipline are in question. And it is when the questioning of our fundamental assumptions are generated by a breakdown in our conventions or ways of making sense of the world that we are in question existentially. Paradigm crises are not just intellectual questions. They are ways of being-in-question. It is in the context of questioning our assumptions while being-in-question that scientists are drawn, according to Kuhn, to philosophy. For philosophy is the investigation of assumptions. Existential philosophy is investigation of assumptions in the context of a disturbance to lived experience.

However, before dealing with the way of being-in-question existentially, it is important to highlight some of the dimensions of the paradigm crisis, the way in which organizational and management studies can no longer rely on their own fundamental assumptions.

In what follows a number of dimensions of the paradigm crisis will be set out.

Crisis of the Relationship between Theory and Practice in Management

Ed Freeman,[1] who, questioning the place of journals in organizational inquiry, said that whereas most medical and legal practitioners need to keep up to date with reading journals in order to maintain their professionalism of practice, one will hardly ever come across a management journal on the desk of a manager or CEO. Managers and leaders cannot even begin to access the language of many of the management journals. This is because of the highly technocratic language of the journals which is not part of the language in use by managerial practitioners. This research community is an inwardly focused community, cut off from the community it is supposed to be researching and thus serving.

There is a direct relationship between medical research and practice. If reading of journals by practitioners (as is the case in medicine) is an indication, there is no—or at best very little—relationship between management research and practice. The theoretical journals are generally written in a language that is inaccessible and of little interest to practicing managers. They certainly do not lie on managers' desks as useful reference sources. If any kind of text does, it is that of the management guru who unfortunately peddles in fads.

The irony of this, of course, is that many of the journals in management have taken what is called a "practice turn," that is, they have focused on management and organizations as practices. Thus one would assume that they are accessible to the practitioner … until one sees that it is a range of theories of practice that dominates these journals.

Indeed, the textbooks used in the range of MBA programs I have taught bear very little resemblance to the research being done by the lecturers. Even though the MBA is a master's course, the textbooks are written in a jargon-infested language that states positions as matters of fact rather than as arguments in need of justification or validation.

Part of the crisis of self-confidence, part of the way in which theory and meta-theory are in question today, concerns what many have called the "relevance" of theory and meta-theory. Part of the question of relevance is the argument that theory does not "speak" or connect with the everyday experiences of managers. The question of "relevance" is a form of questioning that brings the enterprise of theorizing as a whole into question: does theorizing have any

---

1   Stated in a conversation at a Philosophy of Management Conference, Chicago, 2014.

value today? This is not just a question of practices of validity within theorizing, but of the value of management theorizing: for if theory is irrelevant, this is a question that points not at some of the instruments within the enterprise of theorizing but at theorizing as a whole. The question of relevance is a question of the "sense" and "significance"—the meaning—of forms of knowledge in organizational studies. It is not a question of its reliability and validity.

As Steers et al. (1996), at the end of an empirically grounded positivist form of research into leadership and management, say with a sense of confusion and perplexity:

> As we have seen throughout this book, we have learned a fair amount about work motivation and leadership effectiveness in the last few decades. However, when we survey current management practices relating to these topics, we frequently discover a sizeable discrepancy between theory and practice; many contemporary organizations simply do not make use of what we currently know about motivating and leading employees. Why is this so? (Steers et al. 1996, p324).

Their answer to the question that they raise indicates that they are still stuck within a positivist paradigm:

> Some managers continue to hold conservative beliefs about how much employees really want to contribute on the job. They frequently assume that most employees are lazy or indifferent to the organizational needs, and they rely largely on carrot and stick incentives. This is the case despite the large body of data showing that most employees sincerely want to be actively involved in helping organizations to succeed (Steers et al. 1996, p325).

They go on to show that research is concerned with "data" *abstracted* from experience, whereas practice is concerned with decision-making in the *context* of experience. A similar question has been raised in the context of teacher education. Making this point in the context of pre-service teachers entering service for the first time, Herman Widlack (1980) writes of what he calls the "real-life shock" experienced by teachers in the transition from university-based training to the contingent reality of the classroom. He claims that newly qualified teachers often respond to the trauma of transition "by a change in attitude from one which is university based, progressive and liberal to one which is conservative." He also notes that this shock manifests itself in experiences of teacher helplessness, insecurity and a general loss of proportion and perspective, which expresses itself in skepticism towards theory in which newly qualified teachers are advised to "Just forget what you have learnt" (Widlack 1980, p23).

Here we see quite clearly how the uncertainty of the contingent reality of the classroom can transform the explicit "progressive and liberal" beliefs of pre-service teachers to the "conservative" practices of teachers in the "chalk face." Practices are formed, as Argyris and Schon note, under "real-time conditions" (1977, p4), conditions in which teachers have to come to terms with the risk of failure, feelings of helplessness and uncertainties. Argryis and Schon question the relationship between research and practice, noting that research is done under ideal-time conditions while effective action occurs under real-time conditions:

> The old ideal of a working relationship between research and practice has yet to be realized. The technology of rigorous research works best when it does not deal with real-time issues — for example, when scholars take years to study a decision that took several hours to make. This technology ... is based on diagnostic techniques that ignore ... the properties of effective action under real-time conditions (1977, p3).

Whereas research occurs in the safety of ideal-time conditions, practice occurs in the uncertainty of real-time conditions. As Floden and Buchmann have said: "What if [managers] recognize the uncertainty in their work? And what if theorists recognized that intimate knowledge of this uncertainty was exactly what was missing from both their theories and the policies these theories provoke?" (1993, p36).

While many management theorists recognize the role of power in management practice, they do not simultaneously recognize the fundamental role of the lived experience of insecurity, fear and uncertainty in management and the way in which it influences practice and relationships in the workplace. It is left up to the "guru" industry, as Jackson (2001) calls it, to work with the role of fear in organizations. And these are not necessarily the best educated or trained for this activity. Although the role of moods and emotions is coming more and more to be written about, it is still on the margin and there is still the split between cognition and emotion.

Heidegger provides a framework in which to make sense of the relationship between moods, reasoning and body. All three are involved in "understanding." All three are involved in all human activities—even the activity of questioning; questioning has its own mood and it is this mood that gives it its existential significance; its purpose; one that re-enchants its relevance. In a subsequent chapter we will unpack the mood of questioning as the basis upon which to show that theory and practice, praxes, reflection and practice are not separated from each other but belong to the same phenomenon.

Existential Hermeneutics and Reductive Practices of Scientism in Science and Social Science in Management

Martin Eger (1993), a scientist who demonstrates the existential ontological basis of positivism, argues that much of science has lost is existential grounding and that research has been reduced to a methodological formula in which the conclusions are known in advance. He uses the words of Barbra McLintock, who was awarded the Nobel Prize for work in genetics, to describe this reductionism:

> *I feel that much [research] work is done because one wants to impose an answer on it. … They have the answer ready, and they [know what they] want the material to tell them. Anything else it tells them, they don't really recognize as there, or they think it's a mistake and throw it out. …*
> If you'd only just let the material tell you *(quoted in Eger 1993, p27).*

The highlighting of the last point is my own. It is a point central to hermeneutics, existentialism and phenomenology: allowing the phenomena to speak for themselves rather than imposing both a conclusion and a methodology on the subject matter. For both need to emerge out of an attuned relationship to the phenomenon. In his work, *Search for a Method*, Sartre (1968) has made the same phenomenological point in relationship to a Marxist social science. He argues that Marxist social science has lost the flexibility to adapt and develop itself in terms of a response to phenomena. Rather, it imposes itself on phenomena. And because it imposes itself on phenomena, the terms in which phenomena are to be explained are known in advance. Because the terms in which phenomena are to be explained are known in advance, there is no opportunity for new ways of seeing things to emerge in Marxist social science. Rather, he argues that the kinds of explanations that Marxist research will discover can be predicted in advance: "Men and things had to yield to" methodologies of research (1968, p23). Indeed, for him Marxist social science research had become a form of research tyranny which did "violence … to reality" (1968, p22).

Like McLintock and Eger in the context of what I shall call methodological scientism, Sartre believes that when we impose a methodology in advance on to the subject matter of research, we lose touch with or attunement to the everyday experience which is the subject matter of research. We impose a formulaic notion of research onto the subject matter. Marxist social science, he says, has "reduced [research] to a simple ceremony" (1968, p22).

It is this ritualistic, formulaic and ceremonial reductionism of research that Heidegger, Sartre and all existential thinking opposes itself to. Research methods, Sartre claims, "must be born from praxis and must turn back upon it in order to clarify it" (1968, p22). It is in "praxis" that the energy of inquiry lies. As Heidegger notes, for the ancient Greeks this energy was wonder. "Scientistic" ideology has disconnected the energy of research from its context. Tsoukas and Knudsen make this point by stating how abstracted theory has become from the lived experience of practice (2003). Heidegger wants to return theory as an integral part of the lived experience of research. Research questions need to be drawn from the lived experience of managing in a way that befits the mood of existential inquiry.

Without this dialectical relationship between research methods and practice, a sterile empiricism and a rigid and fixed set of concepts develop; ones that are detached from everyday reality (Sartre 1968, p22). As Sartre says: "Marxism has reabsorbed man into the idea, and existentialism seeks him everywhere he is, at work, in his home, in the street." Sartre is arguing that lived experience is reduced by Marxism to an abstract idea, whereas existentialism seeks to stay with the lived experience itself. Back to the phenomenon itself has always been the call of phenomenology and of Sartrian existentialism.

It needs to be emphasized that Sartre is not arguing for the negation of Marxism. Rather, he is arguing for the re-enchantment of Marxism. He believes that Marxism was the governing philosophy of his time, but because it had lost touch with everyday reality it needed to be re-enchanted by existentialism. Existentialism offers a way of revitalizing Marxism through establishing a dialectical relationship between methods of research and subject matter of research. For Sartre this is not a one-way relationship in which research methods shape the way in which phenomena are viewed, but a two-way relationship in which phenomena shape research methods. An existential researcher has the flexibility to allow his or her research methodology and assumptions to be called into question during the research experience.

Indeed, we saw this to be the case with Eger's description of Barbra McLintock in her positivist work in genetics. It was only out of her interaction with the plants that her research attunement developed. She did not impose a research method in advance:

> *I found that the more I worked with them the bigger and bigger [they]
> got, and when I was really working with them I wasn't outside, I was
> down there. I was part of the system. I was right down there with them,
> and everything got big. I even was able to see the internal parts of the
> chromosomes—actually everything was there. It surprised me because
> I actually felt as if I were right down there and these were my friends
> (quoted in Eger 1993, p35).*

Rather than imposing a research method on her "object" of study, it was out of her involvement in the subject matter of study that shaped the way she conducted research and the outcomes of research emerged through this experience. Isaac Newton describes the attunement to real-life experience as a process of allowing the new to "dawn" on the scientist rather than the scientist imposing his or her method on the phenomenon.

In all of the above cases, it is important to note that the examples are drawn not from the qualitative sciences but from the positivist sciences; and that there is a shared sense that the quality of the attunement influences the practice and outcomes of the research.

This phenomenological process of "dawning" is often described best by artists. For example, van Gogh says:

> *But you will ask: What is your definite aim? That aim becomes more
> definite, will stand out slowly and surely, just as the rough draft
> becomes a sketch, and the sketch becomes a picture, little by little, by
> working seriously on it, by pondering over the idea, vague at first, over
> the thought that was fleeting and passing, till it gets fixed (1997).*

Thus we see that it is neither positivism, Marxism nor social science itself that is the issue, but the rigid—almost a priori—application of these research methods in practice.

This practice of imposing either or both methods and conclusions on the phenomena of research is not uncommon in the history of management thought. Indeed, there is research indicating that whether it is in so-called "scientific management" or in the human relations school—both impose conclusions on their subject matter independently and in advance of their subject matter. Kyle Bruce, for example, has argued that while the Hawthorne studies and the Hawthorne effect claimed to be arrived at by Mayo under strictly scientific research practices, in fact he imposed the outcomes in advance on the research and manipulated the subject matter to obtain the conclusions that supported his interests: "there is some doubt," Bruce maintains, "as to whether Mayo's interpretation of the Hawthorne experiments was more reflective of his pre-formed personal views than of the actual empirical results." Indeed, as his argument progresses, Bruce seems to become more convinced that this was the case: "Mayo's theory of human relations was based almost entirely on his own political interpretation of worker motivation" (Bruce and Nyland 2011, p385).

There have been writers who have maintained that scientific management belongs in the same category, that it was a product of pre-formed views of Taylor and that he manipulated situations to get the results that he wanted. Describing Taylor's research practice, Stewart has said:

> *Taylor stormed down to the yard with his assistants ("college men," he called them) and rounded up a group of top-notch lifters ("first-class men"), who in this case happened to be ten "large, powerful Hungarians." He offered to double the workers' wages in exchange for their participation in an experiment. The Hungarians, eager to impress their apparent benefactor, put on a spirited show. Huffing up and down the rail car ramps, they loaded sixteen and a half tons in something under fourteen minutes. Taylor did the math: over a ten-hour day, it worked out to seventy-five tons per day per man (Stewart 2006).*

Continuing his point, he says:

> *When the Hungarians realized that they were being asked to quadruple their previous daily workload, they howled and refused to work. So Taylor found a "high-priced man," a lean Pennsylvania Dutchman whose intelligence he compared to that of an ox. Lured by the promise of a 60 percent increase in wages, from $1.15 to a whopping $1.85 a day, Taylor's high-priced man loaded forty-five and three-quarters tons over the course of a gruelling day—close enough, in Taylor's mind, to count as the first victory for the methods of modern management (Stewart 2006).*

This suggests that in its very origins management research and theorizing was not only manipulated by interests in advance or that it was methodologically flawed, but that it did not have built into its method the hermeneutic, dialectical and phenomenological process of looking at the way in which the interests and paradigms of researchers affect their research. It is the relationship between researcher and researched that needs to be re-examined and revitalized.

This is a point central to hermeneutic inquiry: that the preconceptions in terms of which we inquire affect both the way and the outcome of the inquiry and that we need to be willing to incorporate this into our research attunement. I do not want to say method, because it cannot be reduced to a method. It is not enough to claim to be neutral, objective and detached. These are easily manipulated and often lead to sterile research.

In the sense defined above by Heidegger, the pioneers of management science and social science were not, like the founders of the natural sciences and quantum physics, philosophers. They were not asking originary questions. They were not, like Bohr, Heisenberg or Einstein, interrogating their own way of knowing but imposing it on practice. They were not beginning and returning, as Sartre claimed to praxis. Neither their methods nor their research conclusions were drawn from the mystery of being embedded in the field like Barbra McLintock and as theorized by Eger from a Heideggerian perspective Indeed, from this perspective they did not embody a research attunement. They may have used research methods and techniques to dress up and manipulate their conclusions, but they certainly did not proceed from the mystery of lived experience and there is no indication that they understood research as a lived experience, as an embodied relationship to the subject matter. Indeed, at best, they adopted, in advance, a rigid positivism that separated subject and object—and ironically even this was manipulated for their own advantage.

The philosopher Emmanuel Levinas claims that it is the origins of a way of thought that shape the future of that discipline. This leads us to ask: has management inquiry and research moved beyond this? Certainly there has been very little place for questioning fundamental assumptions of the discipline of management. Ironically, where Heidegger has been used, it is not his originary practice of questioning (disruptions in sense-making) but his instrumental form of questioning (disruptions in the use of items of equipment) that has been highlighted. And even when it is used, it is used as a means towards already established ends or for the sake of an already existent research agenda. There is no indication that it is used to question the fundamentals of management theorizing or the way of doing research in organization studies. While it may be used to look at the subject matter of research in new ways, it is never the researcher or the research attunement that is put in question.

This is not only the case in readings of Heidegger, but it can be argued permeates Marxist and post-Marxist research practices in management studies. For example, Willmott imposes a Marxist reading of crisis on to events rather than drawing the kind of crisis from the events. This is demonstrated in Willmott's paper "Critical Management Learning," where, like Sartre's Marxist, he has his interpretation of the significance of contradictions in management behavior in advance of the actual situation. Indeed, he quite explicitly acknowledges that he has his framework of interpretation in advance (Willmott 1997, pp167–8) and that it did not emerge out of praxis as the empirical data that he is analyzing did not emerge out of his own praxis but, like Bruce's argument in relation to Mayo, he is only interpreting the data in abstraction from the lived experience.

He would need to possess a phenomenological attunement to develop that kind of sensitivity to an event to draw the kind of concept of crisis out of the event.

Need for Phenomenological Sensitivity in Reading of Heidegger in Organizational and Management Studies

The same can be said for the Heideggerian readings in management and organizational studies. The range of authors writing on Heidegger (including Weick, Tsoukas, Sandberg, Chia and Holt, and Zundel) take one dimension of Heidegger's multifaceted understanding of disruption and impose it on all kinds of disruptions. Thus they generalize what Heidegger calls disruptions in the use of equipment to all kinds of disruptions, including disruptions of sense-making. But for Heidegger, as will be demonstrated, there is a qualitative difference between disruptions in the use of equipment and breakdowns in sense-making. Furthermore, where Heidegger has been used, he has been reduced to an already existing organizational discourse. For example, his notion of being-in-the-world has been reduced to a "socio-material practice" and the metaphor of being "interwoven" or "entwined" (Sandberg and Dall'Alba 2009) has been used to describe the latter notion, but there is no evidence in Heidegger for these terms. Indeed, as I shall later show there is sufficient reason to believe that Heidegger would dismiss these ways of reading his work and see them as a reduction of being-in-the-world to metaphors that describe specific forms of relationships and not being-in-the-world as a referential or relational whole.

The reductive and unquestioning nature of theorizing of research in management applies equally to the education of researchers within the field of management. There is, as we have already quoted Sartre as saying, a ceremonializing and routinization of research as a process, set of techniques or methods. These are said to follow a set course: literature review, method, data presentation and analysis, and finally conclusion. Emily Borda has made the point that scientific education leads teachers to present science as a body of "settled facts" and scientific research as a settled way of doing things (2007, p1027). Elaborating, she says:

> *many science courses, … are content-driven, leading instructors to present science as a body of "settled" facts. Such instruction is likely an artefact of reductive positivistic notions of science as objective, static and able to uncover "truths". Because of such instruction, but perhaps also due to developmental restrictions students by and large come to science classrooms with positivistic images of science (Borda 2007).*

Eger has written, in the context of a Heideggerian existential approach to positivist science, of the way in which scientific work has been "decontextualized" and characterized by an "overdependence on formal methods" (1993, p7). He maintains that it is learned and taught "unreflectively yet authoritatively, in the manner of naive realism." It has what he calls a learn-it-and-use-it "tool kit approach" (1993, p4). This, he argues, takes the very mystery and questioning out of the practice of science (1993, p5). Yet it is the mood of curiosity and wonder that has underpinned research and philosophy ever since Plato. Heidegger acknowledges this in his essay "What Is Metaphysics?" where he says that moods of estrangement are central to research (1948).

Eger maintains that a hermeneutics of science emerges out of the way in which scientists are embedded in their practice, attached to their subject matter in what he calls a "feeling for the organism" or subject matter of research (1993, p27). He refers back to the already quoted paragraph from McLintock's reflection on her own research experience, where she was surprised while being amidst the subject matter of her research. In the context of organizational studies this point is again made by Tsoukas and Knudsen (2003), who see research in the latter field as beginning methodologically with abstractions rather than with concrete reality.

From a Heideggerian perspective, research is not just about content, method, technique and epistemology. It is a "way of being concerned" within our world. Research as a way of being concerned needs to be included in an appreciation of the practice of research. For moods of research can overwhelm one—moods such as feeling alone or lost in the research experience.

The danger of leaving mood or the way of being concerned out of the learning and teaching of the research process is that not only does the way of being-in-the-world characteristic of research remain unthought, but it leads to a technocratic, instrumental and reductive scientistic approach to research in which research is more and more being conceived of as just another kind of project to be managed, rather than as a place of re-searching and being compelled by the mystery of the as yet unformulated question.

There is no encouragement of educating future researchers to draw their way of conducting research within the context of practice. And yet ... ironically, there is no better field in which to do this. For management, above all else, is a field of practice. Professional practitioners who enter the field of research bring with them a rich context of lived experience. But the ways of conducting research do not allow for this to be used—except in those forms of action research and in the developing Aristotelian practices of research which encourage a questioning of all kinds of assumptions in the context of practice—and hopefully with the Heideggerian framework that will be sketched out in this work.

I hope that enough has been said from the Heideggerian perspective to justify that research is much more than just a method, a set of techniques for gathering and analyzing data and a literature review. It involves an attunement, a particular kind of sensitivity—just like playing a musical instrument. This was demonstrated in the example of Barbra McLintock, who was absorbed in her subject matter. Researching is a way of being. It involves an identity. A person who does research "is" a researcher and we become researchers by the way in which we are involved in the activity of research. It is a way of living in or inhabiting the world. And we need to pay so much more attention to the practice of inhabiting research and far less on the technical dimensions of research. Technical competence occurs within the research attunement.

Critical Theory as a Form of Reductionism in Management Studies

It is not only in the context of research that the gap between theory and practice has been noticed, but in the realm of management education as well. In many ways, management theory is imposed on students independently of their practice. It provides answers to questions that they are not even asking. Blackman and Benson (2006), in outlining the practice of critical thinking, claim that the latter begins by evaluating the logical soundness of assumptions (p2), but nowhere do they focus on how assumptions or concepts emerge out of everyday practice as themes to be critiqued. It is as though the teacher or educator imposes this on the students. This critique is supported by the work of Ann Cunliffe, who argues that critical theory and thinking approaches to pedagogy focus on "intellectual critique and do not help us cope with more informal, everyday ways of sense making and learning that are the essence of practice" (2002, p37). In this way, even from a critical theorist approach, education for critique is focused around something, "theory text or process" (2002, p39). Critical approaches "do not go far enough in helping managers and students talk in more reflexive ways" (2002, p41) about their practices from within their professional practice.

It is because the "intellectual critique" of critical theory and rationalist approaches to theorizing do not address "everyday ways of sense making and learning" that they are not experienced as valuable by managers engaged in the hurly burly of everyday management practice. Intellectual critique is asking questions and providing answers that managers are neither asking nor experienced as significant.

Jan Blits (1989) has written an interesting critique of modern education in terms of Plato's allegory of the cave. He argues that rather than enabling us to free ourselves from being chained to the floor of the cave, modern education attempts to bring the light of knowledge into the cave; that the more it does this, the more it prevents students from developing a critical and reflexive relationship to the assumptions underpinning their own experience. Blits goes on to say that we can "escape from (Plato's) cave, not by starting with scientific abstractions, but only by properly reflecting on our ordinary or pre-scientific opinions about things" (1989, p293). As is already implied in the above statement, Blits sees scientific forms of education as working in the opposing direction: it denies the value of lived experience as a starting point of inquiry and expects students to begin with already established abstractions of the experts: "The modern scientific understanding is a deliberate repudiation of our natural understanding of the world" (1989, p296). It begins and maintains itself outside of "the categories of everyday speech" (1989, p297). Scientific education begins with "an aggregated body of accepted theories" that are handed down to students as established truths that they are assessed on and thus internalize and apply to practice on the basis of the expertise of the scientist. Blits gives as an example the way in which introductory sociology texts replace the notion of friendship with pseudo technical terms such as the "primary group." Quoting a sociology text which rationalizes replacing friendship with the notion of a primary group, he says: "Friendship is a common sense term but primary group is a more sociological concept" (1989, p297). He gives examples from other fields by saying that a "cursory glance at introductory textbooks shows students in economic classes, for example, are told right from the start that the fundamental economic problem is how a society chooses to use its scarce resources." He also identifies the way in which science is taught as a method abstracted from experience (Blits 1989, p297).

Interesting support for his view comes from science educators such as Borda, who argue that when science is taught as a method outside of and not connected to experience, it is deprived of the embodied passion that characterizes the world of the creative scientist (2007, p1029).

The denial of the value of the common sense in the scientific classroom is, for Blits, the denial of the tacit or intuitive experience in terms of which sense is made of experience. And in denying the basis upon which we make sense of our experience, classroom-based scientific education does not teach us to "understand our world" and our "mode of being in the world," but makes students "the passive recipients of ready-made abstract forms—theories, concepts, definitions, terms, premises, methods, etc" (Blits 1989, p297). It provides a disengaged cognitive knowledge that stands opposed to experience. Ironically, as Blits puts it, it takes us right back into Plato's cave.

Blits does not disagree with the fact that positivist science is critical, but maintains that its critique begins with concepts that are already abstracted from the everyday lived experience of students. In such an education, students are taught to analyze and critique concepts that are not woven into the fabric of everyday experience. The consequence of this is that they end up not developing an appreciation of the assumptions that underpin their own professional practices.

Working with the Phenomenology of Lived Experience in Management Studies

However, there are movements towards working with lived experience in the study of management. For example, for Cunliffe (2002), it is in moments of being "struck" in their practices that managers become reflexively attuned to their practices such that they can firstly see their own practices, critique them or open themselves up to new possibilities. Reflexive learning takes place when in moments of being struck learners are "moved to change our way of being, talking and acting" (Cunliffe 2002). Being struck creates the opportunity for what Cunliffe calls "self rather than meta-reflexivity;" it opens up the possibility for "making taken-for-granted" learning explicit. It opens up the possibility for learning from "within experience," which involves a practice of turning back and making explicit the tacit dimensions of our knowledge.

More than this, reflexive learning through being struck enables us to examine the ways in which we constitute reality rather than looking at the way in which we represent objective reality. For as she points out, even the terms through which we represent reality are constructions that we impose on reality. While we might believe that we are describing reality, we are omitting the fact that we are providing the terms in which we describe it. A reflexive attunement through moments of being struck shifts away from taking the way in which we constitute reality for granted and thus from attempting to represent reality objectively to making explicit and examining the terms in which we describe reality. To look at and examine the way in which we constitute reality means that it is a knowing from within rather than a knowing that is imposed from without. Borrowing from Spinosa et al. (1997), she points to the fact that this kind of knowing is an ontological skill or sensitivity—although she does not develop what goes into making up this sensitivity (Cunliffe 2002, p38).

This approach will be central to this work and will be built on in this writing.

The Limits of Analytic Thought in Management

Another dimension in management thought in which the work of Heidegger can be of service is in terms of the dominance of an analytic logic in management. Perhaps most clearly defined by Descartes, analysis involves breaking things down into their clearest and most distinct parts. The problem with the dominance of an analytic logic is that it produces what Mintzberg calls the "humpty dumpty" logic of organizations. Under the dominance of analysis, management "takes the job apart without putting it back together. Managing thus looks like humpty dumpty, lying in broken pieces on the ground" (2004, p36).

Of course it not only takes the job apart but it takes organizations apart. In a public lecture delivered in 1929, Heidegger maintained that the "calculative rationality" that had taken hold of universities had led to the fragmentation of the university:

> The fields of science are widely separated from each other. Their ways of dealing with the objects they inquire about are fundamentally different. In our time such dissociated diversity of disciplines is held together only thanks to the technical organization of the universities and their faculties, ... But, as a result, close contact among the sciences in their essential common ground has died off (1948).

The same point can be made of organizations in general today, that the different functional specializations have fragmented organizations to the extent that organizations are held together only by the technical organization of the administration. While they may talk about visions and missions, there is a tendency for engineers to be stuck in their own language, finance people in theirs, human resource people in theirs and so on. There is very little sense of the whole in terms of which the parts are held together.

Heidegger's thinking is very useful here because his thinking is one which is concerned with bringing the whole and parts back into relationship with each other. He calls this existential hermeneutic phenomenology. It is based on the principle that the whole can only be understood in terms of the parts and the whole forms the basis in terms of which the parts stand in relationship to each other.

This book explores the value of Heidegger's hermeneutics for moving towards a more holistic reading of organizations. This does not exclude analytical thinking but it does warn against the reduction of the organization to its parts when the latter mode of thinking dominates.

The Notion of Experience in Management

Mintzberg is also most critical and also most focused in his understanding of the role of experience in management education and development. He claims that while many management schools claim to be experientially based, they actually rely on what he calls "second hand experience" in the form of theories and case studies which represent material that is already abstracted from experience. For Mintzberg, central to management education is what he calls "firsthand experience" (2004). The challenge is for educators to develop a pedagogy to enable students to work with firsthand experience. This means not only reflecting on experience but turning the "felt sense" of experience into language, turning the felt sense of experience into—borrowing the Holderlin phrase—a "sign" that is meaningful and readable. Mintzberg argues that the pedagogical processes in management schools do not, either methodologically or intentionally, focus on firsthand experience. It is assumed that firsthand experience is simple to work with, but Mintzberg, quoting a CEO, demonstrates that it is an art or discipline in its own right: "My problem is that when I face a problem, I don't know what class I am in" (2004).

Problems do not appear to us as already defined. We need to define them. Furthermore, the way we define them shapes the way in which we will deal with them. Thus we need to be very clear on our own assumptions or pre-conceptual frameworks in terms of which a problem will be seen.

While Mintzberg does write about the importance of reflection in the context of learning through firsthand experience and while he does speak of some of the conditions in terms of which experience becomes an opportunity for learning, he does not unpack the nature of experience itself and thus of the way in which experience can lead to defensive and prejudicial forms of attunement as well. For just as much as we learn through experience, so prejudices can be reinforced through experience. Furthermore, what Mintzberg does not bring up is the fact that reflection is itself a way of experiencing the world. Indeed, Mintzberg remains stuck within a dualist notion of reflection and experience as though the two are separate and independent of each other. Thus he is in danger of repeating the very problem in which studies in management are caught: the separation of theory and practice without accounting for that through which they are part of the same phenomenon.

John Kotter is another author who calls for a return to experience. In a famous study called "What Effective General Managers Really Do" (1999), he describes the day-to-day experiences of managers. But what is interesting in his description is that he uses what Heidegger calls "clock time" as the basis upon which to describe the day-to-day experiences of managers. Thus he describes the activities of managers in what they do on an almost minute-by-minute basis, as though clock time is the fundamental dimension of experience. But Heidegger calls clock time into question. Indeed, he maintains, that clock time is an abstraction from experience; that more "primordial" is what he calls "familiar" time and "originary" time or what I shall call the "dream time" of "aboriginal time". And if we want to get to the heart of experience, we need to be able to work with all three temporal dimensions of lived experience.

Thus it is important not to take the nature of experience for granted. We need to inquire into the assumptions that we have about experience. We need to inquire into what in Heideggerian terms we call the being of experience. As we have already seen, experience from the existential perspective is characterized by all the dimensions of being-in-the-world. It is this that needs to be opened up for management studies.

Management is not a Law-like Scientific Field

But perhaps the most fundamental challenge to the social sciences in management is the universal assumption that organizing and managing can be understood in terms of law-like generalizations. Henry Mintzberg has maintained that because management is a practice, it cannot be studied in the form of law-like generalizations, and therefore, because it cannot be studied in those terms, a scientific form of research is not what is needed. In fact, he claims that not even a social scientific form of research is needed but, rather, a practitioner form of reflection—one that takes into account the "firsthand experience" of managers rather than the detached empirical observation of managers (2004).

The Marketplace of Creative Destruction does not Operate in Terms of a Law-like Logic

If Joseph Schumpeter was correct in maintaining that the free market is not law-like but underpinned by what he called "creative destruction," then not only do we need to research on creative destruction but we need to look at the way in which research is itself transformed through practices of being creatively destroyed. Indeed, in many ways the paradigm crisis discussed in the last chapter is an example of a practice of creative destruction. One of the fundamental dimensions of positivist forms of research that are called into question through the dialectic of creative destruction is the fundamental principle of law-like generalizations. Whether it be positivist forms of science or positivist forms of social science, creative destruction calls into question the core principles of induction: the idea or belief in the possibility that events repeat themselves. Indeed, Schumpeter points out that the history of the free market is characterized by discontinuities and disruptions in which the new is created in the context of the destruction of the old.

This point is reinforced by those writers who believe that we are managing, leading, educating and conducting research into organizing and management in the context of a free market characterized by creative destruction. Creative destruction renders the marketplace and therefore competition in the marketplace and management of organizations beyond prediction. Neither management nor the marketplace is reducible to law-like behaviors.

An unexpected and unanticipated world is the essence of capitalism. Creating, rather than simply managing, the status quo becomes central to organizing in the context of the free market. Indeed, Spinosa et al. (1997) have defined management as the act of creating what is not yet the case. This is in contrast to science, which reflects what is the case. We need, they argue, to transition from a mentality that simply describes what is to one which creates new states of affairs in the world—new organizations, new businesses, new ways of doing business, new careers and identities and so on. And we need to do so without having a precedent for doing so. Creative destruction implies that we cannot know in advance where we are headed. In Chapter 2 we saw both Christensen and Schumpeter maintaining that the free market is creating industries that do not yet exist. They are creating the rules of the game without any rules to guide them. McDonald's was an example of this.

This in turn means that no method of scientific or social scientific analysis can operate in the realm of creative destruction. For as we have already heard Christensen say, "Markets that do not exist cannot be analysed. ... In known markets, customer needs are understood. In this environment, a planned, researched approach to evaluating, developing, and marketing innovative products is not only possible but desirable. ... However, this is not relevant to disruptive technologies" (Christensen 2000).

Thus both empirical and logical analysis are inappropriate in terms of the phenomenon of creative destruction. This same point was made by the philosopher David Hume over two centuries ago when he claimed that induction was dependent on a regular and stable world in which scientists could assume that the future would repeat the past. While Hume admired this idea, he claimed that it could not be demonstrated. The idea that tomorrow will be like yesterday is central to positivist research. And so if it's very premise is in question, so are the research practices and outcomes drawn from this method.

Unlike the positivist scientist, Schumpeter and Heidegger are concerned with how the new emerges out of the destruction of the old. Rather than description of the world, the phenomenon of creative destruction refers to the practice of creating of new worlds. This is implied in the phrase "create," whereas science is about observing that which is already in place: objects or representations of things.

While we do not want to swing the other way and claim that there is no regularity, Heidegger adopts the position that there is both regularity and times of disruption to the world of regularity. He uses the phrase "average everyday" practical coping to express the role of regularity in human existence. This refers to the habitual and conventional taken-for-granted customs and practices that allow everyday interactions to occur. We all have scripts for getting on with everyday activities. If we did not, we would not be able to get on with things.

The Repetition Compulsion of the Paradigm Crisis in Management Studies

The paradigm crisis has dominated management scholarship for well over twenty years now. Rather than getting beyond it, management scholarship seems stuck in it. Albert Einstein tells us that when we continue to try to solve a problem in the terms in which it was set, we do not open new possibilities for ourselves. What needs to be done is to go beyond the language, assumptions, rules and conventions in which management scholarship has been conducted in order to open new ways of thinking and conducting research into management. It is at this point that existential hermeneutic phenomenology becomes significant, for it deconstructs the language in terms of which a persistent problem arises in order to examine our own ways of thinking such that we can disclose new worlds, new ways of doing research.

References

Argyris, C. and Schon, D.A. (1977) *Theory in Practice: Increasing professional effectiveness*. San Francisco: Jossey-Bass Publishers.

Benner, P. and Wrubel, J. (1989) *The Primacy of Caring: Stress and coping in health and illness*. California: Addison-Wesley Publishing Company.

Blackman, D. and Benson, A. (2006) Can Methodological Applications Develop Critical Thinking? *Electronic Journal of Business Research Methods*. Vol 4, No 1. pp1–10.

Blits, J.H. (1989) Self-Knowledge and the Modern Mode of Learning. *Educational Theory*. Vol 39, No 4. pp293–300.

Borda, E.J. (2007) Applying Gadamer's Concept of Disposition to Science and Science Education. *Science and Education*. Vol 16, No 9–10. pp1027–41.

Bruce, K. and Nyland, C. (2011) Elton Mayo and the Deification of Human Relations. *Organization Studies*. Vol 32, No 3. pp383–405.

Burrell, G. and Morgan, G. (1979) *Sociological Paradigms and Organizational Analysis*. London: Heinemann.

Chia, R. and Holt, R. (2006) Strategies as Practical Coping: A Heideggerian perspective. *Organization Studies.* Vol 27, No 5. pp635–55.

Christensen, C. (2000) *The Innovator's Dilemma*. New York: Harper Collins.

Cunliffe, A. (2009) The Philosopher Leader: On relationalism, ethics and reflexivity—a critical perspective to teaching leadership. *Management Learning.* Vol 40, No 1. pp87–101.

Cunliffe, A. (2002) Reflexive Dialogical Practice in Management Learning. *Management Learning*. Vol 33, No 1. pp35–61.

Dreyfus, H. (1993) *Being-in-the-World: A Commentary on Heidegger's Being and Time, Division 1*. Boston: The MIT Press.

Eger, M. (1993) Hermeneutics as an Approach to Science. *Science and Education*. Vol 2, No 1. pp303–28.

Floden, R. and Buchmann, M. (1993) Between Routines and Anarchy: Preparing Teachers for Uncertainty. In: Buchmann, M. and Floden, R. (eds) *Detachment and Concern: Conversations in the philosophy of teaching and teacher education*. London: Cassel.

Heidegger, M. (1948) What Is Metaphysics? In: Brock, W. (ed.) *Existence and Being*. Indiana: Regnery/Gateway, Inc.

Heidegger, M. (1968) *What Is Called Thinking?* New York: Harper Torchbooks.

Heidegger, M. (1985) *Being and Time*. Oxford: Basil Blackwell.

Hill, L.A. (2003) *Becoming a Manager: How new managers master the challenges of leadership*. Boston: Harvard Business School Press.

Hooks, B. (1994) *Teaching to Transgress: Education as the practice of freedom*. New York: Routledge.

Jackson, B. (2001) *Management Gurus and Management. Fashions: A dramatistic inquiry*. London: Routledge.

Kotter, J. (1999) What Effective General Managers Really Do. *Harvard Business Review.* Vol 77, No 2. pp145–59.

Kuhn, T. (1970) *The Structure of Scientific Revolutions.* Chicago: The University of Chicago Press.

Mintzberg, H. (2004) *Managers not MBAs: A hard look at the soft practice of managing.* San Francisco: Berrett-Koehler.

Sandberg, J. and Dall'Alba, G. (2009) Returning to Practice Anew: A life-world perspective. *Organization Studies.* Vol 30, No 12. pp1349–68.

Sandberg, J. and Tsoukas, H. (2011) Grasping the Logic of Practice: Theorizing through practical rationality. *Academy of Management Review.* Vol 36, No 2. pp338–60.

Sartre, J.P. (1968) *Search for a Method.* New York: Vintage Books.

Scherer, A.G. (1998) Pluralism and Incommensurability in Strategic Management and Organization Theory: A problem in search of a solution. *Organization.* Vol 5, No 2. pp147–68.

Spinosa, C., Flores, F. and Dreyfus, H. (1997) *Disclosing New Worlds: Entrepreneurship, democratic action, and the cultivation of solidarity.* Cambridge, MA: MIT Press.

Steers, R., Porter, L. and Bigley, G. (1996) *Motivation and Leadership at Work.* New York: McGraw-Hill Companies, Inc.

Stewart, M. (2006) The Management Myth: Most of management theory is inane. *Atlantic Monthly.* June. Vol 297, No 5. pp80–87.

Tsoukas, H. and Knudsen, C. (2003) Introduction: The need for meta-theoretical reflection in organization theory. In: Tsoukas, H. and Knudsen, C. (eds) *The Oxford Handbook of Organisational Theory.* Oxford: Oxford University Press.

Van Gogh, V. (1997) *The Letters of Vincent Van Gogh* (selected and edited by Ronald de Leeuw). London: Penguin Books.

Watson, T.J. (1994) *In Search of Management: Culture, chaos and control in managerial work.* London: Routledge.

Weick, K. (1999) Theory Construction as Disciplined Reflexivity: Tradeoffs in the 90s. *Academy of Management Review.* Vol 24, No 7. pp797–806.

Weick, K. (2002) Essai: Real-time Reflexivity: Prods to reflection. *Organization Studies.* Vol 23, No 6. pp893–8.

Weick, K. (2003) Theory and Practice in the Real World. In: Tsoukas, H. and Knusden, T. (eds) *The Oxford Handbook of Organisational Theory.* New York: Oxford University Press.

Widlack, H. (1980) Real-Life Shock: The inapplicability of theoretical knowledge to classroom practice. *Education.* Vol 34, No 1

Willmott, H. (1997) Critical Management Learning. In: Burgoyne, J. and Reynolds, M. (eds) *Management Learning: Integrating Perspectives in Theory and Practice.* London: Sage Publications.

Winograd, T. and Flores, F. (1986) *Understanding Computers and Cognition.* Norwood, NJ: Ablex.

Zundel, M. (2013) Walking to Learn: Rethinking reflection for management learning. *Management Learning.* Vol 44, No 2. pp109–26.

Zundel, M. and Kokkalis, P. (2010) Theorizing as Engaged Practice. *Organization Studies.* Vol 31, No 9–10. pp1209–27

Chapter 8

Heidegger in Organizational Theory and Management Studies

From an Instrumental to an Existential Reading of Heidegger

A question that now needs to be asked is: how does theorizing in the context of management respond to the phenomenon of existential forms of disruption and paradigm crises? Does it embrace and work within and through existential destruction? Is it, able like the theories and practices of leadership discussed in Chapter 6, willing to question itself from within the lived experience of its being thrown into question, discussed in the previous chapter? Or does it claim to stand outside of its own disruption and view it as a phenomenon that it observes from the detachment of a Cartesian scientist? Or in simpler terms, is it able to absorb its own existential crisis, as described in the previous chapter to question its own practices as the basis upon which to disclose new possibilities?

This chapter shall take its cue from the perspective of Heidegger who maintains that knowing is itself a mode of being-in-the-world (1985, p90) and thus not a way of standing outside of being-in-the-world. Just as other aspects of being or practice are questioned, so theory as a practice or way of being needs to be challenged and questioned. Research, education and theorizing are affected, formed and transformed by the world in which they are situated. This is only another way of saying that organizational theory and management learning need to question itself because it is in question—in, as was pointed out in the previous chapter in existential crisis. The question is, does it see its existential crisis as an opportunity for existential reflexivity and hermeneutic questioning?

Within the broad field of what is known as "organizational studies" and "management studies" there is a group of researchers who have begun focusing on the work of Martin Heidegger and so it is possible that we could find a sensitivity to the central role that disruption plays in free market economies and in the lived experience of understandings of organizational and management practice; that not only are management and organizations made up of regularities but irregularities are just as much a part of what it means to be and become.

In acknowledging the role of irregularities this group of researchers turn towards aspects of the writing of Heidegger. And on first readings of their work, it may appear that they do incorporate an ontology of destruction within their writing. This is because they work with a certain form of disturbance. However, on a close reading of their work, they at best work with a limited notion of destruction in Heidegger—one that is not an existential destruction. And at worst, they offer what I shall call a reductive reading of Heidegger and a "repetition"[1] (Malcolm 1988, p28) of a technocratic instrumentalism and Cartesian logic as defined in terms of the work of Heidegger. For while they tend to appropriate aspects of Heidegger to bridge the gap between theory and practice, there is no indication that they see in the work of Heidegger an opportunity to question their own practices of research and theorizing through the ways in which they have been thrown into question (as seen in the previous chapter).

There is perhaps, at least one exception to this point and that is to be found in the work of Sandra Corlett, who, based on Anne Cunliffe's notion of being struck, calls researchers to use experiences of being struck to think through their own particular research projects: "Reframing research as learning, achieved within and through reflexive dialogue [occurring in moments of being struck], might lead us to change the way we talk, act and be in our research dialogues with participants" (2013). However, on this latter view, it is still not research as a practice that is called into question. Rather being struck becomes just another tool within research. Research needs to go beyond this in its hermeneutic and existentially reflexive questioning of its own practices.

The Turn to Heidegger in Organization and Management Studies

There is a small but emerging trend of theorists moving beyond a scientific account of management theorizing, research and education to a Heideggerian existentially based hermeneutic phenomenological reflexive practice of inquiry. This is taking place in a range of management disciplines, including strategy

---

1   The notion of repetition compulsion is based in the work of Freud, where it is considered as a defense mechanism in which a person repeats patterns of behavior (quoted in Malcolm 1988, p28).

(Chia and Holt 2006), management and leadership (Cunliffe 2002, 2009; Zundel 2013) and organizational studies (Sandberg and Tsoukas 2011; Weick 2003).

All these Heideggerian-oriented authors agree that it is in moments of interruption, breakdown or experience of being struck that reflection and reflexivity from within occurs. Disruption also places theory in relationship to practice. As Sandberg and Tsoukas, quoting Winograd and Flores, remark, "a breakdown is not a negative situation to be avoided, but a situation of non-obviousness" (2011, p165)—the recognition that something is missing or is not quite right, with the result that some aspects of the relational whole come to the fore.

Sandberg and Tsoukas (2011) and Weick (2003) start off with a critique of a Cartesian rationality that assumes that the human being is ontologically separated from the world such that there is no need to account for either the lived conditions under which the research question emerges or the ways in which the questions are responded to and elaborated. Summarizing the significance of this point, Weick says that the starting point for research or "investigation should not be the assumption that people are detached, contemplative and theoretical, but rather they are involved, concerned and practical" (Weick 2003, p467).

Using a Heideggerian logic, he says that it is from experiences of interruption in practice that theorizing becomes an existentially significant activity for the practitioner: "Practitioners are best able to spot those theories that matter most when their world is interrupted." In the same way, he maintains that in order for theorists to work effectively with practitioners, they need to begin from the lived experience of interruptions to their everyday practices: "And theorists are best able to spot the situations of situated action that they should be puzzling over in their world of theory in the presence of interruptions" (Weick 2003, p468).

It is in the context of interruptions to practice that the theorist and the practitioner can meet each other rather than living in two separate worlds: "It is in the moment of interruption that theory relates most clearly to practice and practice most readily accommodates the abstract concepts of theory" (Weick 2003, p470).

The significance of interruptions, Weick maintains, is that they allow both theorists and practitioners to catch a glimpse of the background horizon or context in terms of which the everyday is made intelligible: "When everyday projects suffer a breakdown of action, theorists and practitioners alike share a common vantage point from which they can glimpse thwarted potentialities embedded in networks of projects" (Weick 2003, p469).

In accounting for the role that interruption plays in enabling reflexivity, Weick makes use of a Heideggerian distinction between "ready-to-hand" and "present-at-hand" modes of being involved within the world. Both modes of involvement refer to different ways in which the human being stands in relationship to its world. Entities are said to be "ready-to-hand" when the human being is involved in a pragmatic relationship to "entities" within the world. Entities, in this mode, are items of equipment to be used. Thus the "hammer" is for "hammering," the guitar is for playing. In this mode of involvement the human being has what Heidegger calls a non-thematic awareness of the instrument, that is, rather than being conscious of the instrument, the human being has an embodied relationship to it. Thus when it is using the hammer, it is not positing the hammer as an object of observation or even of thought. It is in the flow of getting its work done. Its body has a felt sense for using it. Dreyfus (1993) translates Heidegger as calling this flow "absorbed practical everyday coping." The human being is in this mode proximally and for the most part.

The "present-at-hand" refers to a different kind of relationship to entities within the world. Entities are said to be "present-at-hand" when the human being stands in a relationship of observation to entities. At this point entities become "things," "objects" or "substances" and the human being becomes a subject that stands outside of and removed from the entity as object. The entity as object is something that we can observe, dissect, analyze. It has properties which can be measured and quantified. Heidegger makes it clear that it is not only discrete and particular objects that manifest themselves in this way, but the workshop in which the items of equipment are situated, the environment in which the workshop is situated and, in broader terms, the referential whole that is constructed through the human being.

For Weick, it is in the moments of interruption of everyday coping, in those moments when the human being is made to stand back from its everyday practical coping, that the art of theorizing and research begins. For in these moments of interruption, practices for doing things are placed in question in such a way that we come to notice the practice. So when a plane crashes, instead of just using the plane, we can come to think about the plane and the causes of the crash. It is at this point that researchers and practitioners can enter into a dialogue with each other. For the interruption creates the space for the practitioner to stand back and theorize.

Sandberg and Tsoukas (2011) share a similar but more nuanced view. Based on Hubert Dreyfus's reading of Heidegger, they make a distinction between two modes of standing back that occur in breakdowns, each of which disclose objects in the world in slightly different ways. They make a distinction between what they call "involved thematic deliberation" and "theoretical detachment" (2011). The difference between the two is that in pure "theoretical deliberation" a person is so detached from their "everyday absorbed coping" in such a way that they are simply spectators, no longer able to engage in their practices. They are able to view the objects of their world from a pure distance—like a scientist who is disengaged. Indeed, Sandberg and Tsoukas' (2011) critique is that much of management theorizing science takes place in this space such that it is so detached from the practitioner and is experienced as having no relevance. Quoting Dreyfus, they say: "Once our work is permanently interrupted, we can either stare helplessly at the remaining objects or take a new detached theoretical stance toward things and try to explain their underlying causal properties. Only when absorbed, ongoing activity is interrupted is there room for such theoretical reflections" (Sandberg and Tsoukas 2011).

Note that Dreyfus makes a choice in the response to breakdown possible: we can either just stare at it or we can affirm the detached attitude of a scientist; indeed, of a curious scientist. I will have more to say about choice later.

"Involved thematic deliberation" (Dreyfus 1993), on the other hand, presupposes some detachment from the world but not to the extent that a person becomes a disengaged spectator of their world. Rather they are able to observe themselves and participate simultaneously in the network of activities that make up their world. They give the example of a teacher in a classroom who, in her practical coping, has been using a PowerPoint presentation without explicitly thinking about PowerPoint. However, at a certain stage in the lecturing, the computer breaks down. At this point, the computer which was in the background of her awareness now comes to the foreground of her awareness. Her mind shifts from one of being immersed in the lecture to thinking about either fixing or replacing the computer and how she will continue with the lecture. Rather than simply being involved in delivering the lecture, she catches sight of delivering the lecture. It becomes an explicit theme of thought. Assuming that she finds a strategy for continuing with the lecture by fixing, replacing or even doing without the computer, she has demonstrated a practice of being simultaneously absorbed in lecturing and watching herself being absorbed in lecturing such that she can recalibrate the lecture to go beyond the disruption. They call this involved thematic deliberation: "although the faulty PowerPoint presentation forces the lecturer to pay deliberate attention to it momentarily, he or she is still involved in teaching—the teacher is in the mode of involved thematic deliberation" (Dreyfus 1993).

The difference between involved thematic deliberation and theoretical deliberation has nothing to do with the "personality" of the person but it has to do with the extent of the breakdown or interruption in practical coping: the one is a temporary breakdown and the other is a permanent breakdown. Based on this distinction, Sandberg and Tsoukas (2011) maintain that it is the role of the theorist to tune into and work with practitioners in the context of temporary breakdowns in their practices. They mention three categories of breakdowns in which researchers and practitioners can collaborate: when the expectations of practitioners are thwarted; in the context of an awareness of differences; and in the emergence of deviations and boundary crossings.

The Limitations of Readings of Heidegger in Organization Theory and Management Studies: A Dreyfusian Perspective

The basis for arguing that readings of Heidegger in the broad field of organizational studies is a repetition of a Cartesian reading of Heidegger is based on a distinction of a writer on Heidegger that seems to be recognized in organization studies as a central source for understanding Heidegger. In his work *Being-in-the-World: A Commentary on Heidegger's Being and Time, Division 1* (1993), Hubert Dreyfus argues that Heidegger articulates two types of inquiry: a scientific one in which the "the scientist is detached from and is so able to thematize and objectify his object, nature" (1993, p82) and, we can add, even himself.

The second form of inquiry he calls a "hermeneutic ontological" form of inquiry which "makes his theme precisely the shared background understanding in which he dwells and from which he cannot detach himself" (p83). Dreyfus goes on to maintain that the hermeneutic ontological form of inquiry is a "special form of involved deliberate attention—an authentic response to anxiety, a special form of disturbance."

Developing the distinction between these two modes of inquiry further, Dreyfus maintains that the hermeneutic ontological form of inquiry refers to those forms of disturbance that allow *Dasein* or the being of the human (recall we need to distinguish between the human being and the being of the human) to catch sight of existence from within. It reveals existence as "that in which we already are" (1993, p83).

In contrast to this, the scientific forms of inquiry, "from physics to factual history," are studied from a detached and outsider's perspective (1993, p83).

This detached and outsider's perspective is also identified by Heidegger and by Dreyfus's reading of Heidegger as being the place in which Cartesian subject-object based thinking is appropriate. Indeed, it is disruption of equipment ready-to-hand that the relationship between being and world becomes that of a subject standing over an object. Even the environment, which, for Heidegger, is a referential whole, is understood in the mode of detachment and objectivity rather than from within.

Furthermore, I shall argue that there is a qualitative difference between deliberate forms of reasoning and what Dreyfus calls the special form of involved deliberation in hermeneutic ontology. In fact, I shall show that hermeneutic phenomenology is qualitatively different from deliberation as practiced in the sciences and in being deliberate. Rather than being calculative, it allows beings to be. It is a *thinking through* or a *working through* in contrast to a *thinking about*. Cartesian and scientific thinking is a *thinking about*, while hermeneutic attunement is a *working through*. Thinking about assumes an object to be thought about, whereas thinking through is a more meditative thinking which allows thinking to emerge. It is what the psychoanalyst Adam Philips calls the "side effects" of deliberation—allowing these to emerge. I will look at the works of Flores, Gendlin and even some forms of psychoanalysis to demonstrate this hermeneutic kind of reflexivity.

I see no reason not to place the many of the current readings of Heidegger in organizational studies on a par with physics and factual history (albeit one characterized by what van Manen calls "physics envy") rather than a hermeneutic ontological inquiry. I have and will elaborate Heideggerian reasons for arguing this to be the case. Firstly, the logic of the breakdowns, disruptions or interruptions that are dealt with by authors in the broad field of organization studies is not a breakdown in meaning or sense-making; not a hermeneutic and existential form of anxiety but a disturbance or breakdown in the use of equipment or the network of equipment "ready-to-hand." As is clear in Dreyfus's reading of Heidegger and Heidegger's own early writings, the latter breakdowns lead to the detached, objectifying stance of a subject in which subject and object are separated from each other and which characterize those disciplines from "physics to factual history."

Secondly, they do not make use of the hermeneutic phenomenological forms of reflexivity that arise in anxiety or in any breakdown *of* the familiar.

At best they are breakdowns *within* the familiar. The familiar is the basis in terms of which a referential whole becomes a whole. It is through familiarity with a referential whole that we come to know our way about it and we come to be at home in the circle—knowing our way about without having to think about it. We ourselves emerge as the beings that we are in the hermeneutic circle, that is, our way of being emerges from within the hermeneutic circle, as do the embodied roles that we play as well as the whole which holds the roles together.

Thus they are a thinking about rather than the allowing of the meditative attunement of a thinking through. Let me give some examples to indicate the point I am raising.

Instrumental Disruption in Organizational Thinking

As several authors in organizational studies have argued, this Heideggerian instrumental logic applies not only to physical activities, but theorizing is itself a practice that we inhabit by being involved in the world and it is when there is a breakdown in our practice of theorizing that we come to think about the background context in which we theorize. In their article "Theorizing as Engaged Practice," Zundel and Kokkalis (2010) give an example of this from a disruption in their practice of writing a paper for a journal. They say: "We have experienced a 'breakdown' in the form of the revisions suggested to us by the editors and reviewers in response to our submission. These revisions represent an event which stands in the way of achieving our projected ends, rendering obstinate (*aufsässig*) that with which we are primarily concerned" (2010, p102).

They go on to maintain that in the breakdown the background context for writing was made manifest to them:

> In our case, what was brought to presence was our context of equipment. This entails not merely the "theoretical" assumptions and arguments that we presented in our paper, but also the review procedures of academic journals, the impact of a publication for our careers, the structures of promotion at our educational establishment and our work schedule, as well as the impact of teaching hours on our research capacity and thus on our ability to produce the revisions requested (2010, p102).

Indeed, the breakdown experienced in writing does allow one to come to grips with the background context of writing, the standards of research, the demands placed on researchers by institutions and even the sense of self-worth of the particular researchers.

However, what I would like to emphasize is that there is another kind of breakdown that is central to Heidegger's writing, that this kind of breakdown deprives the world of sense and meaning, that in having a resolved attitude towards the loss of sense and meaning, new worlds are disclosed.

What Zundel does not consider is a breakdown in the meaning of the network that he has caught sight of. Thus he catches sight of the linkage between career, standards of research, teaching hours, and so on, but their meaning is still intact. He has caught sight of them but they still "make sense," to use a phrase that Zundel (2013) also uses.

At best, the breakdown enables him to reflect on the way he can improve the means for achieving his ends, but because the sense of meaning of the ends has not broken down, this is not the kind of crisis for questioning the ends. The meaning of research is not at all in question. And the authors do not demonstrate that they address themselves to this kind of questioning. In fact, they caution against this kind of questioning. Zundel quite explicitly points out that he would be weary of any role for anxiety in Heideggerian reflexive inquiry. As he says:

> While, for instance, Segal (2010) suggests that this Heideggerian form of resolve can be found and demonstrated in the ways in which the anxiety of a breakdown transforms possibilities for being in leadership practice, I would suggest a more cautionary approach. Only once we have learned to be attuned to the wonder of the usual, being as whole can be thought (2013, p121).

What is interesting is that one of the texts that he used to justify his response to the connection between anxiety, resolve and wonder that I have made based on Heidegger is Heidegger's text "What Is Metaphysics?" (Zundel 2013, p121). One does not need to do a particularly detailed reading of this text to see the connection that Heidegger makes between anxiety and inquiry. Indeed, Heidegger makes it quite clear that anxiety, the dynamism of nothingness or the presence of absence is very closely linked to the wonder of inquiry. He makes this clear repeatedly in this text such that it is amazing that Zundel could make such a claim.

The same point applies to Sandberg and Tsoukas' description of the teacher whose PowerPoint presentation has been interrupted. This does disrupt her in an instrumental way. It gets her to rethink the way in which she does the teaching or the lecture, but it does not get her to rethink teaching or lecturing as an end in itself. That teaching or lecturing is worthwhile is something that is taken for granted. Its sense is not thrown into question.

Existential Questioning in Organizing and Management

In contrast to this is the researcher or lecturer who begins to question the significance or value of research itself. Or the scientist who begins to question the paradigm out of which they are operating. Or the business person who is challenged to reinvent their way of doing business. Or the person whose kind of career has been made redundant by practices of creative disruption—these are all crises in ends. They are all crises in ways of being.

Let me give a more detailed example of this. It is the existential questioning of an MBA student of mine who was a project manager. The context is a conversation that he is having with a friend of his while they are driving from Germany to Denmark. I will quote him verbatim so the tone and sense gets across:

> I really struggled to explain to him what does it mean to be a project manager and it was not the first time that I struggled with that. I am pretty sure that my mother never understood what I am actually doing in my role as an IT project manager. Maybe I don't know it either?
>
> OK—I am quite good in selling myself, so I was able to build some fancy sounding sentences around some catchwords such as "project plans," "board meetings," "strategy meetings," "workshops," "GANTT charts," "change requests" and "project controlling," as I always do when I was asked by outsiders about my job. This gave him the impression that it is a quite important job with a lot of responsibility but also a lot of freedom. And from time to time I really believe that it is a wonderful job, that it gives me a lot of satisfaction and that I should be really happy. But can you be happy if you are not even able to describe what you are doing?
>
> A couple of hours later, we were already close to the border to Denmark, he was telling me about his latest projects and pointed at an impressive bridge spanning a strait in the Baltic Sea. I was impressed—not only by the bridge itself—rather by the simplicity of illustrating what he did the last 16 months. There was no need for any further explanations. Even my mother would be able to understand what he did the last 16 months simply by looking at the bridge.

> *My mood changed a bit and from this moment onwards I had the feeling that I rather would like to have a job where you can see, feel and touch what you have done over the last 16 months than working in such a virtual business and non-tangible business such as IT project management.*

In this rather large extract of an essay it is not the particular tools of project management that are in question and need refining, but the very meaning of what it is to be a project manager. This is an existential rather than an instrumental question.

Heidegger's existential dimension of questioning occurs when the meaning, sense or ends themselves rather than the means to the ends are breaking down. In this sense, it can be said that the understanding of the breakdowns which would open up the meaning of activities has not yet occurred in organizational and management theorists. It is refining the means and not questioning the ends that matter. Weick is quite insistent in his belief that it is on an "instrumental" rather than existential level that theorizing is in crisis; that theorists need to drop and question what he calls their "heavy tools of paradigms" and retain what he calls their "light gear," which consists of theorists' "intuitions, stories, experience, awe, vocabulary, and empathy" (1991, p804). He writes of what he calls the need for "instrumental reflexivity" (1991, p803), claiming that the advantage of instrumental reflexivity is that it is more structured and thus does not lead to a kind of anarchy of being "open ended and harder to shut down" (1991, p803).

The Heideggerian point is that it is precisely in the disruption of meanings that the question of the meaning of an activity arises. It is in the breakdown of the sense and meaning of research that we come to ask the question of the meaning of research.

Thus at the very least there is a disruption *within* research practices and a disruption to the significance and meaning *of* research as a whole. Zundel and Kokkalis (2010) are concerned with the former and not the latter; so too are Sandberg and Tsoukas (2011) and Weick in his 2003 article on Heidegger. All are concerned with instrumental and not existential disruptions; with disruptions in the use of items of equipment ready-to-hand and not the background sense and meaning of activities. It is not research as such that is in question in their work but the technology of research.

Metamorphosis and Existential Questioning.

In a paper by Cornelissen and Holt published in *Management Learning* (2014) we do see the beginnings of an acknowledgment of the role of mood, and therefore existential disruption, in Heidegger. They (2014, p532) make the claim that "Moods leave us open" for being-in-questioning and disclosure.

However they do not work with the process through which the uncertainty experienced in anxiety is transformed into the openness of being-in-question and disclosure. They do not see that we are "within" and all consumed by the openness of being-in-question. Moods such as anxiety may, according to Heidegger close us off from the practice of questioning when they trigger off a defensive mode of fleeing into a "tranquilized familiarity" (1985, p234) of everyday habits of practice.

How do we respond to an existential anxiety that embraces us as a whole? How do we remain open rather than defensive when we are enveloped by such anxiety? Instead of dealing with what Gellner (1964) calls the metamorphosis from a defensive to an open response to anxiety in one person, Cornelissen and Holt (2014, p535) use the response of two different authors to the Mann Gulch fire to characterize a defensive and open response: Karl Weick's description of the fire is seen by them as exemplifying a defensive response and Norman Maclean's description of the fire as exemplifying an open response.

Like Kafka's metamorphosis of man into beetle, it would have been more precise and true to Heidegger for Cornelissen and Holt to focus on the metamorphosis in one person. This is how Ernst Gellner re-describes Kafka's metamorphosis in existential terms (1964). He says that the crucial challenge existentially is the space of metamorphosis between "man" and "beetle"; the space where Kafka's "man" is no longer a "man" and is not yet a "beetle". He is in between both. In the space in between both he has neither the way of being or conventions of man nor beetle to hold onto and to give him a source of identity or orientation in the world. In other words his way of being within the world is itself in the process of metamorphosis. He has neither the way of being of the old way nor the way of being of the new way.

An organizational example of this is the experience of Mort Meyerson where, in response to the existential anxiety of technological disruptions he was challenged to change his way of being a leader. He describes the transformation as a metamorphosis: "I told myself I was having the same experience as a caterpillar entering a cocoon. The caterpillar doesn't know that he'll come out as a butterfly. All he knows is that he's alone, it's dark, and it's a little scary. I came out the other end of the experience with a new understanding of leadership. I don't have to know everything. I don't have to have all the customer contacts. I don't have to make all the decisions. In fact, in the new world of business, it can't be me, it shouldn't be me, and my job is to prevent it from being me" (1996).

It is important to note that Meyerson is within the metamorphosis. There is no "Meyerson" outside of and watching the metamorphosis. So it is with anxiety from a Heideggerian perspective. It consumes and transforms our way of being as a whole. We are "in" the transformation. In *What Is Called Thinking?* Heidegger defines the lived experience of such metamorphosis: "What withdraws from us, draws us along by its very withdrawal, whether or not we become aware of it immediately, or not at all. Once we are drawn into the withdrawal, we are drawing toward what draws, attracts us by its withdrawal. And once we, being so attracted, are drawing towards what draws us, our essential nature already bears the stamp of "drawing towards". As we are drawing towards what withdraws, we ourselves are pointers pointing toward it" (1968, p7).

As stated "we" are "in" the withdrawal. For Heidegger the condition of possibility of metamorphosis is that in anxiety there is no longer a coherent "I" or "me" or "you" with which to face the world. There is only "one". And in this sense of "one" the distinction between subject and object collapse; indeed all binary opposites cease to make sense: "At bottom therefore it is not as though 'you' or 'I' feel ill at ease; rather it is this way for some 'one'. In the altogether unsettling experience of this hovering where there is nothing to hold onto, pure Dasein is all that is still there."

This breakdown in the distinction between the subject and object is not an end in itself but is the basis the disclosure of being-in-the-world as being-in-the-world. For in anxiety all binary oppositions disappear such that being-in-the-world discloses itself to being-in-the-world: "Here the disclosure and the disclosed are the self same" (1985, p233).

Entwinement and the Referential Whole of the Hermeneutic Circle

Because of the circular nature of being-in-the-world the metaphors that presuppose a separation between subject and object in understanding this notion need to be discarded; for example, "entwinement" (Sandberg and

Tsoukas 2011, p343; Sandberg and Dall'Alba 2009). For Heidegger, being-in-the-world is neither a metaphor nor is it a form of "entwinement" (the latter suggests that they can be either separate or entwined, whereas being-in-the-world is such that it can neither be separate nor entwined but is that in which separation and entwinement occur). Being and world for Heidegger are co-constitutive of each other. As demonstrated in Part I, the language that Heidegger uses to describe the relation between them is that of a "referential whole." Being is "already and always" in a world and world always implies being. They are simultaneously the same and other, what Heidegger also calls the "ontological difference."

Entwinement presupposes at least two objects that are logically separate from each other to begin with. For Heidegger being-in-the-world is ab-originally an indivisible whole within which we always and already find ourselves. Any "beginning" is always in this referential or relational whole. Being and world are simultaneously the same and other—what Heidegger calls "equiprimordial." Entwinement is just not such a whole.

Rather than being "entwined," being-in-the-world has a circular nature. This circle is a hermeneutic rather than a vicious circle. The parts and the whole are co-constitutive of each other. Just as the artist, the artwork and art are co-constitutive parts that make up a hermeneutic whole, so being-in-the-world is a hermeneutic whole without being entwined. Furthermore, being-in-the-world is a lived experienced. It is experienced in moments of anxiety in which *Dasein* comes "face to face" with itself. Putting it in what sounds like a tautology, being-in-the-world *experiences* itself as being-in-the-world (Heidegger 1985, p233). For example, if one takes climate change seriously, its logic has a circular nature: our way of being in the world is destroying our way of being in the world. If this is the case, there is nowhere to turn, no place to hide. Yet, for the most part, this is still dealt with as a technical rather than a hermeneutic issue. We try to respond to it with the very way of being that generated it in the first place.

Being-in-the-world is also not primarily a socio-material (Sandberg and Tsoukas 2011, p343) practice. While the latter may be a part of being-in-the-world, it does not describe it ontologically, that is, as a hermeneutic circle. Indeed, a socio-material practice is closer to what Heidegger calls "average everyday" ways of being within the world. But even then it is not Heideggerian; for average everydayness contains very much the dimension of a tension between being and not being at home in the world, a dimension that is not expressed in the notion of socio-material practice—as is the notion of being-towards-death, which is a central ontological category.

Existential Questioning in Karl Weick's Work

Interestingly enough, in a paper not connected to his work on Heidegger, Weick (1993) does write about existential rather than instrumental forms of disruption. Examples of this can be found in the now often quoted paper on the Mann Gulch incident: the fact that the firefighters were unfamiliar with the kind of fire they were confronting and were unfamiliar with each other in a fire that they were not able to handle meant that they had no shared taken-for-granted background of sense-making. This sent most of them into a panic state in which they could no longer trust their way of being as firefighters. Their very existence was at stake and threatened. Indeed, for the majority it was the end of their existence. Weick also identified this experience of panic as a loss of sense and meaning and as the basis for disclosing what he called a "cosmological order":

> As Mann Gulch loses its resemblance to a 10:00 fire [the expected form of the fire], it does so in ways that make it increasingly hard to socially construct reality. When the noise created by wind, flames, and exploding trees is deafening; when people are strung out in a line and relative strangers to begin with; ...and when the temperature is approaching a lethal 140 degrees (p220), people can neither validate their impressions with a trusted neighbor nor pay close attention to a boss who is also unknown and whose commands make no sense whatsoever (1993, p636).

Weick points out that in this case, there is a total lack of meaning, both for the individuals and a shared or inter-subjective meaning for the group as a whole. They experienced that "the more basic, the more frightening feeling that their old labels were no longer working. They were out-stripping their past experience and were not sure either what was up or who they were" (1993, p636).

As David Jardine (1994) points out, the power of the familiar to ensure existential or ontological security should not be underestimated. The familiar is "the world wherein one felt at home and able (playing as this does with the wonderful etymological link between *habilite* and ability)." Unlike in unfamiliar situations where we may need to rely on others, the familiar is a place in which we are enabled and thus empowered. To lose the familiar is thus to lose the horizon which allows us to be powerful. And to lose power is to be helpless.

Weick acknowledges that his description of the firefighters depicts the breakdown of an existential sense dimension and not just a breakdown in equipment ready-to-hand. Yet Weick does not seem to account for this when he reads and writes about the importance of Heidegger for organizational theory.

This loss of familiarity or existential, rather than instrumental, disruption is often experienced when going to a new and unfamiliar culture for the first time: we just have no sense as to how things get done. This is not a breakdown of something ready-to-hand. It is a strangeness and unfamiliarity in ways of doing things. This experience is often called "culture shock" because it is an anxiety experience in which we, in Heideggerian terms, have nothing—no set of conventions upon which to hold. We just do not even know how to begin knowing our way about—at least with the breakdown experienced in writing a paper we have a background context in which to make sense of and critique the journal or our own perspective. As Zygmunt Bauman has said, hermeneutic forms of uncertainty or anxiety emerge in those moments in which we do not know how to read situations within which we are. He says that "hermeneutic problems ... arise when the meaning is not unreflectively evident. ... Unresolved hermeneutical problems mean uncertainty as to how the situation ought to be read and what response is likely to bring the desired results. At best, uncertainty is felt as discomforting. At worst, it carries a sense of danger" (1990, p146).

Existential anxiety occurs in those moments when we have no set of conventions on which to hold. It is a breakdown in our set of conventions rather than in instruments or items of equipment ready-to-hand and instead of lighting up our particular background context, it deprives it of all meaning. However, it deprives it of meaning not as an end in itself but as the condition for disclosing new worlds—just as was the case for Weick in reshaping the sense of the cosmological order.

The Creative Destruction of Organizational Theory and Research

Organizational inquiry needs to go through its own experience of creative disruption before it can develop an attunement to creative disruption. It is caught in and attempts to reduce Heidegger to a logic of instrumentalism. It uses only one aspect of Heidegger's work without acknowledging it and thus without situating it in the context of its whole. If I were to do a psychoanalytic reading of organizational theorists' work on Heidegger, I would be suspicious that it is operating in terms of defense mechanisms such as splitting and repetition compulsion, that is, they split off one part (the good) and leave out the remainder of Heidegger. Yet this ends up in repeating the very problem they are trying to overcome in organizational inquiry. If I were to go on with this line of inquiry, I would suggest that such splitting and repetition compulsion occur because organizational studies shows no signs of deconstructing its own history in the face of its acknowledged paradigm crisis, which I dealt with in section. Under such conditions it is bound to repeat its mistakes.

For Heidegger there are scientific, reflective and existentially reflexive forms of inquiry, theorizing, research and education, each of which arise out of different kinds of disruption in our everyday practices as managers, researchers and educators.

There is a danger in most of the theorists of using a very general form of disruption and thus ignoring the development of a phenomenological sensitivity to different kinds of disruption. As Sartre has pointed out (1968), the danger of not developing this sensitivity to disruption is the failure to listen to what is being made manifest or explicit through the disruption. The danger of not developing the sensitivity to nuances in disruption is that management researchers and educators impose their preconceived notions of theorizing onto disruption, whereas disruption understood hermeneutically and phenomenologically is an act of enabling both the researcher and researched, theorist and student to question their own theoretical assumptions from within. Indeed, Sartre critiques Marxist methodology for having the answer before the questioning in crisis even occurs (1968). In organizational theory, Willmott (1997), for example, elaborates a notion of disruption and crisis as a basis for reflection but he has decided in advance that the language to construct the breakdown is a Marxist materialist language. Weick (2003) and Sandberg and Tsoukas (2011) are on the margins of doing this when they reduce Heidegger's notion of disruption to one form of disruption—the disruption of items of equipment ready-to-hand.

The power of phenomenology is that it does not decide the language of a breakdown in advance. Rather it follows the researcher to see what possibilities are opened up and revealed through the breakdown. It allows the being of breakdown to be. This is the phenomenological "sensitivity" to anomaly that Spinosa et al. (1997) refer to. To follow the path of a disruption is to be reflexively attuned to the way in which one's own assumptions are affecting judgment. A management researcher or educator accomplished in the "practical wisdom" of reflection and reflexivity, like a musician with a keen ear, is able to listen to the melody of the disruption as it unfolds.

Furthermore, this group of Heideggerian-based management theorists do not develop the Heideggerian existential basis for going beyond the distinction between theory and research on the one hand and practice on the other hand.

While Sandberg and Tsoukas (2011) make a move in this direction by claiming that their Heideggerian-based rationality aligns theory and practice, Heidegger goes further by using a horizon to bring the distinction between theory and practice into a relationship with each other. He does this by demonstrating that just as much as practical coping has its mood, so theorizing and research have their moods—that each are forms of concern, ways in which the human being is attuned to the world and thus ways of mattering. By understanding both theory and practice as moods and ways of being concerned, Heidegger provides a framework within which to undercut the reification of the distinction between theory and practice and brings them into relationship with each other. They are different ways in which the world is revealed as mattering.

References

Bauman, Z. (1990) Modernity and Ambivalence. In: Featherstone, M. (ed.) *Global Culture: Nationalism, globalization and modernity.* London: Sage Publications.

Chia, R. and Holt, R. (2006) Strategies as Practical Coping: A Heideggerian perspective. *Organization Studies.* Vol 27, No 5. pp635–55.

Corlett, S. (2013) Participant learning in and through research as reflexive dialogue: being "struck" and the effects of recall, *Management Learning.* Vol 44, No 5. pp453–69.

Cornelissen, J. and Holt, R. (2014) Sense Making Revisited. *Management Learning.* Vol 45, No 5. pp525–39.

Cunliffe, A. (2002) Reflexive Dialogical Practice in Management Learning. *Management Learning.* Vol 33, No 1. pp35–61.

Cunliffe, A. (2009) The Philosopher Leader: On relationalism, ethics and reflexivity—a critical perspective to teaching leadership. *Management Learning.* Vol 40, No 1. pp87–101.

Dreyfus, H. (1993) *Being-in-the-World: A commentary on Heidegger's Being and Time, Division 1.* Boston: The MIT Press.

Eger, M. (1993) Hermeneutics as an Approach to Science. *Science and Education.* Vol 2, No 1. pp303–28.

Gellner, E. (1964) *Thought and Change.* London: Weidenfeld and Nicolson

Heidegger, M. (1968) *What Is Called Thinking?* New York: Harper Torchbooks.

Heidegger, M. (1985) *Being and Time.* Oxford: Basil Blackwell.

Jardine, D. (1994) Student-Teaching, Interpretation and the Monstrous Child. *Journal of Philosophy of Education.* Vol 28, No 1. pp17–24.

Malcolm, J. (1988) *Psychoanalysis: The impossible profession.* London: Pan.

Sandberg, J. and Dall'Alba, G. (2009) Returning to Practice Anew: A life-world perspective. *Organization Studies.* Vol 30, No 12. pp1349–68.

Sandberg, J. and Tsoukas, H. (2011) Grasping the Logic of Practice: Theorizing through practical rationality. *Academy of Management Review.* Vol 36, No 2. pp338–60.

Sartre, J.P. (1968) *Search for a Method.* New York: Vintage Books.

Spinosa, C., Flores, F. and Dreyfus, H. (1997) *Disclosing New Worlds: Entrepreneurship, democratic action, and the cultivation of solidarity.* Cambridge, MA: MIT Press.

Tsoukas, H. and Knudsen. C. (2003) Introduction: The need for meta-theoretical reflection in organization theory. In: Tsoukas, H. and Knudsen, C. (eds) *The Oxford Handbook of Organization Theory.* Oxford: Oxford University Press.

Weick, K. (1999) Theory Construction as Disciplined Reflexivity: Tradeoffs in the 90s. *Academy of Management Review.* Vol 24, No 7. pp797–806.

Weick, K. (2002) Essai: Real-time Reflexivity: Prods to Reflection. *Organization Studies.* Vol 23, No 6. pp893–8.

Weick, K. (2003) Theory and Practice in the Real World. In: Tsoukas, H. and Knudsen, C. (eds) *The Oxford Handbook of Organizational Theory.* New York: Oxford University Press.

Willmott, H. (1997) Critical Management Learning. In: Burgoyne, J. and Reynolds, M. (eds) *Management Learning: Integrating Perspectives in Theory and Practice.* London: Sage Publications.

Zundel, M. (2013) Walking to Learn: Rethinking reflection for management learning. *Management Learning*. Vol 44, No 2. pp109–26.

Zundel, M. and Kokkalis, P. (2010) Theorizing as Engaged Practice. *Organization Studies*. Vol 31, No 9–10. pp1209–27.

Chapter 9

Existential Philosophical Reflection

Existential Inquiry within Management

Given that the last two chapters established that management inquiry is in an existential paradigm crisis, and that its ways of dealing with the way in which it is in paradigm crisis are themselves part of the problem, the next question that can be asked is, what kind of inquiry allows for moving beyond paradigm crisis? Is this crisis a case for clinical intervention? Or is it the basis of philosophical intervention? Based on Kuhn's view of the link between paradigm crises and Heidegger's view of the link between philosophical research and existential anxiety, this chapter will maintain that a paradigm crisis is the basis for existential philosophical research and inquiry. Paradigm crises are ways in which the being of those who were housed in that paradigm are thrown into question. Existential philosophical research and inquiry is that form of inquiry that allows the questions that are generated in paradigm crises to emerge, be articulated and worked through with the aim of disclosing new worlds or new possibilities for research and ways of being as a manager and professional in general.

An existential form of philosophical inquiry is closer to a therapeutic form of philosophy than it is to philosophy as an academic form of inquiry. It sees paradigm crises as opportunities through which to transform ways of being-in-the-world, disclosing new worlds or new paradigms through which to conduct research and be and do in the world. It is not focused primarily on textual analyses or on representational knowledge of the texts of philosophers.

Drawing out an implication of this logic, we may say that even some forms of emotional "dis-ease" experienced by members of a paradigm are part of a paradigm crises. As we will see, Kuhn furnishes us with several examples of the way in which scientists were thrown into a kind uncertainty and anxiety which was not personal but based on the fragmentation of their paradigm.

This would suggest that to understand and work productively with the dis-ease experienced by individuals, we need to inquire not only into their—or our—own psycho-histories but to develop an understanding of how the practices of emotional dis-ease are shaped by the socio-historical and cultural contexts in which the subject is situated. Modernist forms of psychotherapy have developed languages in which to explore the effect of early childhood experiences, the role of the family system and the environment on the formation of individual subjectivities but they have not developed a language in which to articulate the effects of social, historical, cultural and ontological contexts on the being of individuals.

How can we explore the ways in which the social and cultural contexts of individuals contribute to their emotional dis-ease? Is there a dimension of the dis-ease of individuals that arises out of our cultural contexts? And is there a process to work in productive ways with individuals on the ways in which their emotional dis-ease is shaped by their social and cultural contexts?

In this chapter I will use a contrast between "existential philosophical practice" and "psychotherapeutic" interpretations of dis-ease to bring out the nature and significance of a philosophical approach to making sense of everyday life. I will show that just as in the case of psychotherapy, philosophical practice becomes vital in moments of dis-ease and that just as in the case of psychotherapy, so in the case of philosophy, dis-ease is experienced as a withdrawal or dissociation from being absorbed in the everyday world. However, I will argue that philosophy and psychotherapy differ in terms of the focus of the withdrawal. I will show that unlike psychotherapy, philosophy does not focus on the disruption of the personality, psyche or self but on the breakdown in the conventions which structure everyday life and thus that a philosophical crisis is one in which the conventions for everyday living no longer give everyday life structure or meaning. From this perspective the aim of philosophical practice is not to heal the self but to explore the disruption in conventions and to open alternative frames for making sense of everyday life.

Crucial to this chapter is that questioning of conventions is to be distinguished from questioning of "selves" or even of sense of self. In questioning our conventions we are not questioning something within us but, on the contrary, are questioning the context that we are already in. This shift from questioning something within us to questioning that which we are already in is a shift from psychotherapeutic to philosophical questioning. But it is not a disengaged or scientific questioning of conventions. It is a personal and passionate questioning of conventions, a questioning within the midst of a dis-ease in everyday living.

Central to existential philosophical questioning is the willingness to stay with the question. Rather than trying to answer the question, it is developing the curiosity in questioning. Rainer Maria Rilke phrases this curiosity as allowing the question and the response to emerge:

> *Try to love the questions themselves as if they were locked rooms or books written in a very foreign language. Don't search for the answers, which could not be given to you now, because you would not be able to live them. And the point is, to live everything. Live the questions now. Perhaps then, someday far in the future, you will gradually, without even noticing it, live your way into the answer (Rilke 1993).*

The process of allowing both the question and answer to emerge is central to existentialism. The way we ask a question shapes the framework within which it is addressed, so it is central to listen to and even critique the way in which we are asking a question. As Epicurus said: "Empty are the words of that philosopher who offers therapy for no human suffering. For just as there is no use in medical expertise if it does not give therapy for bodily diseases, so too there is no use in philosophy if it does not expel the suffering of the soul" (Grafton et al. 2010).

In this chapter the way in which questions emerge existentially out of the paradigm crises in management will be explored. It will explore the notion of existential anxiety as opposed to clinical anxiety, existential philosophical forms of education, the way in which certain attitudes towards this anxiety close down the vision or sight of leaders and managers, and the attitudes that allow for the disclosure of new possibilities, new ways of seeing, doing and being in organizations and the free market. In other words, we will be exploring the way in which theories of existential anxiety provide a framework for turning existential forms of uncertainty into opportunity.

Uncertainty in Management Today

One may well ask: what has existential anxiety got to do with management and uncertainty? We will make three claims in this chapter:

Firstly, there is, if not conclusive evidence, at least support for the belief that much of the uncertainty experienced in technological change, organizational change, the changes in the conventions of doing business, the experience of difference in the context of globalization, the challenging of very core beliefs, is an existential form of anxiety. Indeed, even the act of becoming a manager or leader involves experiences of existential anxiety for they involve "leaps into the unknown." This is highlighted by the way in which managers and leaders need to immerse themselves in experiencing management and leadership before they have an embodied or felt sense of how to be and do management and leadership. Habits develop only through being habituated. This point is shared by Aristotle and existentialism: our habits of practice are developed by practicing our habits.

This chapter will also contribute a second dimension: that of existence. While many theorists have explored the role of practice in management, there has not been a tendency towards exploring the phenomenon of existence which, from an existential perspective, underpins the notion of practice. Even those scholars who make use of the work of Heidegger in management tend to highlight the dimension of practice (Weick 2003, Zundel and Kokkalis 2010, Sandberg and Tsoukas 2011) rather than the existential and *existentiell* dimensions (Heidegger 1985) in terms of which Heidegger grounds practice. Yet, as will be maintained in this chapter, both leadership and management are more than practices; they are ways of existing, ways of being within the world. And being-in-the-world is characterized by existential uncertainty, the uncertainty of developing an identity or way of being through action and not through advanced theorizing or developing of a blueprint.

There is a third dimension to this chapter: it will conclude by suggesting that existential forms of education, research and inquiry are appropriate for management studies in times where the uncertainty is such that the foundations of a paradigm or way of being and doing cannot be taken for granted. Indeed, it is a form of education for those experiences of uncertainty in which the way of being or inhabiting the role of a professional manager or leader cannot be taken for granted.

The chapter is divided into the following sections:

1.   the existential dimensions of paradigm crises;

2.   existential anxiety as an illness to be cured or existential anxiety as the basis for existential hermeneutic forms of inquiry?;

3.   the existential distinction between anxiety as focusing on the "I" and anxiety as reflexive inquiry into the way of being in which the "I" is situated;

4.   individuality as an abstraction;

5.   using an ambiguity in Rollo May's concept of anxiety to show how existential philosophical forms of anxiety focus on ends and ways of being, whereas psychological theories focus on the disruptions of the "internal" means of achieving the ends and not on the ends themselves;

6.   existential hermeneutic forms of anxiety: the conditions for becoming inquirers into our own ways of existing and practicing;

7.   defensive and disclosive responses to existential anxiety;

8.   existential anxiety in the context of the free market;

9.   existential anxiety in the context of changing leadership paradigms;

10.   bewilderment of leaders in the face of existential anxiety;

11.   existential anxiety in the face of globalization;

12.   existential anxiety and the hermeneutics of management education;

13.   existential education as the basis for experiencing uncertainty as the basis for inquiry and opening of new opportunities.

The Existential Dimensions of Paradigm Crisis

Thomas Kuhn (1996) demonstrated how philosophical questioning emerges in times of paradigm crisis when scientists can no longer take their basic assumptions for granted. He maintained that in their everyday activities, scientists are puzzle-solvers who must presuppose the rules of science in order to continue in their everyday activities. They do not need to make these rules explicit. In fact, making them explicit is an obstacle to successful puzzle-solving because it shifts the attention of the scientist from puzzle-solving to the rules of puzzle-solving. Concern with puzzle-solving and with the rules of puzzle-solving are two different kinds of activities (1996, p47). The former is a scientific and the latter a philosophical activity.

It is only in times of paradigm insecurity (1996, p47) or crisis that the rules and assumptions underpinning the everyday activity of puzzle-solving become explicit themes of concern. In experiences of paradigm crisis, scientists are said by Kuhn to experience "acute personal crisis" (1996, p112) and "pronounced professional insecurity" (1996, pp67–8). Einstein reported feelings of having no secure ground or foundation upon which to stand (cited in Kuhn 1996, p83). In the face of the uncertainty caused by paradigm crisis, some scientists are reported to leave the field of science, while others become dogmatic, clinging in a defensive and blind way to the principles and practices of the old paradigms. Yet it is also in times of paradigm crisis that scientists come to reflect on their paradigms and practices which they tend to take for granted during the normal course of scientific activity. Summarizing these points, Kuhn has said:

> It is, I think, particularly in times of crisis that scientists have turned to philosophical analysis   Scientists have not generally needed to or wanted to be philosophers. ... To the extent that normal research work can be conducted by using the paradigm as a model, rules and assumptions need not be made explicit. ... But that is not to say that the search for assumptions ... cannot be an effective way to weaken the grip of a tradition upon the mind and to suggest the basis of a new one (1996, p88).

From the Kuhnian perspective, it is philosophical reflection that paves the way for the emergence of a new paradigm, and thus a new way of seeing and experiencing the world. In the case of paradigm crisis, the trauma experienced in the rupture of paradigms does not lead to reflection on the personality or psychology of the individual. It leads to reflection on the standards of truth, the metaphysical assumptions, methods and language of the paradigm; that is, rupture of the everyday activity of the scientist leads the scientist to become philosophical. Kuhn thus holds the view that a rupture in a paradigm is the condition of the paradigm itself becoming explicit and a theme for deconstruction.

This deconstruction is the basis for the emergence of a new paradigm or set of scientific practices. Such philosophizing performs a therapeutic, rather than an epistemological, role because it is not about representing the truth in statement-like form but about paving the way for new paradigms and thus new sets of practices, ways of experiencing and seeing the world.

Heidegger and Kuhn appear to hold similar views on this point. Heidegger says:

The greatness and superiority of natural science during the sixteenth and seventeenth centuries rests in the fact that all the scientists were philosophers. They understood that there are no mere facts ... Where genuine and discovering research is done [today] the situation is no different from that of three hundred years ago ... the present leaders of atomic physics, Niels Bohr and Heisenberg, think in a thoroughly philosophical way, and only therefore create new ways of posing questions and, above all, hold out the questionable (1993, p272).

In order to pose questions in new ways, these scientists questioned the very assumptions of the paradigm in which they were habituated. This was not just an intellectual or cognitive mode of questioning but an existential one which involved their whole being. Thus Wolfgang Pauli says:

I remember discussions with Bohr which went through many hours until very late at night and ended almost in despair; and when at the end of the discussion I went alone for a walk in the neighboring park I repeated to myself again and again the question: can nature possibly be so absurd as it seemed to us in these atomic experiments? (quoted in Kuhn 1996, p86).

Questioning here is existential in that the scientists question because their way of being is in question; their sense of purpose, meaning and identity is invested in the paradigm. The latter is more than a set of rules or conventions. It is a way of life which includes interests, identities, politics, aspirations and achievements. When these break down it generates a sense of anxiety; that kind of anxiety which has no "measure," no set of conventions to guide one in making sense of the world. This is existential anxiety where there is "no-measure," "no-thing" to ground one's practices.

But, as Kuhn points out, it is not only the individuals that are in crisis; it is the community of scholars that can no longer share a paradigm that hold them as a community. They are fragmented and at war with each other: "the proliferation of competing articulations, the willingness to try anything, the expression of explicit discontent, the recourse to philosophy and ... debate over fundamentals" (1996, p91).

From a sociological perspective, Ernst Gellner has reiterated this point by maintaining that philosophical questioning, the question concerning the meaning of our activities, emerges where a "stable identity is not available" (1964, p52). According to Gellner, philosophy as an existential activity emerges where there are no stable rules of the game or where the rules of the game are constantly shifting. The absence of a set of stable rules gives rise to an experience of existential anxiety. For existential, unlike psychoanalytic, forms of anxiety occur where we cannot take the rules which regulate our practices for granted anymore. For Gellner, the anxiety that is generated in this instability is the source of meta-theoretical and philosophical questioning. Indeed, for Gellner, existential philosophy is orientation in a crisis. Zygmunt Bauman calls those forms of insecurity that revolve around crises in paradigms "hermeneutic insecurities" (1990, p146). Hermeneutic insecurities are insecurities that are focused around the inability to read or make sense of the meaning of a situation.

Paradigm shifts are qualitative changes in the way in which the world is experienced. This means that it cannot take place in a linear and quantitative way. It also suggests that it is not a rational process, as reasoning takes place within a paradigm. It thus presupposes a kind of *Gestalt* shift or what Heidegger calls a "a blink of the eye" (*eine augenblick*) or *gestalt* switch to begin to see the world in a new way. This is a shift in what Gendlin calls a "felt sense," from the disturbing "felt sense" that things are not quite right to a focus of conviction in which new worlds are disclosed. For example, prior to the discovery of the role of paradox in quantum physics, Niels Bohr was overwhelmed by a sense of uncertainty and self-questioning regarding science. However, in the words of Heisenberg, once Bohr embraced the role of paradox in quantum physics, "He felt so strongly that even when one had the final answer, there will remain a completely paradoxical situation which could not be handled by any of the usual concepts so that the whole philosophy of natural science should probably be changed in order to understand what happened here" (Kuhn 1996).

This "felt sense" is not unique to discoveries in quantum physics. Even in the field of mathematics it is central to paradigm switches. This is evidenced in the words of Henri Poincaré:

> For fifteen days I strove to prove that there could not be any functions like those I have since called Fuchsian functions. I was then very ignorant; every day I seated myself at my work table, stayed an hour or two, tried a great number of combinations and reached no results. One evening, contrary to my custom, I drank black coffee and could not sleep. Ideas rose in crowds; I felt them collide until pairs interlocked, so to speak ... making a stable combination. By the next morning I had established the existence of a class of Fuchsian functions, those which came from the hypergeometric series; I had only to write out the results, which took but a few hours (1946).

Poincaré goes on to say that the most that rationality could do was to help him work out what he had already resolved through "felt sense":

> Then I wanted to represent these functions by the quotient of two series; this idea was perfectly conscious and deliberate, the analogy with elliptic functions guided me. I asked myself what properties these series must have if they existed, and I succeeded without difficulty in forming the series I have called theta-Fuchsian (1946).

To summarize, in existential terms, to be in a paradigm crisis is to be caught between the collapse of an old paradigm, or way of doing things, and the coming into being of the new way of doing things. This space is an extremely insecure space, but from a Heideggerian perspective, it is also the basis of existential philosophical questioning. Quoting one of his favorite poets, Holderlin, Heidegger says "There where the danger is, so the saving power grows." And in a similar fashion, Niels Bohr says: "Every great and deep difficulty bears in itself its own solution. It forces us to change our thinking in order to find it."

The paradoxical logic of existential philosophy is that by embracing that our way of being is in question, we open up the possibility for disclosing worlds in new ways.

However, we can be defensive in response to existential anxiety, in which case we close off new worlds and retreat into the traditional paradigm. This has an air of resignation about it. In contrast to this resignation and despair, both Heidegger and Kuhn call for an active rather than passive destruction of the tradition. For the tradition blocks our access to new possibilities: "Tradition takes what has come down to us and delivers it over to self-evidence; it blocks our access to those primordial 'sources' from which the categories and concepts handed down to us have been in part quite genuinely drawn" (Heidegger 1985, p43).

Is Existential Anxiety an Illness to be cured or is it the Basis of Existential Hermeneutic Inquiry and Questioning?

Neither the hermeneutic or reflexive phenomenon of existential anxiety nor existence *per se* have been explored in much depth in management discourse. Yet the pervasiveness of anxiety in organizations is indicated by Tony Watson. This point is made by Watson, who chooses one company to exemplify his point:

> *The more I saw of the managers at Ryland [organization], the more I*
> *became aware of human angst, insecurity, doubt and frailty among them.*
> *I observed managers being rude to their staff … losing their tempers …*
> *spreading malicious gossip … failing to turn up to meetings. … I found*
> *myself mediating between managers who had fallen out with each other*
> *(2006, p68).*

So powerful can a sense of fear be that it prevents managers and reports from working for the greater good of the company. As Menon and Thompson claim, "In one technology company we studied, managers who felt threatened by another group's idea simply ignored it" (2010, p76).

While emotions are a core topic in organizational theory today, it is a specific form of attunement that this chapter focuses on: existential anxiety and its relationship to management, leadership and organizations in the context of the free market. This is not to deny that non-existential forms of anxiety have been explored in organizations. The work of Yiannis Gabriel is an example of looking at anxiety from a psychoanalytic perspective, but this is not anxiety and its relationship existence in organizations. Similarly, the name of Manfred Kets De Vries is associated with exploring anxiety in organizations from a psychodynamic perspective. Indeed, the debate between existential and psychoanalytic views of anxiety has a long and intricate history.

Furthermore, there are many other theories of anxiety, including Gestalt, cognitive behavior, rational emotive and existential forms of anxiety. The former three tend to focus on the individual while the latter focuses on the way of existing in which human beings are situated.

As Peter Koestenbaum claims, existential anxiety is the basis of hermeneutic reflexivity, the basis for becoming attuned to, learning about and transforming one's own conventions for doing things in response to changing circumstances In a more general way, Ernst Gellner, the sociologist, claimed that existential anxiety is the basis of existential philosophical research and education. For, as Gellner claims, because they do not stand on "some rock like, firm position, but … have had the skids put under them," existential thinkers are able "to communicate a transition, a genuine uncertainty of vision" (1964, p54). They dwell in the space between what Heidegger poetically calls the loss of the old gods and the not yet of the new gods.

Indeed, even Thomas Kuhn (1996) has maintained that scientists turn to philosophical inquiry when they cannot take the conventions of their paradigms for granted anymore and are exploring new conventions and rules for conducting science. And Heidegger writes not only of the way in which anxiety is central to research but of the way in which pioneering scientists were not simply embedded within an already existing framework but were philosophers able to reflect on their assumptions (1993, p272).

The theme of connecting reflexivity, anxiety, existence and existential philosophical paradigm reframing underpins all the writers who have been identified as existentialist. From Kierkegaard to Heidegger, anxiety, questioning, inquiry, research and education are connected to each other. In all these thinkers, anxiety is a condition of disrupting the taken-for-granted conventions of our habitual ways of doing things and paving the way for the disclosure of new possibilities, new worlds and new ways of doing things.

Indeed, anxiety is the condition of existential questioning, that form of questioning that occurs in those forms of uncertainty in which we can no longer take our familiar practices and interpretations for granted. In this sense, anxiety is not an illness to be cured but the existential basis of asking questions. What a philosophical practice needs to do is not so much look at the causes of anxiety—as does a scientist—but at the questions that are being asked in anxiety. Anxiety is a way in which our being is in question such that we are called to ask questions.

Professional and research psychologists write as though anxiety were a problem outside of and independent of them—as though it were "objective." In contrast to this, in some if not all of these existential writers, we find that anxiety is an integral feature and even a condition of possibility of their own thinking practices. This is most visibly the case in the writing of Nietzsche and Kierkegaard. The former not only maintains that all thinking is autobiographical but that much of his thinking was a response to the pain of his existence—and he went on to say that his pain is not of the type than can be cured but it does make him more philosophical.

In the same way, it is not difficult to see the connection between Kierkegaard's description of his own lived experience of anxiety, his theorizing of anxiety and the way he understands anxiety to be the condition of possibility of an existential education. Although not an existentialist, Ludwig Wittgenstein writes about the connection between the pain of his existence and his activity of philosophizing.

Indeed, this theme is not new in the history of Western thought. As Thomas Kuhn points out, scientists like Einstein, Heisenberg and Bohr become reflexive in the context of the existential uncertainty that is experienced between the breakdown of old paradigms and the not yet of new paradigms. In Plato's work, *Phaedrus*, he writes quite unequivocally about the relation between states of madness and philosophizing. It can also be argued that the perplexity Socrates saw as so central to his philosophical being is more than an intellectual perplexity. He asked fundamental questions because his *being* was "in question." Rather than just a form of intellectual or cognitive questioning, questioning was a way of life for Socrates. It was a state of being, and it was this state of being that opened up the possibility of examining life itself. In the same vein, Montaigne's melancholia is the basis, as Screech notes, for his philosophizing. In fact, in his work on Montaigne, Screech (1991) reported that states of mania and melancholia are central to becoming philosophical. It is not hard to see the connection between mood states of anxiety and depression in the work of Kierkegaard (1958) and Nietzsche (Jaspers 1965). Both make the connection between these mood states and being philosophical quite explicit. It is also quite evident in the way in which Wittgenstein (Finch 1995) thought about the activity of philosophizing, namely that there was an intimate connection between his philosophizing and the angst of his being. Indeed, in writing about Heidegger, Wittgenstein has said: "I can readily think what Heidegger means by Being and Dread. Man has the impulse to run up against the limits of language. Think, for example, of the astonishment that anything exists" (Finch 1995, p63).

Running up against the limits of language was central to the philosophies of both Wittgenstein and Heidegger. Heidegger saw existential anxiety as the mood for pushing beyond the conventions of everyday language. It was the basis for seeing the world in new and different ways. For in anxiety nothing makes sense anymore; even the language with which we describe the experience of anxiety loses its sense of significance.

In the *Phaedrus*, Plato wrote explicitly about the way in which the madness of scientists discloses worlds in new ways: "The ancients … who gave things their names did not regard madness as shameful or a matter for reproach; otherwise they would not have connected this very word with the finest of the sciences" (1968, p245).

Furthermore, unlike writers who claim to be scientific in the narrow and reductive interpretation of positivism and thus claim to be writing about objects independently and separate from themselves, the existential writers are writing about what they are already within. They are writing from within the lived experience of their anxiety about the meaning and significance of existence. This is a reflexive mode of writing and research which places a way of being in the broader context of existence.

The Existential Distinction between Anxiety as Focusing on the "I" and Anxiety as Reflexive Inquiry into the Way of Being in which the "I" is Situated

We see not only a general reflexive and hermeneutic practice in these philosophers but a very specific one: it is not that their anxiety leads them to become attuned to the inner world of their individual existence, their personality or psyche *per se* but the context of conventions in which they are situated. Anxiety leads not to a focus on self but on existence; that in which the self occurs. Heidegger says that anxiety is not about "I" or "you" or "me" but about the way of being-in-the-world in which both the I and its relationship to the world and others is situated. Through anxiety and being-in-question the world context in which I exist is discovered. Through exploring the way in which my being is in question I do not discover an "I" or a "me" but the paradigm or average everyday context in which I am situated. As Dreyfus says, "Anxiety reveals Dasein as dependent upon a public system of significances that it did not produce" (1993, p177). Continuing his point, he says that it is through anxiety that the human being "understands itself in terms of the system of roles, goals and equipment which make up the world" (1993, p128).

Thus rather than the subject matter being outside and an independent object of investigation, it is an exploration of the way of being from within the way of being. This is a hermeneutic as opposed to a reductive positivist way of understanding. It is as players from within the game that we are playing that we explore the game rather than as neutral and distanced spectators.

From an existential perspective, this is the case because there is no separation between an "I" or "me" and the world of which I am part. There is no separation of being and world, subject and object. The human being is by definition "always and already" situated in the world. The inseparability of being and world is expressed in the phrases being-in-the-world and *Da-sein* or being-there. The human is always and already "there." There is no I independent of a world or a spacio-temporal context. A human being is "always and already" in a way of being or is inhabiting a network of roles, practices, habits—professional and otherwise.

Individuality as an Abstraction

To see the being of the individual primarily as an individual is to have abstracted them from the context of their existence. Heidegger sees the latter as a central fault in the history of Western thought. It assumes the view that abstracted individuals are ontologically primarily and thus looks at the way in which individuals are constituted: for example as psychosexual drives and stages or as a will to power. It also gets caught in scandalous debates; for example between nature and nurture and freedom and determinism. For Heidegger, because the human being is always and already part of the world, "it," the "human being," is not independent of its environment such that it can be determined by it; nor is it free of its environment.

Using an Ambiguity in the Work of Rollo May to bring out the Distinction between Existential Philosophical and Psychological Forms of Anxiety

The difference between a psychological and a philosophical level of anxiety can be seen in terms of an ambiguity in Rollo May's concept of anxiety, in which anxiety is seen to arise in response to both a threat to live out what one values and as a response to a lack of values at all. This ambiguity is implicit in May's definition of anxiety as a threat to a value that an individual holds vital to their existence (1996). Exemplary of what May means by a threat to a value is the case of Nancy and Tom: "Nancy illustrates the identification of the love of another person with her existence when she said, speaking of her fiancée, 'If anything went wrong with his love for me, I'd break down completely.' Her security as a self depended upon this other person's love and acceptance of her." And writing about Tom, he says:

> The identification of a value with one's existence as a personality is dramatized in the remark of Tom in his anxiety over whether he would be retained in his job or be forced to resort again to government relief: "If I couldn't support my family, I'd as soon jump off the end of the dock." He thus tells that if he could not preserve the self-respecting position of being the responsible wage-earner, his whole life would have no meaning and he might as well not exist (May 1996, p206).

It is Nancy's and Tom's ability to attain or live out what they value that is in question rather than the values themselves. They are sure of what they value and are overcome by anxiety because they cannot achieve what they value.

The desirability of these values is itself not in question. Nancy's need for love and Tom's desire to be a breadwinner are themselves not in question. The values themselves are taken for granted. For May the problem with both Nancy and Tom is that there is some conflict within themselves that is making it very difficult to attain what they value. It is this conflict within themselves that is the source of their anxiety. Neurotic anxiety is the name given by May to those anxieties that have their source in internal conflicts within the self: "Neurotic anxiety is that which occurs when the incapacity for coping adequately with threats is not objective but subjective—that is, due not to objective weakness but to inner psychological patterns and conflicts which prevent the individual from using his powers" (1996, p215).

But May makes room for another type of threat, a threat not only to the attainment of what is valued but a threat experienced in the absence of specific values, purposes and meanings. In another context May does make room for the second sense of values being in question when he says:

> *I here propose that the quantity of anxiety prevalent in the present period arises from the fact that the values and standards underlying modern culture are themselves threatened. ... The threats involved in the present social changes are not threats that can be met on the basis of the assumptions of the culture but rather are threats to those underlying assumptions themselves. The threat is experienced not as a threat to subsistence, nor even chiefly to the prestige of the individual concerned, but is rather a threat to basic assumptions which have been identified with the existence of the culture, and which the individual, as a participant in the culture, has identified with his own existence (1996, p238).*

May thus allows us to think of at least two levels of threats to one's values, namely, when the actualization of what we value is in question and when we lose sense of what we value in the first place. These two may be thought of as a "psychological" and (what I shall still tentatively call) a "philosophical" level. In the terms of May the psychological level expresses itself when a conflict or tension within ourselves prevents us from attaining what we value. As he himself puts it, neurotic anxiety occurs where a conflict within the subjectivity of a person frustrates them from attaining their goals. Philosophical anxiety occurs where we are not sure of the conventions, the purpose or the goals that we aspire to in the first place, when we have lost sense of our values. When the basic assumptions of a culture are, as May suggests in the above, threatened, we are called to become philosophical.

We become philosophical when the basic assumptions of a paradigm or culture can no longer explain our world to us. In such situations these assumptions cannot be taken for granted. They become explicit themes of concern and examination.

May does not develop an understanding of the experience of threat that arises in the context of the rupture of the assumptions of a culture. Indeed, the language of modernist forms of psychotherapy in general do not seem to have a framework through which to reflect on, deconstruct and examine crises in values or ends. This point is indicated by Charles Guignon, who maintains that "therapists may feel poorly equipped by their training" (1993, p217) to respond to the question of the relationship between anxiety and ends or values. As Guignon notes, psychotherapy tends to take the question of the relationship between crises in living and ends or values for granted by seeing values as being unchangeably centered in a commitment to satisfy "those basic needs dictated by our biosocial makeup or as matters of personal preference. Psychotherapy, seen as a technique designed to help people attain their ends, remains indifferent to the ends themselves" (1993, p219).

This is clearly the case in a humanistic psychology which is concerned with enabling clients to actualize their potential. The goal—actualization of potential—is not in question in the therapeutic context. It is the client's means or path towards actualization that is the focus of therapeutic activity. Similarly, a psychotherapy which aims at growth or health or happiness has fixed the goal in advance of therapy. In these cases therapy is about developing the means to achieve these goals. Guignon feels that even Rollo May is caught within the discourse of means rather than ends because, according to Guignon, May believes that "values can be justified only if they are treated as means to achieving non-moral ends [such as] personal satisfaction or fulfillment or 'empowerment'" (1993, p221). The example which I, in the above, drew from May confirms this because for both Tom and Nancy the ends are not in question (supporting the family and love), but the way in which they are blocked from achieving their ends is in question.

But it is not only humanistic psychologists who are concerned primarily with means and not ends; so too are depth psychologists. In the context of organizations, Yiannis Gabriel claims that much, if not all, of psychoanalytic thought is focused on working with organizational inhibitions and dysfunctions: "The majority of depth psychologists, however, would view emotion itself as vital in breaking out of dysfunctional processes that inhibit performance and exacerbate anxieties and discontents" (1998, p210).

From an existential perspective, existential anxiety is not primarily about breaking out of dysfunctional processes, as Gabriel maintains, but is the condition of existential questioning and the basis of disclosing new worlds.[1] It is about meaning-making and sense of purpose. As Heidegger claims, the human being questions because its being is in question. And the ultimate form of being-in-question is anxiety. Existential anxiety is the condition of inquiry, research, education and philosophy. It is also not about means but about disclosing new ends—new purpose and meaning.

The language of psychotherapy thus tends to operate within the framework of means rather than ends, freeing patients from inhibitions and enabling patients to develop the means that would allow them to achieve their ends, but it does not bring the issue of ends into focus itself.

However, as has already been indicated, the experience of anxiety cannot be limited to the experience of means to the exclusion of ends. As our depiction of the ambiguity in the work of May indicates, there are experiences of anxiety, pain, uncertainty and insecurity which are focused around the way in which we are shaped and structured by our sociocultural and historical context. It is this context that defines the ends that we pursue. We need to develop a discourse or language that can address the pain, uncertainty and trauma experienced in the way in which we, our subjectivities, are produced by our context or average everyday practices. What are the conditions under which our ends, context, culture, horizon or background become an explicit theme of questioning?

Existential Hermeneutic Forms of Anxiety: the Conditions for Becoming Inquirers into Our Own Ways of Existing and Practicing

Historically, philosophers have been concerned with the question of ends. In the name of the notion of the "good life" or the "meaning of existence," philosophers have sought to raise the question of ends by an analysis of, amongst others, the concepts of the good, happiness, justice and virtue. However, it is not this form of questioning that this chapter wishes to develop. Generally such questioning has taken on a disembodied form, a form in which concepts rather than situated concepts have been the primary theme of focus. As I will show, in the context of anxiety we are concerned not with a decontextualized asking of the question of ends but with a form of questioning that arises in the rupture

---

1   The relationship between psychoanalytic and existential concepts of anxiety has a long history and would need a separate paper in itself to explore.

of the tranquility of the everyday. It is when we experience an absence of the sense or meaning of the good life that the question of the meaning of such a life becomes an existentially explicit theme of concern. Furthermore, as I will show, in anxiety, we ask the question of ends not by analyzing disengaged concepts of happiness or justice, but in the context of reflection on our own practices. It is through accounting for the way in which our identities are formed by our everyday practices that we pose the question of the meaning of our activities, existence and the question of the good life. For it is only as we make explicit and deconstruct the taken-for-granted average everyday meanings which have structured our practices within the everyday world that we can pose the question of the good life—otherwise we are still caught within a taken-for-granted web of meanings.

Exemplary of a hermeneutic insecurity is the insecurity of a migrant who is unable to make sense of the unfamiliar language and values of a strange culture or way of life. The anguish of hermeneutic forms of insecurity is demonstrated by Hermann Hesse in his description of the experience of being caught between cultures or ways of life:

> There are times when a whole generation is caught in this way between two ages, between two modes of life and thus loses the feeling for itself, for the self-evident, for all morals, for being safe and innocent. Naturally, everyone does not feel this equally strongly. A nature such as Nietzsche's had to suffer our present ills more than a generation in advance. What he had to go through alone and misunderstood, thousands suffer today (Hesse 1974, p28).

The loss of feeling for itself which Hesse refers to in the above would today be called an anxiety of meaninglessness and emptiness, an affliction which, as Hesse notes, is no longer limited to an isolated few but has become a central concern of what it means to exist today. Indeed, as Ian Lennie points out, for the entire twentieth century, management theory and practice was dominated by what he calls the "disembodied head." He asks: "How does this come to be an acceptable representation of management, evoking identification from managers, rather than repulsion, fear or incomprehension?" (Lennie 1999, p15).

Defensive and Disclosive Responses to Existential Anxiety

Existential anxiety does not necessarily lead to inquiry, reflexivity or questioning. It can just as easily lead to a defensive response. Different existentialists write about these two forms of response in different ways. For example, Kierkegaard writes about the way in which embracing existential anxiety leads to a disclosure of new possibilities, while refusing the pain of anxiety leads to the despair of resignation or defiance. Nietzsche writes of a passive nihilism which is an attempt to insulate oneself in one's conventional ways of doing things. He also writes of an active nihilism which is the philosophical activity of accepting anxiety by asking kinds of questions that would not even begin to surface in the taken-for-granted common sense of everyday life; for example, in active forms of nihilism, we are challenged to ask the question of the value of all values. This is not the question: "what are your values?" It takes this a level further and asks about the construction of the notion of value itself—something we assume in everyday life. Sartre writes of bad faith as a defensive response to anxiety. The latter manifests itself either as a withdrawal into the world of abstraction or a total identification with the roles and routines of everyday life.

Heidegger writes of an authentic and inauthentic response to anxiety. The inauthentic response is what he sees as an attempt to fall back into or hold onto the conventions or paradigms that have been thrown into crisis. It is an attempt to hold onto the past in the form of, for example, idealizing the past. An authentic response to anxiety is one which embraces the anxiety and uncertainty of a future that cannot be objectified. It is a form of living into the world of possibility and the basis for disclosing new worlds. It is the world in which, according to Spinosa et al. (1997), the entrepreneur and entrepreneurial leader dwells.

And according to Heidegger, an authentic response to anxiety is the existential basis of research. The wonder for research begins with the anxiety of the destruction of one's taken-for-granted ways of making sense:

> *Only when the strangeness of beings oppresses us does it arouse and evoke wonder. Only on the ground of wonder—the revelation of the nothing—does the "why?" loom before us. Only because the "why" is possible as such can we in a definite way inquire into grounds, and ground them. Only because we can inquire and ground is the destiny of our existence placed in the hands of the researcher. The question of the nothing puts us, the questioners, in question (Heidegger 1993).*

I would like to emphasize Heidegger's last point: it is when our being is in question that we begin to question. It is when our way of being, our professional practices, are in question that we begin to question and inquire into them. This kind of questioning is the basis for hermeneutic and reflexive research.

But there is still a point that needs to be dealt with: what is it that enables a person to embrace an authentic rather than an inauthentic response to existential anxiety? Rather than speaking about resilience, Heidegger writes about what he calls resoluteness. In contrast to resilience, which is popularly defined as the power to bounce back, being resolute is the willingness to stay in the uncertainty, to allow it to speak through one in such a way that it discloses new possibilities and new ways of being. Resoluteness is a letting oneself be rather than a resisting of anxiety. Its archetype, for Heidegger, is the figure of Socrates, who "All through his life and right into his death … did nothing else than place himself into this draft, this current, and maintain himself in it. This is why he is the purest thinker of the West. This is why he wrote nothing" (1968, p17).

The details of the two types of responses to anxiety can be brought out by looking at them in terms of Victor Frankl's notion of "paradoxical intention." In the context of anxiety, this principle would state that the more we try to escape anxiety by willing ourselves to be free of it, the greater the anxiety becomes. For we are willing ourselves to do kinds of things for which the will is inappropriate. Just as we cannot will ourselves to sleep or to stop being embarrassed, we cannot will ourselves to feel or stop feeling anxious or nervous. An example given by Frankl refers to the notion of pleasure: "The more a man aims at pleasure by way of a direct intention, the more he misses his aim" (1967, p17).

For Frankl, we do not overcome anxiety by intending or willing its overcoming, but it is by letting ourselves be overwhelmed by the anxiety that we are experiencing that we are able to surpass it. By accepting rather than resisting it, we are able, as he maintains, to take the wind out of its sails (1967, p224). It loses its power to dominate us. Speaking, as he does, in the context of neurotic illnesses, he says: "If we succeed in bringing the patient to the point where he ceases to flee from or to fight his symptoms, but, on the contrary, even exaggerates them, then we may observe that the symptoms diminish and that the patient is no longer haunted by them" (1967, p224).

Translating this into the language of the Heideggerian perspective, it is by accepting, rather than fleeing or willing to overcome, the anxiety of nothingness that the human being begins to inquire into the nature of being-in-the-world itself. The more the human being accepts anxiety, the more it "deconstructs" its average everydayness, and the more it "deconstructs" average everydayness the closer it comes to an attunement to being-in-the-world itself. As Dreyfus says: "The ultimate choice … is no choice at all. It is the experience of transformation that comes from Dasein's accepting its powerlessness" (1993, p319). Accepting such powerlessness is the basis of becoming clear sighted. Sometimes it is better to do nothing!

The process underpinning the notion of resoluteness is not unique to Heidegger but can be found in the writing of Kierkegaard. In his book *The Concept of Anxiety* (1980), he sees the resolute affirmation of anxiety as the basis of Socratic education. For Kierkegaard, the resolute person:

> *does not shrink back, and still less does he attempt to hold [anxiety] off with noise and confusion; but he bids it welcome, greets it festively, and like Socrates who raised the poisoned cup, he shuts himself up with it and says as a patient would say to the surgeon when the painful operation is about to begin: Now I am ready. Then anxiety enters his soul and searches out everything and anxiously torments everything finite and petty out of him, and then it leads him where he wants to go (1980, p159).*

Socrates, represented in an existential and hermeneutic way, was resolute because, rather than fleeing in the face of not knowing, he accepted that he did not know anything. This acceptance was not only an intellectual or cognitive one but permeated his entire being. He was a stranger to himself. He would not have said that the "unexamined life is not worth living" if this were not the case. He saw in himself the possibilities of being many "dark" and sinister beings. For example, as Frankl maintains, he saw in himself the possibility of being a criminal (1967, p20). Rather than denying this possibility in himself, he saw it as a basis upon which to inquire into himself; to ask himself the question, "who am I such that I can be a criminal?" On the Heideggerian and Franklian logic, it was precisely by accepting that he could be a criminal that he was ready to inquire into his being.

Heidegger uses the word "destroy" to characterize the activity of being resolute. The activity of "destroying" takes place in the context of being freed from tradition, for, as Heidegger puts it:

> *Tradition ... blocks our access to those primordial "sources" from which the categories and concepts handed down to us have been in part quite genuinely drawn. Indeed it makes us forget that they have had such an origin, and makes us suppose that the necessity of going back to these sources is something which we need not even understand (1985, p43).*

It is only as we "destroy" that which is already in question that we pave the way for new possibilities. For we cannot build new ways of doing things on embedded heritages or histories. We need to deconstruct the history to open the way for dealing with uncertainty. Being resolute in the face of anxiety is the basis for doing this.

Being resolute in the face of anxiety is the basis of existential education. It is as we are willing to accept that our way of being, our professional practice, is in question that we can begin to open up new possibilities and disclose new worlds.

References

Bauman, Z. (1990) Modernity and Ambivalence. In: Featherstone, M. (ed.) *Global Culture: Nationalism, globalisation and modernity.* London: Sage Publications.

Douglas-Mullen, J. (1981) *Kierkegaard's Philosophy: Self-deception and cowardice in the present age.* New York: A Mentor Book.

Dreyfus, H. (1993) *Being-in-the-World: A commentary on Heidegger's Being and Time, Division 1.* Boston: The MIT Press.

Finch, H.L. (1995) *Wittgenstein.* Dorset: Element.

Frankl, V. (1967) *Psychotherapy and Existentialism: Selected papers on logotherapy.* London: Penguin Books.

Gabriel, Y. (1998) Psychoanalytic contributions to the study of the emotional life of organizations. *Administration & Society.* Vol 30, No 3. pp292–315.

Gellner, E. (1964) *Thought and Change.* London: Weidenfeld and Nicolson.

Grafton, A., et al. (2010) *The Classical Tradition.* Boston: Harvard University Press.

Guignon, C. (1993) Authenticity, Moral Values and Psychotherapy. In: Guignon, C. (ed.) *The Cambridge Companion To Heidegger.* Cambridge: Cambridge University Press.

Heidegger, M. (1968) *What Is Called Thinking?* New York: Harper Torchbooks.

Heidegger, M. (1985) *Being and Time.* Oxford: Basil Blackwell.

Heidegger, M. (1993) *Martin Heidegger: Basic writings.* San Francisco: Harper Collins.

Hesse, H. (1974) *Steppenwolf.* London: Penguin Books.

Jaspers, K. (1965) *Nietzsche: An introduction to his philosophical activity* (trans. C.F. Wallraff and F.J. Schmitz). Tucson: University of Arizona Press.

Kierkegaard, S. (1958) *The Journals of Kierkegaard.* http://www.archive.org/details/journalsofkierke002379mbp.

Kierkegaard, S. (1980) *The Concept of Anxiety.* Princeton: Princeton University Press.

Kuhn, T. (1996) *The Structure of Scientific Revolutions.* Chicago: University of Chicago Press.

Lennie, I. (1999) *Beyond Management.* London: SAGE Publications.

May, R. (1996) *The Meaning of Anxiety.* New York: W.W. Norton and Company Inc.

Menon, T. and Thompson, L. (2010) Envy at Work. *Harvard Business Review.* Vol 88, No 4. pp74–9

Plato (1968) *Phaedrus* (translated by C.J. Rowe). England: Aris and Phillips.

Poincaré, H. (1946) *Science and Method: The foundations of science.* Lancaster: The Science Press.

Rilke, R.M. and Kappus, F.X. (1993) *Letters to a Young Poet* (in an edition by M.D. Herter Norton, translator). New York: W.W. Norton & Co.

Sandberg, J. and Tsoukas, H. (2011) Grasping the Logic of Practice: Theorizing through practical rationality. *Academy of Management Review.* Vol 36, No 2. pp338–60.

Screech, M. (1991) *Montaigne and Melancholy: The wisdom of the essays.* London: Penguin Books.

Spinosa, C., Flores, F. and Dreyfus, H. (1997) *Disclosing New Worlds: Entrepreneurship, democratic action, and the cultivation of solidarity.* Cambridge, MA: MIT Press.

Watson, T. (2006) *Organising and Managing Work* (2nd ed.). Harlow: Prentice Hall.

Weick, K. (2003) Theory and Practice in the Real World. In: Tsoukas, H. and Knusden, T. (eds) *The Oxford Handbook of Organisational Theory.* New York: Oxford University Press.

Zundel, M. and Kokkalis, P. (2010) Theorizing as Engaged Practice. *Organization Studies.* Vol 31, No 9–10. pp1209–27.

PART IV
An Existential Hermeneutic Approach
to Management Research

Chapter 10
Existential Crises as the Basis of Research Questions

Finding the Gap, Problematization or Existential Questioning as the Basis of Research Inquiry

Alvesson and Sandberg (2011) argue that management research is at a crossroads in which researchers need to develop a novel approach to generating research questions. They argue that research inquiry needs to move from what they call a "gap spotting" (2011, p247) to a "problematization" (2011, p247) notion for generating research questions. Their argument is based on the idea that the traditional approach to research is based on spotting gaps or extending the literature in the area or on extending empirical research (2011, p247). The virtue of a gap-spotting approach to research is, they claim, that it allows for rigor in the practice of research but it does not allow for novelty or the generation of interesting research. The difference, they argue, between gap-spotting and problematization as bases for generating research questions is that the former is focused on spotting gaps in existing literature and aims to fill the gaps that are spotted. This is the traditional expectation in higher degrees research.

The problematization approach, on the other hand, is concerned with questioning the assumptions of a tradition or way of doing research so as to arrive at novel or new ways of seeing phenomena (2011, p247). This is a very interesting but unacknowledged turn in management research. For the idea of examining and questioning taken-for-granted assumptions is the very definition of philosophy that Plato gives in *The Republic*, where he calls philosophy an act of destroying assumptions until the philosopher comes up with first principles (1968). Furthermore, one of the forms of problematization that they refer to is questioning the assumptions of a paradigm. As already alluded to in this work, Thomas Kuhn claims that the questioning of the assumptions of a paradigm is a philosophical activity. His claim is that in times of normal science, scientists have no time for philosophy, but when they are met with persistent anomalies, they are, if they embrace the anomalies, challenged to question their assumptions. This point is reinforced by the sociologist Ernst Gellner, who says that questioning of assumptions "happens to be the principle origin of philosophy" (1964, p51).

Although philosophy is defined as the activity of questioning assumptions and although there is over 2,500 years of history to practices of questioning assumptions, or what they call "problematization," Alvesson and Sandberg take none of this history into account in their paper. Indeed, they go about re-inventing the wheel and write about a particular process of questioning assumptions which they call a "dialectical process" (2011, p252).

Alvesson and Sandberg are to be applauded for questioning the traditional and taken-for-granted point of doing research, that is, spotting a gap in the literature and replacing this with a notion of problematization. Furthermore, they are to be recognized for unwittingly and possibly even unknowingly situating philosophy in the context of management research. However, they are to be questioned on their own review of the literature concerned with examining the phenomenon of questioning assumptions and even of a dialectical process for doing this. Plato also saw the art of dialectic in the form of dialogue between people who held different positions as the foundation of philosophy. In contrast to Alvesson and Sandberg, Platonic dialogues did not begin with metatheories but moved from everyday lived experience to metatheories (Blits 1989).

However, this is not the main aim of this chapter. The main aim of this chapter is to demonstrate, through a critique of the work of Alvesson and Sandberg, that an existential form of questioning assumptions, developed in this work and in the range of existential philosophers, is a fruitful basis for professional practice research. It allows the professional practitioner to question the assumptions of their own way of being as a professional practitioner from the experience of being a professional practitioner. Furthermore, through using Heideggerian forms of disruption, existential philosophical practice displays the conditions under which questioning from within a professional practice occurs. The latter is something that Alvesson and Sandberg do not do. They do not offer an account of the lived experience of questioning and of how people come to be researchers. This chapter will develop the conditions for questioning in the context of practitioner research.

This chapter is not concerned with scientific philosophy. It is concerned with developing the research philosophical practitioner, the professional that questions and abstracts from within their practice to see their own practice in new ways, and to disclose new ways of seeing their own practice.

The chapter is divided into three sections:

1.   an existential critique of Alvesson and Sandberg's position;

2.   existentialism as the basis for professional practice research;

3.   examples of lived experience of research questioning from within the context of existential disruptions to practice.

An Existential Critique of Alvesson and Sandberg's Position

Alvesson and Sandberg call the process for problematizing – and thus for generating a kind of questioning that allows for the exploration of taken-for-granted assumptions – a "dialectical process" in which we not only compare and contrast paradigms with each other, but we actually learn to see our own assumptions through the paradigm of the other and create the space for allowing the paradigm of the other to be seen through our assumptions. It is in the dialectical interplay between seeing our own perspective in terms of the perspective of the other and creating the space for the other to see themselves in terms of our perspective that questioning and novelty occurs in the research process. Describing this process, they say: "a key task in generating research questions through problematization is to enter a dialectical interrogation between one's own and other metatheoretical stances so as to identify, articulate, and challenge central assumptions underlying existing literature in a way that opens up new areas of inquiry" (2011, p256).

In order to engage in such dialectical problematization as the basis of research and metatheorizing, they claim that a domain of literature needs to be identified, the assumptions supporting this domain need to be identified and evaluated, and developing alternative assumptions and considering them in relation to their audience are all central parts of the dialectical process of problematization (2011, p256).

However, from the existential perspective being outlined in this work, there are three more fundamental questions that they fail to address: why should we want to do research in the first place? From a Heideggerian perspective we cannot take our way of being as researchers for granted. Indeed, research occurs only under certain existential conditions. In our everyday modes of practical coping, we are absorbed in the world. We get on with the activities of everyday doing. Research is just not significant.

Secondly, what is to prevent us from becoming defensive rather than open in the dialectical interplay of the perspective of the gaze of the other? Indeed, the very idea of the "paradigm wars" in cross-cultural management research is testimony to the fact that rather than being open in the face of difference, there is a tendency to become defensive, insular and defend our own assumptions and turf at the expense of the kind of curiosity required for inquiry based on problematization. Thus Alvesson and Sandberg would need to address the question: how do researchers allow themselves to be open in the face of the unfamiliarity or strangeness of the perspective of the other? How do they allow themselves to be questioned and question themselves in terms of the gaze of the other?

But perhaps I am wrong. For there is a very strong suggestion in Alvesson and Sandberg's work that they are actually not interested in the other. Rather, the way they frame their interest is in terms of the metatheory (2011, p25?) of the other. This is suggested in the quotation above, where they explicitly say they are concerned with juxtaposing metatheories.

Thus, is it just the theories of the other that they are talking about? It is not what writers such as Bauman, Derrida, Levinas, Homi Bhabha and other post-colonial writers have called the otherness of the other, the fact that the other cannot be reduced to a perspective or framework but is always more than the metatheoretical or paradigm perspective. Summarizing this perspective, Bauman makes a distinction between enemies and strangers. He maintains that an enemy is someone who accepts the same terms of reference as I do but who takes an oppositional stance to me. A stranger, on the other hand, is someone who does not share the same horizon of intelligibility. Whereas "enemies are flawed friends," strangers are "undecidables," which, quoting Derrida, Bauman maintains "can no longer be included within philosophical (binary) opposition, resisting and disorganizing it, without ever constituting a third term" (1990, pp143, 147).

Continuing his point he says: "One meets friends at the other side of one's responsibility. One meets enemies (if at all) at the point of a sword. There is no clear rule about meeting the strangers" (p152). Strangers are, as Bauman maintains, "a constant threat to world order" (p149) or to my way of ordering the world.

The significance of this for research is brought out by Rorty: "The attempt to edify (ourselves or others) may consist in … the attempt to reinterpret our familiar surroundings in the unfamiliar terms of" our encounter with other "culture[s] or historical period[s]" (1980, p360).

It is not the existential experience of otherness that Alvesson and Sandberg are concerned with. It is the epistemological problem of the relationship between metatheories that forms the center of their attention. From an existential perspective, it is when our way of being rather than our metatheory is estranged through the meeting with the other that a dialectical and dialogical play across different fields of assumptions can begin. This is because when we are estranged from our own assumptions we can begin to see them for the first time (Segal 1998).

Existential questioning arises when our taken-for-granted way of making sense of the world is fragmented. We question because our way of being is in question. Alvesson and Sandberg do not account for the conditions under which research questioning arises. They assume that we are already within the world of research. They simply assume that we want to engage with sets of literature such that we will create a dialectical interchange between them. They do not address the question as to why we should begin to read the literature in the first place: what makes anyone want to inquire?

It is not a question that Heidegger omits. Rather than assuming that we just turn up as researchers, Heidegger is very particular about the conditions under which inquiry comes about. I have already quoted Heidegger on this, but it is worth quoting again:

> *Only when the strangeness of beings oppresses us does it arouse and evoke wonder. Only on the ground of wonder—the revelation of the nothing—does the "why?" loom before us. Only because the "why" is possible as such can we in a definite way inquire into grounds, and ground them. Only because we can inquire and ground is the destiny of our existence placed in the hands of the researcher (1948, p52).*

This very fundamental existential question is the key, from a Heideggerian perspective, to the purpose and passion for doing research. We do research because our way of being is in question and even if we do not know the questions that we want addressed, there is a passion that drives us into research. There is, as Heidegger maintains, a wonder of why which is generated by being in question in our way of being in the world.

It is the existential hermeneutic framework created in this thesis that enables us to address this question; the question of the lived experience conditions under which we come to want to do research or find ourselves already involved in the activity of researching before we are consciously aware of it. Within this context research rises out of interruptions within everyday living.

From the existential perspective, research does not begin by investigating the literature or in the way we approach the literature. The latter occurs when we are already emerged in the practice of research. Transitioning from everyday practical coping to research needs to be accounted for and occurs, as has been said and as will be shown in more detail in this chapter, when our everyday practical coping is distracted. It is when we are in question that we begin to ask questions. And one of the ways of responding to the questions that we are asking is through research.

Furthermore, a distinction which has run through this work allows us to see two different kinds of research: research into the world of objects present-at-hand and research into the meaning or sense-making of the conventions behind our practice for doing things. The former is a scientific form of research within our traditional set of assumptions, while the latter is a research into the fundamental assumptions that have guided us in our everyday practices

Both can be novel forms of research. Novelty is not only dependent on questioning fundamental assumptions. It occurs where research arises out of everyday lived experience. That which prevents research from being novel is where, as we have already said, research is reduced to a ritual in which the method and the solution are known in advance.

Existentialism as the Basis of Professional Practice Research

It is the contention of this chapter that hermeneutic research as a research that begins through the existential experience of having the sense or meaning of our everyday ways of doing things disrupted is central to the research of professional practice. For professional practitioners often begin to inquire into their practices when their practices no longer make sense for them. This is the occasion upon which they can begin to question their assumptions. This is also the occasion for the possible emergence of novelty, or as Spinosa et al. (1997) call it, disclosing new worlds. For when we question our assumptions, we open up the possibility of seeing, doing and being in new ways (Spinosa et al. 1997).

Heidegger claims that what is "most closest" to us is also "most furthest" from us (1985). It is only through this existential encounter with otherness that the familiar is itself made explicit for questioning and examination. Our own paradigms become explicit when they are existentially challenged. In a sociological context this point is expressed by Bourdieu, who says "The sociologist who chooses to study his own world in its nearest and most familiar aspects should not as the ethnologist would domesticate the exotic but ... exoticize the domestic ... through a break with his initial relation of intimacy with modes of life and thought which remain opaque to him because they are too familiar" (Bourdieu 1988, pxi).

As already demonstrated, from a Heideggerian perspective we conduct research from within pre-thematic understanding or, to put it in the words of Kuhn, we live and conduct research from within paradigms. Being-in a paradigm is a way of being-in-the-world. To become attuned to our paradigm is to become attuned to our way of being in the world. This is not the form of attunement presupposed in subject–object logic in which a subject examines an object that is separated and distanced from it. Rather, it is a hermeneutic form of reflexivity in which we examine what we are already in from being within it. This logic needs to be developed and specified.

As already detailed, for Heidegger and Kuhn, when our paradigms begin to collapse, our world is threatened. For Kuhn we move into a state of paradigm crisis and for Heidegger we are thrown into a state of existential anxiety where we have no conventions in terms of which to make sense of the world.

Following on from this, for both Kuhn and for Heidegger, research into the taken-for-granted assumptions of a paradigm begin where we are thrown into a paradigm crisis. This is a crisis in which our way of being-in-a-paradigm or being-in-the-world is in crisis. It is when we can no longer make sense of the world that we have so taken for granted that research into fundamental assumptions begin.

In contrast to the tradition that has dominated Western thought between Descartes and positivism, Heidegger does not take the phenomenon of questioning for granted. Rather, he makes it a matter for inquiry in its own right. He questions what it means to question: to inquire, observe and conduct research. In this respect he maintains that questioning is not primarily or only a cognitive, intellectual or detached rational activity but is a fully embodied activity conducted in a mood of mattering. Questioning is a way of being concerned for and within our being in the world. In this way it occurs within a circular rather than a linear relationship to practice. It is this circular relationship between theory and practice that allows Heidegger to provide a framework for going beyond the separation between theory and practice that has so dominated management studies, practice and education.

While in *Being and Time* Heidegger writes in a language that is difficult to access, Nietzsche often makes the same points in everyday language in a way that strike one immediately. In his insight called "Moral for psychologists," he offers us insight into the existential basis not only for psychologists *but for researchers, inquirers, educators and thinkers.* He warns the psychologist: "Not to go in for backstairs psychology. Never to observe in order to observe! That gives a false perspective, leads to squinting and something forced and exaggerated. Experience as the wish to experience does not succeed" (Nietzsche 1974, p62).

His reason for pointing out the dangers of observing for the sake of observing are expressed in just as devastating a manner: "One must not eye oneself while having an experience; else the eye becomes 'an evil eye.' A born psychologist guards instinctively against seeing in order to see; the same is true of the born painter" (1974, p62).

Deliberate observation is a form of faked inquiry from a Nietzschian perspective. One must not, as he puts it, "lie in wait for reality." Rather authentic inquiry begins in those kinds of moments in which the inquirer—whether as scientist or artist or philosopher or manager in practice—finds their very way of being in question. Thus Nietzsche says that the researcher or inquirer "never works 'from nature'; he leaves it to his instinct, to his camera obscura, to sift through and express the 'case,' 'nature,' that which is 'experienced.' He is conscious only of what is general …" (1974, p62).

The moral for psychologists applies just as much to researchers. Researchers need to move from faked forms of observation to questioning that emerges out of interruptions in practice. For both Heidegger and for Nietzsche, it is in experiences of chaos, wonder, anxiety, nihilism, interruptions in our everyday functioning that define the conditions for questioning and becoming. Nietzsche makes this clear in a range of ways: he talks about the role of pain in making him more profound. He writes about chaos giving rise to a shining star and about the role of pain in making us stronger. Heidegger also talks about the role of moods in inquiry and in research in a range of ways, but before detailing Heidegger's ways of conceptualizing this relationship, I would like to give a detailed exemplar of this Heideggerian-Nietzschean practice.

Thus what needs to be explored is the way in which research develops in and through breakdowns in sense-making. Not all breakdowns in sense-making, managing or practical coping express themselves as a naked existential anxiety. There are less extreme interruptions in practical coping. Eugene Gendlin, a philosopher and psychologist heavily influenced by Heidegger, has developed the idea of "felt sense" to describe a continuum of breakdowns or interruptions in everyday sense-making or practical coping. The phrase "felt sense" was initially used in the context of psychotherapy and refers to the "noise" or feelings of dissonance, fragmentation—even anxiety—that a patient or client brings to therapy but which they themselves cannot initially name or embrace. It is a feeling that things are not quite right but that which is not quite right cannot be pinpointed. It is a process of turning what we are intuitively aware of but cannot yet articulate into something that is articulated. It is the experience of connection that is made when, for example, a word that has been on the tip of your tongue suddenly jumps into your mouth.

Just as anxiety functions as the basis of inquiry and questioning for Heidegger, so the notion of felt sense functions as the basis of inquiry through for Gendlin. It is important to highlight that it is a process of thinking through or focusing (as Gendlin calls it) rather than thinking about. Focusing is the discipline of tuning into these thoughts and feelings as they pop up and encouraging their expression and development. In contrast to the focusing of felt sense, "thinking about" is a process of seizing on the object, analyzing it, arguing about it and observing it. In therapy Gendlin found that people who came in thinking about their problem—their felt sense—did not actually come to grips with their felt sense. It is a process of listening to and bringing out the chain of thoughts/feelings that pop up in us. It is a practice of allowing thinking to occur rather than imposing thinking on the world.

The process of focusing on felt sense is an existential, hermeneutic and phenomenological process. It is phenomenological in that it is focused on lived experience and it is hermeneutic in that it is concerned with making sense of our way of being within a situation. It is existential in that it involves an interruption in our way of making sense in situations.

Examples of Lived Experience of Research Questioning from within the Context of Practice

In what follows I will look at a series of examples of breakdowns in felt sense in order to bring out the existential basis of questioning and to address the existential conditions under which inquiry as the basis of research begins. In a book entitled *What Do You Do for a Living?* Stephen Johnston (2007) describes how it was a sense of being existentially struck by the question of leadership that led him into the exploration of leadership:

Have you ever stopped to ask yourself the question "What do I do for a living??" It is such a simple, innocuous—even clichéd—kind of question, don't you think? But while it may seem wholly unremarkable at first, it's not a question to be underestimated; in fact, it's a slippery little sucker and one that in all my forty-three years I had never really stopped to contemplate—that is, until now. This question popped into my head, completely uninvited, one sunny morning while I was taking a shower—and it wouldn't pop back out again. I even remember the date—14 April 1999—because it marked my first day of employment as managing director of a business organization.

Note that he says that in all his forty-three years he had not asked this question. In Heideggerian terms, he was absorbed in his practice. Note also that he did not simply choose in a rational and deliberative way to ask the question. As he says, it "popped" into his head and would not leave him alone—or, to put it in Heideggerian terms, his being was being "called" (1985) to question his practice. He did not want this question, but he was overwhelmed by a sense of the strangeness and, in the language of *Being and Time*, "uncanniness" of his own work. He simply wanted to go back to work, but he was overwhelmed by what he called "a niggling doubt" in which his work lost all sense and meaning for him. He speaks about not understanding what he himself is doing: "Here I was, on the threshold of what might be the most exciting day of my career, and I intuitively knew that, just when I needed it most, I simply had no real insight into what I did for a living" (Johnston 2007).

He goes on to confirm that this is not a question of his competence or ability. Indeed, he feels quite comfortable in the fact that he has proved that he is a "can do" person. Rather, he has lost all sense of the purpose and meaning of his action:

I just felt in my gut that achieving financial results and co-ordinating tasks, no matter how complex, was not what my personal purpose was all about. Moreover, I was mighty annoyed that, after a twenty year career of doing all sorts of "important stuff", much of which I knew like the back of my hand, I couldn't come up with six lousy words of my own about what I did for a living!

This sense of estrangement from his practice did not lead him into a state of despair, but to a sense of wonder, which became the basis for reflexive research into leadership as a practice: "Were there other organizational leaders like me … but lacking that burning insight into exactly what purpose they served—

what they *really* did for a living?" And so he began research into and wrote a book called *What Do Leaders Really Do for a Living?*

Note that the existential conditions under which he became a researcher were a disruption in his everyday practice; not a disruption in equipment ready-to-hand but in a rupture in the felt sense of what it means to be a leader. He did not simply choose in a rational way to become a theorist or researcher.

Following on from Thomas Kuhn (1970), anomalies are forms of breakdown in sense-making which lead to questioning the way of doing things or conventions of the old paradigm as a way of opening up possibilities for a new paradigm and new possibilities for research.

The way in which Spinosa et al. (1997) write about the way in which Flores came to do a PhD thesis called "Conversations in the Office of the Twenty-First Century" and develop a business practice around this thesis exemplifies the power of existential questioning in generating research and practice. In their book *Disclosing New Worlds*, they refer to the case of what they call a "composite entrepreneur" (1997, p45). Within the context of work, this entrepreneur found himself in a state of contradiction. On the one hand his role description was focused on producing the "best model of the economy" (1997, p45). Indeed, his whole training and thus "mindset" or habitual way of making sense of the world predisposed him towards this.

However, in practice, he found himself "constantly talking; he explained this and that, to that and this person." He went into a kind of existential vacuum in which it "seemed to him that he was doing nothing substantial" (1997, p45).

However, Spinosa et al. point out that rather than leading to a state of resignation, their "composite entrepreneur" was prepared to dwell or stay in the state of contradiction in which he developed a playful attitude such that he could work in the space between his expected role description of producing models of the economy and yet continue talking at the same time. Rather than being resigned, he was fascinated by what he called "this oddity" in his life and lived it out as what he called an "anomaly," that is, as a state of being caught between differing interpretations of his work.

He allowed himself to continue working but at the same time remained sensitive to the anomaly. He was simultaneously involved in his work and watching his way of being involved in his work: "The entrepreneur remained sensitive to the fact that his work was not producing any concrete or abstract thing but that he was working nonetheless" (1997, p46).

It is important to note that he neither tried to produce insights nor did he will or force insights out of this experience of being in contradiction. He was much more playful in this space, allowing himself to be drawn through the contradiction. In Heideggerian terms, the paradoxical willingness to suspend the need to will a conclusion or an answer is called resolve. It is the openness to wonder that emerges out of existential emptiness and being in a state of anomaly. It is a space in which he "came to realize" (1997, p46).

There were a number of realizations that he had, all culminating in disclosing a new way of seeing his way of being at work. Firstly, he realized that he had grown up with certain preconceptions regarding work, that is, managing was about doing. He allowed this assumption or preconception in himself to be questioned through the act of dwelling in the anomaly, that is, the anomaly became the existential condition for questioning his practice while being in his practice. Through existentially questioning this assumption, he began to worry less and liberate himself from the way it shaped his expectations of himself at work.

More than this, his questioning began to open new possibilities or disclose new ways of seeing the way of being at work that was required of him. By both allowing and following the anomaly, he came to realize that "this anomalous aspect of work [holding conversations] was actually its central feature: Work never occurs in isolation but always in a context created by conversation" (Spinosa et al. 1997).

Without the anomaly and existential vacuum, he would have, as he himself says, "passed over the conversation" and focused on the production of things or even standards. But, through the existential questioning, detached and attached questioning, he came to see that even the production of standards occur in conversation. In fact, while work in organizations does involve doing, all these doings take place in the context of conversations. As Spinosa et al. put it, "In Western culture, which has always emphasized the production of things, this insight appears as a startling innovation" (1997, p46).

As a result of this reframing of work, he went on to conduct research and write a thesis, which in a sense integrated both the conversational and doing dimensions of work. He developed the theory and practice of what he came to call "conversations for action" in which he saw the latter as the central function of management, that is, being able to hold and look after a network of conversations. This became the basis for a consulting business called Business Design Associates.

Thus what we see is a particular form of reflexivity taking place; neither a simple detachment nor a simple involvement but a simultaneously involved and existential detachment—a sighting of what we are ourselves involved in. This simultaneous detachment and involvement has a long history in philosophy. We must be very careful in simply identifying detachment with what is in fact a specific kind of reading of Descartes.

Furthermore, what we also see is that this simultaneous detachment and involvement requires a refined sensitivity to the lived experience of anomaly, senselessness and contradiction within a workaday world in particular and in being within the world in general. From a Heideggerian perspective, the paradox of being willing to accept the limits of the will as the basis for questioning requires resolve. Resolve is the basis of allowing questioning to occur while living and working within a state of anomaly, contradiction or existential senselessness.

Thus an existential view of management education emphasizes education from within practice. It is a kind of education that emerges out of the contradictions that a manager finds themselves in. It is about creating the space for allowing them to follow the "signs that are not yet read" through embracing contradiction.

While existential questioning as forming the basis for research may not yet have been explored in the context of management, it has of course been explored in the context of hermeneutics and phenomenology. A very good example of this is a paper written by Clark Moustakas (1981) reflecting on his practice of allowing a research topic to emerge. He demonstrates how his practice of research arose in a non-deliberate way out of disruptions in everyday living. Rather than being drawn to research, he was attuned to looking after his daughter. However, an existential challenge in this process led him into research. The particular experience that he refers to revolved around an experience of loneliness that emerged when he was confronted by the need to make a decision regarding life and death surgery for his daughter. Although he had many friends around him, people that he could talk to, he was alone in making the final decision regarding the surgery.

The experience of being alone made him very sensitive to loneliness. It is not that he saw loneliness everywhere, but he did begin to see it in many places that he had not been attuned to before. He came, for example, to see "loneliness is often experienced by men who must make crucial decisions that will have major consequences in the lives of other men" (Moustakas 1981, p209). He began to see loneliness in the hospital: in the faces of the children separated from their parents. He began to see the relationship between the technical ways in which the medical fraternity "treated" children in the hospital without being in touch with the loneliness of the children and the effects of their loneliness on their well-being: "I began to see how children separated from their parents underwent a period of protest and resistance against separation, against the mechanical actions and fixed faces and gestures of the hospital combine" (1981). As he also claims, he began to see the children losing their sense of will in the face of this loneliness. And again, he began to see that the medical teams neither saw this loneliness nor the effect of it on the well-being of the children. As he says: "I witnessed a basic, pervasive feeling of dehumanization, which sought to repress lonely feelings and the whole range of human emotions that characterize the alive and growing child."

It was at this point that his research attunement opened up:

> When I saw that these dimensions of loneliness were almost totally ignored, misunderstood, and misinterpreted by hospital aides, nurses, and doctors, I decided, using the hospital situation and my own intuitive awareness as a beginning, to try to understand loneliness, how it fitted into the perceptions and behavior of hospitalized children, and the way in which it existed in myself and others (Moustakas 1981).

Here we see quite clearly that his research emerged out of a disruption in his everyday coping. He makes it quite clear that he did not intend to do research. He intended to make a decision about his child's surgery but found himself very much alone in this experience:

> My study of loneliness had no design or purpose, no object or end, and no hypotheses or assumptions. While I was faced with a question or problem (whether or not to agree to major heart surgery which might restore my daughter to health or result in her death) in the beginning, I was not inquiring into the nature or meaning of loneliness and its impact on the individual in modern society (Moustakas 1981).

Given the disruption in him, the relationship between loneliness, being in hospital and well-being began to emerge for him as a theme for research.

He began to explore the experience of loneliness in himself, in the experience of patients in hospitals, in literature in general and in hospital-specific experiences until he came up with both a pattern and methodology in terms of which to write up and describe the research he was doing. In other words, it is not the case that the literature and methodology preceded the research. They co-evolved. They evolved in the form of a hermeneutic circle, going forward and backward until the parts began to be identified, the parts formed into a whole and the whole allowed the parts to be situated in relationship to each other. Once this occurred he had a coherent whole, a pattern which formed the research project on which he was working.

Thus we see that existential research begins not with gap-spotting or problematization. In a sense the latter is already too late. It occurs once we are in research. The question is: what brings us into research in the first place? What this chapter has demonstrated is that from an existential hermeneutic perspective, it is conditions of disruption of our fundamental assumptions that we are drawn into reflexive attunement to our ways of doing things, our habits of practice and thus to questioning our fundamental assumptions.

This form of questioning is a questioning from within the conventions in terms of which we are involved in practical coping. We are thus questioning our being-in-a-practice from within our being-in-a-practice. Such a form of questioning is a hermeneutic form of inquiry. For hermeneutic inquiry is focused on questioning the assumptions of what we are already in.

Not only is this a source of novelty; it is also an effective basis for professional practice research. For the research of professional practice is a questioning of professional practice from within professional practice. If we want to understand the assumptions and even transform the assumptions that shape the way we do things, we need to be able to reflect on them from within the practice of doing them. We will see several examples of this in Part V of this book.

References

Alvesson, M. and Sandberg, J. (2011) Generating research questions through problematization. *Academy of Management Review*. Vol 36, No 2. pp247–71.

Bauman, Z. (1990) Modernity and Ambivalence. In: Featherstone, M. (ed.) *Global Culture: Nationalism, globalisation and modernity*. London: Sage Publications.

Blits, J.H. (1989) Self-Knowledge and the Modern Mode of Learning. *Educational Theory*. Vol 39, No 4. pp293–300.

Bourdieu, P. (1988) *Homo Academicus*. Cambridge: Polity Press.

Gellner, E. (1964) *Thought and Change.* London: Weidenfeld and Nicolson.

Heidegger, M. (1948) What Is Metaphysics? In: Brock, W. (ed.) *Existence and Being.* Indiana: Regnery/Gateway, Inc.

Heidegger, M. (1985) *Being and Time*. Oxford: Basil Blackwell.

Johnston, S. (2007) *What Do You Do for a Living? A bold new vision for leaders.* Melbourne: Hardie Grant Publishers.

Moustakas, C. (1981) Heuristic Research. In: Reason, P. and Rowan, J. (eds) *Human Inquiry*. New York: John Wiley & Sons.

Nietzsche, F. (1974) Twilight of the Idols. In: Karl, L. and Hamalian, L. (eds) *The Existential Mind: Documents and fiction*. Greenwich, CT: Facett.

Plato (1968) *The Republic* (translated by Lee, D.). London: Penguin Books.

Rorty, R. (1980) *Philosophy and the Mirror of Nature.* Oxford: Basil Blackwell.

Segal, S. (1998) Philosophy as a Therapeutic Activity. *Inquiry*. Vol 17, No 3. pp36–47.

Spinosa, C., Flores, F. and Dreyfus, H. (1997) *Disclosing New Worlds: Entrepreneurship, democratic action, and the cultivation of solidarity.* Cambridge, MA: MIT Press.

Brad's PhD as a Case Study in the Role of Mood in Existential Questioning

Creating the Space for Asking a Research Question

Heidegger is a notoriously difficult philosopher to read and one who, out of context, ironically, sounds rather abstract. I say ironically because Heidegger's is very much a philosophy of the relationship between the abstract and the concrete; one in which instead of seeing them as separate and distinct from each other, he sees them both as integrated parts of the human being's way of being within relationship to the world.

This is in at least two senses: both theory and practice are ways of relating to the world. But more than this, they are parts of the same phenomenon connected to each other in that they are both moods in which existence matters to us. They are ways in which we care for, are attuned to and are concerned about existence. They reciprocally inform and transform each other in the form of what Heidegger calls a hermeneutic circle.

That theory and practice are both moods, or ways of caring for existence, or ways in which existence matters allows us to use the work of Heidegger to reframe the relationship between theory and practice in management studies. There a number of writers in the field of organizational studies who have, based on the work of Heidegger and secondary readings of Heidegger—including Tsoukas and Knudsen (2003), Sandberg and Tsoukas (2011), Chia and Holt (2006) and Weick (2003)—noted that Heidegger provides a language for overcoming the separation between observer and observed, spectator and player reinforced in Descartes' distinction between subject and object.

However, to my knowledge, no writer within the field of organizational studies has noted that Heidegger allows us to see what is referred to as mood, concern, mattering or care as the basis upon which to overcome the split between theory and practice that has bedeviled not only organizational studies but a range of disciplines. Sandberg and Dall'Alba (2009) do discuss the notion of being-in-the-world, and they do mention the notion of mood but they do not bring out the fact that questioning occurs in a mood and that mood is the basis of the significance of questioning.

In a paper by Cornelissen and Holt we do see the beginnings of an acknowledgment of the role of mood in Heidegger. They (2013, p532) do make the claim that "Moods leave us open" for being-in-questioning and disclosure. However they do not work with the process through which the uncertainty experienced in anxiety is transformed into the openness of being-in-question and disclosure. Moods such as anxiety may, according to Heidegger, close us off from the practice of questioning when they triggers off a defensive mode of fleeing into a "tranquilized familiarity" (1985, p234) of everyday habits of practice.

How do we embrace the uncertainty inherent in anxiety as the basis for questioning and disclosure? Instead of dealing with the metamorphosis[1] from a defensive to an open response to anxiety in one person, Cornelissen and Holt (2013, p535) use the response of two different authors to the Mann Gulch fire to characterize a defensive and open response: Karl Weick as a defensive response and Norman Maclean's as an open response.

Like Kafka's metamorphosis of man into beetle, it would have been more helpful for them to focus on the metamorphosis in one person. This is how Ernst Gellner redescribes Kafka's metamorphosis in existential terms: beetle-into-man or man-into-beetle (1964). And the lived experience with which he is essentially concerned is the no man's land between being a man in transition to a beetle or vice versa. For in this space, the being has neither the language of man nor the language of beetle through which to make sense of existence. It is responding to the anxiety of having been deprived of the old identity and not yet having the new identity that is crucial.

For the crucial challenge is the resolve to transform defensiveness into an openness in the face of anxiety or the vulnerability of the between. It is in the mood of this transformation that resolute questioning arises.

---

1   This metamorphosis is dealt with in my 2010 article published in *Management Learning* in which anxiety presupposes a fragmentation of the being of the self for Dasein to be open to and disclose new possibilities.

As will be demonstrated in this chapter the mood of resolute questioning arises from listening to the way in which the being of the self is fragmented in experiences of senselessness. Questioning, from a Heideggerian perspective, is very challenging. It arises out of and creates uncertainty because the sense of self and world, the sense of relationship between subject and object is fractured.

Questioning, from a Heideggerian perspective, is very challenging. It arises out of and creates that uncertainty in which the self has lost sense of itself. Both theorizing and practices are moods for Heidegger. In contrast to the tradition that has dominated Western thought between Descartes and positivism, Heidegger does not take the being of questioning for granted. Rather, he makes it a matter for inquiry in its own right. He questions what it means to question. In this respect he maintains that questioning is not primarily or only a cognitive, intellectual or detached rational activity but is a fully embodied activity conducted in a mood of mattering. Questioning is a way of being concerned for and within our being-in-the-world. In this way it occurs within a circular rather than a linear relationship to practice. It is this circular relationship between theory and practice that allows Heidegger to provide a framework for going beyond the separation between theory and practice that has so dominated management studies, practice and education.

Furthermore, for Heidegger, explicit questioning is an activity that takes place under certain mood conditions. It is in the context of the surprise or uncertainty experienced in interruptions or disruptions of our absorbed ways of coping with our everyday activities that explicit questioning occurs and becomes a significant or meaningful activity. Research, theorizing and inquiry are, for Heidegger, not always an explicit, significant or meaningful activity in their own right. It is not even the primary activity in which the human being is involved. For the most part the human being is a practical being that is concerned with building a home in the world.

It is in this sense that Heidegger contrasts himself with the history of philosophy. For the history of philosophy does not account for the conditions under which questioning becomes explicit. This is especially but not only the case since the philosophy of Descartes, who seemed to assume (ironically or paradoxically) that the human being is primarily a creature of doubt (Taylor 1993) and that while everything else needs to be accounted for, the activity of doubting does not need to be accounted for. As Taylor claims, Descartes ontologized rationality, reading it "into the very constitution of the mind and made part of its structure" (1993, p318).

Even Plato provides in his allegory of the cave an understanding of the conditions under which some forms of questioning become explicit, that is, the moment of disruption and perplexity experienced by the prisoners when they turn around and see the light of the fire for the first time. However, he takes for granted that the natural position of the prisoners in the cave is one of observation of the shadows on the wall and does not account for the practices through which a person would become an observer.

Heidegger sees himself as unique in the history of thought for calling into question the conditions under which the human being does come to be an observer, ask and respond in an explicit way to questions. For Heidegger a question does not present itself as already formulated. We need to learn to embrace the uncertainty of anxiety and learn to listen to the question that is emerging through the anxiety.

An understanding of these conditions will also enable us to understand the conditions under which questioning and thus theorizing, philosophizing, research and inquiry become existentially meaningful and significant acts. Or, in the language of management today, the conditions of bringing relevance and rigor of thought together. For this relationship has been so problematic in the history of not only management thought but the relationship between theory and practice in general.

Thus the question that this chapter will seek to address is: what are the existential conditions under which a professional becomes a researcher?

Rather than beginning by describing research inquiry or questioning, searching and researching conceptually, I would like, in the spirit of the philosophy of Heidegger, to begin by describing it phenomenologically, that is, by describing it in the context of lived experience. After having described the lived experience of questioning and the circular relationship between theory and practice in this experience, I will draw out the Heideggerian implications in a conceptual framework.

Thus in this chapter we will question in an existential hermeneutic and phenomenological manner the lived experienced of research questioning in order to disclose questioning and disclosure as parts of the same way of being in relationship to the world.

The Lived Experience of Doing a Thesis: The Experience of Brad

Let me begin with what Thomas Kuhn (1970) calls an exemplar, a person whose practice embodies this mode of inquiry. I will start with a completing PhD student of mine named Brad. Before beginning his PhD Brad had been—and still is—a highly successful and sought-after project manager, recognized in the industry for his project management performance.

However, approximately seven years ago Brad became quite frustrated with project management. His initial frustration was not so much with project management but with himself as a project manager. Although he was recognized as highly successful, he realized that he failed on numerous occasions to complete within the given conceptual framework of project management, that is, complete the project on time, budget and on cost. Initially he believed that he was not trained well enough in project management and so he took further courses in project management. But this did not have the impact of significantly improving completion on time, on budget and to specification. In the name of continuous improvement Brad undertook to enhance his understanding of project management by immersing himself in the literature of project management. However, even a refinement of his theoretical knowledge of the literature on project management did not enhance his excellence in practice.

At this point Brad had nowhere within the framework of project management to turn. And so he turned to doing an MBA at the Macquarie Graduate School of Management. One of the units offered in this program was called "The Foundations of Management Thought," which turned out to be an abridged version of a journey through the history of Western philosophy. In this unit Brad came to recognize that philosophy was and is an activity of questioning the assumptions that ground a discipline, practice or program such as project management.

As a teacher of this unit, Brad turned to me to read for the degree of PhD in the area of project management. I must confess that I knew very little about project management; Brad knew that I knew little about it but wanted to work with the philosophical practice of questioning the assumptions in which project management had historically been grounded. And so we agreed to work together.

Initially neither Brad nor I knew what the structure of the thesis would look like. We did not know the precise nature of the question/s that he would be asking. We did not have a sense of the literature that he would work with in examining the assumptions of project management. And we did not have a sense of the methodology that he would be working with.

All he had was his frustration with existing practices of project management. And all I had was the practice of what I will call existential philosophical questioning—a kind of questioning of assumptions in the context of moods such as frustration, uncertainty, anxiety and disruption in general.

And so Brad and I agreed that we would set up a conversation between us in which we would examine what Eugene Gendlin (see Todres 2007) calls the "felt sense" behind his disruption. Gendlin describes the experience of felt sense in a number of ways. One of them is the idea that a person has an experience of something being or feeling not quite right but actually cannot yet put into language that sense. It is like the word is on the tip of one's tongue but, try as one might, the language just does not come to one. It is a feeling that things are not quite right but that which is not quite right cannot be pinpointed.

Existential philosophical questioning is a practice for working with giving language to a felt sense, so that it begins to open up a world or field of inquiry in which a person can immerse themselves. Heidegger claims that language is the house of being. Part of what he means by this is that language discloses a world. Our world comes into being through language. What we were therefore searching for was a language in which Brad's frustration would be the basis for disclosing a world.

We agreed to explore Brad's felt sense of frustration around project management. Central to the practice of working with felt sense is to look at what resonates (see Todres 2007) with the felt sense. So we began to explore the resonance between Brad's felt sense of frustration with project management. We did not want to start off with a conceptual understanding of project manager, but with what it felt like to be a project manager and what was frustrating within this lived experience of being a project manager. In the course of the conversation we covered many themes: the range of projects that Brad had worked on, the paradox of failure as success in his practice as project manager, meanderings around other project managers' experience of the relationship between the espoused ideal of project management and the practices of project management. Without intending to, we looked at Brad's experience of his parents' careers, conversations that he had had with friends and other members of his family.

And so our conversation went forward and backward, turning and returning to the same feelings and themes. A theme that we kept returning to, something that resonated very deeply for Brad, was a felt sense of being unable to say in a common-sense way what project management was/is. This inability to describe the phenomenon or practice of project management in a common-sense way popped up in different terms: in one context, he compared himself with his parents, who, as teachers, had long and stable careers through their identities and their place in the community was defined. However, Brad was a project hopper who did not stay in any project for longer than six to eight months at a time. And so he had no stable community through which to form his identity. If he was anything, it was more like a nomad, moving between places. Actually, he had recently read Zygmunt Bauman on liquid modernity and saw himself both as constructed by and constructing the liquidity of modernity—the fact that there were no stable conventions or ways of doing things in modernity.

Initially Brad responded to this with an experience of despair. There was no-thing, no convention upon which he could ground or hold himself. However, rather than concluding with this experience of despair, we explored his felt sense around the despair. In these conversations he came to embrace the despair. And ironically and paradoxically, the acceptance of the despair allowed him to catch sight of another way of seeing his way of being as a project manager. Instead of seeing the "gypsy" image in a negative light, he came to see it in a positive light. It began to disclose a new way of seeing project management.

He began to see project management as a practice or phenomenon that was nomad-like in that it involved the activity of moving between and coordinating people of different functions, departments, silos or language games within an organization. As a project manager he needed to be able to listen to and talk to people of different functional and disciplinary languages in a language that each of them understood. Furthermore, he had to bring them together in a shared language.

The felt sense now began to formulate itself in language for Brad. He began to see project management, or a part of project management, as an activity of coordinating projects through the activities of translating and re-describing projects for the range of stakeholders involved in the project. These stakeholders, because of their functional or disciplinary backgrounds, had different sets of assumptions, different ways of speaking to each other, different perceptual blindnesses and ways of framing situations. The essential challenge of project management, as he began to see it, was to be the translator or re-describer that brought all of these qualitatively different stakeholders together.

Through these conversations Brad developed a sense of excitement and energy; a world had opened up for him. Interestingly enough, this experience belonged to the same category as Helen Keller's (1903) discovery of the way in which language discloses a world. Describing her experience, she says:

> *Have you ever been at sea in a dense fog, when it seemed as if a tangible white darkness shut you in, and the great ship, tense and anxious, groped her way toward the shore with plummet and sounding-line, and you waited with beating heart for something to happen? I was like that ship before my education began, only I was without compass or sounding-line, and had no way of knowing how near the harbour was. "Light! give me light!" was the wordless cry of my soul, and the light of love shone on me in that very hour.*
>
> *We walked down the path to the well-house, attracted by the fragrance of the honeysuckle with which it was covered. Someone was drawing water and my teacher placed my hand under the spout. As the cool stream gushed over one hand she spelled into the other the word water, first slowly, then rapidly. I was at first annoyed. I did not know what she was doing. As she persisted I stood still, my whole attention fixed upon the motions of her fingers. Suddenly I felt a misty consciousness as of something forgotten— a thrill of returning thought; and somehow the mystery of language was revealed to me. I knew then that "w-a-t-e-r" meant the wonderful cool something that was flowing over my hand. That living word awakened my soul, gave it light, hope, joy, set it free! There were barriers still, it is true, but barriers that could in time be swept away.*
>
> *I left the well-house eager to learn. Everything had a name, and each name gave birth to a new thought. As we returned to the house every object which I touched seemed to quiver with life. That was because I saw everything with the strange, new sight that had come to me.*

Although not nearly as fundamental as Helen's, Brad's experience of being able to name his phenomenon disclosed a world to him. However, at this point Brad's revelation could not be counted as a thesis. It was nothing more than a personal or private disclosure. The question became: how could we assess whether this was nothing more than a personal experience arising out of Brad's own already existing taken-for-granted understanding of the world? How could we assess whether it had public relevance such that it could be generalized beyond Brad to the community of practitioners known as project managers?

It was in response to this series of questions that we could begin building the thesis. But we still did not have a pre-ordered process for proceeding.

We did not immediately know what literature we would turn to, whether we would do empirical study, what methodology we would use and so on. In other words, we were going without knowing exactly where we were going — we were exploring.

In the process of exploration Brad started off by playing seriously with the writings of three philosophers: Richard Rorty, Alistair McIntyre and Charles Taylor. He studied their original works and wrote papers on each of the authors but through a process of evaluating we eliminated two of the authors: Taylor and McIntyre. We came to agree that Richard Rorty would be the central author of his work, that Richard Rorty would be the basis of the logical coherence of his work. In retrospect it was easy to see why: Rorty had articulated the notion of philosophy as a process of re-description and Brad was re-describing project management as a practice of re-description. Furthermore, Richard Rorty provided Brad with the language to critique project management from within, demonstrating how the theory and practice of project management are in contradiction with one another. It is this contradiction which forms the basis for the re-description in Rorty's terms and in Brad's thesis.

Now Brad had a logic for critiquing project management and a basis for re-describing it as the practice of re-description. Once again, this logic did not occur in advance but it was only by working through Rorty, the literature in and on project management and the relationship to Rorty that this logic became clear.

While finding it was an agonizing process, having found it was an ecstatic process. It was Kant who claimed that the experience of the sublime is an experience of simultaneous joy and pain. In this sense a thesis that is not outlined in advance in a formula is an ecstatic and sublime experience.

However, the agony and ecstasy of Brad's thesis was not about to stop. Brad's aim has never been only to make a theoretical contribution to the literature on project management but to inscribe the re-description of project management into the practice of project management. In this sense Brad still wanted to do two things: check his newfound understanding of project managers in the context of experienced project managers and to test his understanding in his own practice as a project manager. In terms of the former he undertook a series of interviews with experienced project managers to test his own understanding and he observed himself in the process of transforming his own practice as a project manager. However, his observations were not simply passive, for it was not only his new way of seeing his practice that transformed his practice but his practice involved a process of transforming his way of seeing his practice. There was thus a circular experience occurring in which practice and theory were transforming each other from within.

Together all of these pieces became part of his thesis: the existential dimensions of raising the question of project management, the imminent critique of project management in Rortian terms, a description of Rorty's notion of re-description, an inscribing of Rorty's notion of re-description in the context of re-describing project management as a practice of re-description, challenging of his own pre-conceptions of project management through interviewing others and a practice of reflexively being attuned to the transformation in his practice through seeing project management in a new light as well as transforming this new light in the context of his practice of project management.

At the risk of repeating myself, this structure was not pre-defined. It emerged only through the experience of doing the thesis. I am repeating it a number of times for two reasons: it contradicts much of the espoused wisdom about project-managing a thesis, that is, that first you begin with the question, then you go on to the literature review, outline the methodology, analyze the data, discuss and conclude. It is only once Brad developed a handle on doing a thesis, that he could develop a sense of the structure and timing involved. But even then, the structure and timing were subject to continuous reiteration.

The second point is directly related to the first point: instead of seeing a thesis as a linear sequential process, it is in fact circular in a hermeneutic sense: it involves a continuous forward and backward movement until the parts and whole begin to fit together. While a thesis may have the appearance of being written in a linear way, both the actual sense-making of a thesis and the writing of a thesis occur in the form of a hermeneutic circle—in a constant turning and returning until the parts form a whole and the whole allows the parts to be situated in relationship to each other.

Brad has now completed his thesis.

Heidegger's Hermeneutics

There are several dimensions of Heidegger's existential hermeneutic phenomenology that are exemplified in Brad's experience of being involved in a PhD.

Firstly, I would like to highlight the notion that undertaking a PhD or higher degrees research is a form of lived experience. This may sound superfluous—until we realize that so much of the preparation for a PhD and the practices of being involved in a PhD do not teach or even theorize it as a form of lived experience. Rather, in learning to do research, most effort goes into the technical dimensions of research: quantitative and qualitative methods, review of literature, posing of a question outside of the felt sense of the question, data analysis and conclusion.

The lived experience of research, the form of attunement involved in research, the way of being attentive, noticing, thinking, embracing the unknown, going backward and forward, joining the parts and the whole, sense of inquiry or wonder, are in general not seen as dimensions worthy of inquiry or teaching in the context of research. Research has been reduced to the formulaic of a method where, as Heidegger puts it, it has become "material for reworking" (1985, p43). In broad and general terms, this is the essence of Gadamer's book *Truth and Method* (1975): that research understood hermeneutically is much more than a formulaic method. It is a way of being attuned and a way of inhabiting the world.

Furthermore, both research as an attunement and as a way of inhabiting the world are not accidental or coincidental to research; they are at the heart of research as a practice or as a lived experience. We see this quite clearly in the case of Brad described above. For him research is a way in which his practice matters to him. It is a way in which his world matters to him. It is not out of idle curiosity that he conducts research but because his way of being as a project manager is at stake and in question that characterizes his involvement in research.

Furthermore, the way in which his practice or way of being as a project manager is in question interrupts his everyday practice of project management—interrupts it in the sense of not preventing him from getting on with performing but with taking the meaning out of his performance. He is simultaneously involved in managing projects and is withdrawn from the activity of managing his project. As Heidegger frames this, the thinker is distracted from everyday being by the question of the "truth" (or in Heidegger's terms, "world disclosure"). This does not mean that he or she cannot continue in their everyday activities. They are both players and spectators of their own playing at the same time.

An example of this is to be found in John Stuart Mill's description of the way in which his practice as a philosopher was brought into question by an existential crisis, a crisis in meaning, but he was able to continue performing.

So too for Brad it was an existential questioning, one in which he had lost or did not have the felt sense of the meaning of what it means to be a project manager, that brought him to question the phenomenon called project management. And, ironically or paradoxically, it was in the experience of having lost a felt sense for the meaning of his activity that the meaning of this activity became an explicit theme to be questioned.

The logic of this form of existential questioning is central to the philosophies of both Heidegger and Nietzsche. For Nietzsche, for example, it is only in nihilism, the felt sense of a breakdown in values, that the question of value becomes a question to be asked. Outside of the experience of nihilism, we may speak about valuing this or that value but we do not question the meaning of value itself—not what are your values, but what does it mean to "value" in the first place? How do we get the phenomenon of "valuing"? Similarly for Heidegger, it is only in the breakdown of the conventions through which "average everyday life" is held together that we come to question the conventions of average everyday life.

Putting this in the form of a paradox: when everyday living is felt as meaningful, when we are preoccupied with it, we do not even stop to ask the question of meaning. In fact, it is a meaningless question. We just want to get on with the job and do not understand why anyone would want to raise the question of the meaning of existence. However, when the felt sense of meaning evaporates, the question of meaning becomes a question that focuses our existence. It becomes a question of ultimate concern.

There are a number of other examples of this. Clark Moustakas, for example, calls his research "heuristic research" and describes it as a form of research which begins with a disruption in practice as a basis upon which to conduct research into practice. The example that he chooses to demonstrate the way in which research arises out of practice is the experience of loneliness. It was through the experience of his own loneliness in making a decision as to whether to give his child life-saving but death-risking surgery that he accidently came across the phenomenon of loneliness in hospitals. Through his own experience the phenomenon of loneliness opened up to him and he wrote a research piece based on loneliness.

This brings us to the lived experience of questioning for Heidegger. It should be clear that, for Heidegger, questioning is not only a cognitive or intellectual activity conducted with part of our being but involves and is itself a way of being within the world. This was certainly the case with Brad. Questioning or inquiring into project management as a practice was and is a lived experience. It is an activity within which he is involved. It is a way of being attuned.

To paraphrase Heidegger and to situate him in the context of management, it can be maintained that management researchers, educators and practitioners have, in general, forgotten and need to recollect and re-connect with the art of inquiry. Inquiry, from a Heideggerian perspective, begins not with intellectual questions or even questioning. It begins with the experience of our being being-in-question. It is when our beings are in question that the possibility of questioning discloses itself. Questioning becomes possible not as primarily an intellectual or cognitive activity but as an existential attunement that is fully embodied. It involves our whole being, including body, mood and language. Questioning existentially is a way of being in relationship to the world. It is the way of being in relationship to the world that is characteristic of questioning that needs to be disclosed. And as part of the way of relating to the world that is called questioning, is the way of world disclosure—the way of opening up new worlds.

Existential questioning, questioning when our way of being is in question, does not need to always be as ultimate as it was for Tolstoy, Mill or Brad. It is a kind of questioning that occurs at many points of transitions in our practices and lives. Linda Hill, in her book *Becoming a Manager* (2003), has brought this kind of questioning out well in her description of the transition made by a group of technical experts into becoming managers. She writes of the surprise or shock of the unexpected which called into question their own assumptions about management.

Furthermore, what is in question is Brad's own existential practices for being in the world. It is not just an abstract and cognitive questioning but one which emerges out of the way in which his practice is disrupted. This disruption expresses itself initially in a felt sense that things are not quite right, but Brad cannot quite put his finger on or bring to language that which is not quite right. He needed to go through a process of turning the felt sense into language and into an explicit form of questions. Thus the questions emerged out of the way in which his own practice was in question for him.

This is the first sense of the "hermeneutic circle": it is an activity of working through the felt sense of disruption in an act of turning back on and making explicit of his own practice as a theme of inquiry from within the experience of his practice. As already stated, he conducted the inquiry into project management from within the experience of being a project manager. He was simultaneously involved in and withdrawn from his practice in such a way that he could question it while continuing to perform. This is expressed in the notion of estrangement: estrangement from what one is involved in allows the practitioner to catch sight of what they are involved in. To think in a hermeneutic phenomenological way from within one's practice means to reflect from a position, as Eger says, of "'being in' that which one is interpreting" and requires a "state of [existential] detachment and attachment: detachment from the everyday self (*mood*) required for an attachment to the subject matter or to the instrument that brings one closer to the subject matter" (Eger 1993, p17).

Eger's point is exemplified in Brad, who was existentially estranged from but part of his practice at the same time. Douglas-Mullen sees this as an ontological dimension of being human: "One feature peculiar to humans is the ability to detach ourselves from our lives and see ourselves as if we were 'just one of them.' For some of us the thought of this comes more often and stays longer. This type of person is described as 'reflective,' 'self-conscious,' 'neurotic,' 'ironic,' 'pensive,' 'deep' etc." (Douglas-Mullen 1981, p11).

But it would be a mistake to say that Brad was only questioning his practice as a project manager. Rather, his very way of existence manifested itself for questioning. This was especially the case when he viewed himself in the context of the stability of his parents' identity through being part of a contiguous sense of community, whereas he was more like a gypsy moving from project to project without a stable ground. Moreover, like Tolstoy, Brad was perplexed through his own existentially reflexive questioning. As he often said, he had everything that he wanted, was married to his best friend and was doing very well in his career; yet what he was doing made no sense to him.

It is this kind of questioning that occurs in the face of there not being any reason, cause or trigger for questioning which is existential in the most ultimate sense of the word. It is a form of questioning that occurs when, as Paul Tillich, the existential theologian, put it, our ultimate concerns no longer provide us with purpose and thus guidance in our lives.

Interestingly enough the range of theorists in organizational studies who draw on the work of Heidegger do not bring up the existential dimensions of questioning. They may bring up the notion of questioning a practice but do not make explicit that a practice is itself situated in the context of existence and so the existential dimensions of a practice need to be made a theme of inquiry. This limitation can be found in the works of Weick, Tsoukas, Knudsen and Sandberg.

However, it is ultimately with the existential dimensions of a practice that Heideggerian questioning is concerned. For Heidegger is concerned with the structures of existence and not primarily with practice. Or putting it in another way, his primary concern would be with the being of practice and not only or simply with practice. And even this dimension is a hermeneutic circle: it is existence that calls us to question existence. It is in the very essence of the being of the human being to be in and question its existence.

This is once again where some writers in organizational studies misread Heidegger as primarily a philosopher of practice when he is a philosopher of existence.

Thus we have one dimension in which the thinking of Heidegger is purposefully and explicitly circular: through the being of the human being, the being of the human being is placed in question. Another way in which he says this is that because it is part of the essence of the human being to question its existence, it is when its existence is in question that the question of the essence of its existence is made explicit for questioning.

As has been seen in the case of Brad, what this means is that it is when our practice or way of existing is placed in question that we come to question our practice. For Heidegger, for the most part, we do not come face to face with the question of our practice. We are far too busy coping with the everyday tasks of existing to question existing itself. And Heidegger says that this is rightfully so. However, when in states of meaninglessness or emptiness or nihilism, our everyday way of existing breaks down; we come face to face with our everyday way of existing. We are drawn into the attunement of questioning. We become questioners. It is important to note that it is not just that we are asking questions in a detached or intellectual way, but our being is thrown into question in such a way that we are questioning with our whole being.

The image of the sculpture of *The Thinker* exemplifies this notion of questioning, for what we see in him is that his whole being—his body, mood and thinking—is withdrawn into an attunement of questioning.

Perhaps I am projecting, here but what is great about *The Thinker* is that his thinking is not about anything in particular. He certainly is not thinking about or observing and analyzing an object at a distance from himself. We cannot even say that he is thinking about himself. Indeed, if I may project a Heideggerian interpretation onto him, he is allowing thinking to come to and pass through him. Rather than seizing on an object of thought, trying to force it into a box or pattern, he is allowing thinking to occur. This kind of practice of thinking is exemplified not only by existential philosophers but even in scientists. For example, Newton in writing about his practice of reflection has said that rather than seizing on a concept, he allowed the concept to dawn on him.

This process of allowing thinking to dawn on us is central to a hermeneutic practice of reflexivity. It can be seen in the way in which Brad, as Heidegger would put it, "dwelled" in his thesis. As has been said, we did not always know in advance where we were going with the thesis. In many ways both he and I allowed the thesis to take us on a journey. Insights and methods, the logic of the thesis, the empirical and the conceptual parts dawned on us. They dawned on us in what Heidegger calls *"eine augenblick,"* a blink of the eye, in moments of resonance through which Brad then drew the parts and the whole together.

The practice of drawing the parts and whole together is central to hermeneutics. For Heidegger, hermeneutics is not only a practice of turning back on our way of being in practice but it is a constant practice of returning to the relationship between the parts and whole of the practice. Hermeneutically a practice is formed like a jigsaw puzzle: as the parts are brought together, so the whole begins to emerge and as the whole begins to emerge, so it becomes easier to see how the parts stand in relationship to each other.

Brad's thesis was written in this way. It was by throwing himself into the question of his practice that he began to explore his felt sense of his practice, and as he began to explore the felt sense of his practice, so the parts began to emerge. As the parts began to emerge, so the whole began to take shape, and as the whole began to take shape, so the relationship between the parts began to fit together. This writing of a thesis was not a linear and sequential activity of beginning with the end in mind, as Stephen Covey likes to recommend. If anything, the beginning only emerged at the end. As Foucault has said of writing, if he knew what he was going to write, it would not be worth writing. It is only at the end that he realizes both the beginning and the end. How often is it that an introduction is written as the last or one of the last parts of the thesis. This is because the parts inform the whole and the whole informs the parts; the end informs the beginning, which in turn informs the end.

However, there is a third sense in which Brad's thesis was hermeneutic: through the way in which he embraced the way in which his being in practice was in question, Brad began to question the pre-conceptions, or what Heidegger calls the pre-thematic awareness, that had shaped his frustration without him initially even knowing that he had a pre-thematic understanding of project management.

From a Heideggerian perspective, we can only become frustrated about a phenomenon in terms of a set of background conventions or tacit beliefs and assumptions that we have of a phenomenon. In the case of Brad, Brad's frustration was not born out of thin air but emerged out of a set of background conventions through which he experienced the incongruity between the espoused vision and practice of project management on the one hand and his own implicit or background conventions which shape his understanding. Heidegger calls this background understanding an "average everyday" understanding. It is average and everyday because it guides our everyday practice, but we only have a very dim attunement to it. For the most part, we have not thought about it, examined or critiqued it. We have a very "average" understanding of it. For example I might believe that going out on Saturday night is a source of joy or relief, but I have not examined this convention for doing things.

So too Brad's frustration is in terms of a set of "average everyday" background conventions for doing things. It is only when he feels frustrated that he can begin to unpack these conventions of which he has an average everyday understanding. An essential part of his inquiry and thus his thesis is the process of unpacking these background sets of pre-thematic conventions which have shaped his practice without him having been explicitly aware of these as shaping his practice.

The practice of developing an explicit attunement to the background pre-thematic conventions that have shaped his practice constitutes a dimension of the hermeneutic circle. It is a process of turning back from within his practice on the historical conventions that have shaped his practice. It is an existential form of reflexive attunement in which Brad is coming face to face with the conditions that have shaped his practice. Putting this in explicitly Heideggerian language: "*Dasein* ... is ontically distinguished by the fact that, in its very Being, that Being is an *issue* for it. ... [Thus] there is some way in which *Dasein* understands itself in its Being." On another occasion in *Being and Time*, Heidegger says: "Understanding is the existential Being of *Dasein*'s own potentiality-for-Being; and it is so in such a way that this Being discloses in itself what its being is capable of" (Heidegger 1985, p144).

Stolorow (2011) has made sense of these Heideggerian quotations in the following way: "an unthematized, pre-ontological understanding of our Being is constitutive of our kind of Being, we humans can investigate our own kind of Being by investigating our understanding (and lack of understanding) of that Being." Continuing, Stolorow has said: "Heidegger's analytic of Dasein is a hermeneutic phenomenology aimed at disclosing or unconcealing the basic structures of our kind of Being, its *existentiality*, which lie hidden within our understanding of it" (Stolorow 2011).

In the history of philosophy the practice of turning back on your practice from within your practice has been called a practice of remembering or recollecting or even, as Burbules (1995) points out, a process of reconnecting and recognizing. Heidegger calls this practice a *"wiederholing,"* a repetition of the historical conventions in terms of which our way of being is shaped.

What is also crucial in the history of philosophy is that the conditions which create the possibility of such recollecting or reconnecting is an experience of disruption. Socrates referred to it as a state of perplexity. Burbules (1995), reading Socrates through the lens of Derrida, sees it as an experience "aporia," which means an experience in which one has existentially lost one's way. The Frankfurt school wrote about the role of estrangement in establishing a class consciousness. Wittgenstein writes of experiences of being struck and Heidegger, along with a range of other existential thinkers, describes a whole range of disruptions which form the basis for recollection. For example, the experience of existential anxiety is central to such recollection from an existential perspective; so too are experiences of boredom, alienation and Heidegger even includes homesickness as a disruption which opens up the possibility of hermeneutic questioning.

All of the above trigger the hermeneutic circle of understanding—that kind of understanding in which it is, as mentioned earlier, only in the breakdown of meaning that meaning is explored or, in Nietzschean terms, it is only in the nihilism of values that we can begin to explore the historical origin of value in the first place. For where we can take the question of value for granted, we are not thrown into making the issue of value an explicit theme of questioning. We go on living. However, when value is disrupted in the form of nihilism, the question of value and its historicity becomes an explicit attunement, as Nietzsche courageously demonstrated.

So too with Brad it is in the frustration of project management that the question of the conventions which shape the being of the practice of project management become an explicit theme for attuned questioning and inquiry.

The process of recollection, or *wiederholing*, is a process of moving from the particular to the general. Although the existential hermeneutic practice of research may be new in management studies, it is certainly not new in other fields. In the field of psychology, for example, Moustakas has demonstrated how it was his lived experience of loneliness which became the existential basis for his research into loneliness. He calls his form of research "heuristic" and, in describing the lived experience of this form of research, he notes that he does not begin with an initial and explicit intention to do research. It is not until he has a disruption in his everyday way of being that he begins to ask questions and it is in the context of beginning to ask questions that the possibility of research opens up for him. In describing one example, the example of doing research on loneliness as a way of being, he says that it was the loneliness that he experienced in needing to make a decision that would either lead to better health for his daughter or could culminate in her death that created in him an explicit awareness of loneliness. Although he could consult and take counsel from others, he was ultimately alone in bearing responsibility for the decision to have his daughter operated on. Through his own experience of loneliness, the phenomenon of loneliness was disclosed to him. He began to see loneliness in his daughter, in the way in which children were in hospitals, in the way in which people were treated in bureaucracies. This led him to explore literature on loneliness and then to write a phenomenologically grounded thesis on loneliness.

And thus, in existential terms, we see that as his being was called into question through the experience of loneliness, so he began to question loneliness as a way of being. Furthermore, it was from within his own experience of being lonely that he explored the question of loneliness. It was not from an outsider's perspective, not from a scientifically neutral and objective distance, but from a player's perspective—a player who has a perspective of his own way of being as a player.

This form of research is not new to feminist studies. It is exemplified in the work of Bell Hooks, who writes of the way in which her being's being-in-question formed the basis for questioning conventional ways of being in the context in which she lived. This kind of experience is described by Bell Hooks, who says: "I came to theory because I was hurting—the pain within me was so intense that I could not go on living. I came to theory desperate, wanting to comprehend— to grasp what was happening around and within me" (Hooks 1994, p59).

The hurt was a specific kind of hurt. It was the experience of being estranged from the very family(iar) environment in which she lived:

*I did not feel truly connected to these strange people, to these familial
folks who could not only fail to grasp my worldview but who just simply
did not want to hear it. As a child, I didn't know where I had come
from. … I was desperately trying to discover the place of my belonging.
I was desperately trying to find my way home (1994, p60).*

It was in the context of her estrangement that the norms and standards of
the way of life into which she had been thrown became explicit themes of
questioning. She began to challenge male authority, "rebelling against the very
patriarchal norm" of her parental house.

Even though it was through the pain of a disruption of her everyday
experiences that she came to theorize or philosophize, Bell Hooks' commitment
to philosophizing was unshakable. The same can be said in the case of Tolstoy.
His pain became a passion which gave his life a central purpose and focus that
he could not set aside but in fact affected all his other activities.

Brad's resolve in questioning his existence as a project manager was a
questioning of the same form.

What is perhaps new is that the Heideggerian form of existential
hermeneutic and phenomenological research is now being introduced in
a management context. In this respect there are a number of PhD research
candidates at the Macquarie Graduate School of Management who are in the
process of engaging in this form of research. The way in which their research
is existential, hermeneutic and phenomenological will be exemplified by them
in Part V of this book.

Research as Inhabiting a Way of Being

But it is not only a thesis that can be written in this way; research as a way
of being in practice is inhabited in this way as well. Although the reductive
positivists amongst us believe that we first learn the theory of research and
then put it into practice, it is only in the context of practice that research is
fully embodied. And the journey of embodying research as a way of being is
one in which we do not know in advance where we are headed. We need to be
able to go without knowing where we are going until such time as we embody
research as a way of being.

References

Burbules, N. (1995) Reasonable Doubt: Toward a postmodern defense. In: Kohli, W. (ed.) *Critical Conversations in Philosophy of Education*. New York and London: Routledge.

Chia, R. and Holt, R. (2006) Strategies as Practical Coping: A Heideggerian perspective. *Organization Studies*. Vol 27, No 5. pp635–55.

Douglas-Mullen, J. (1981) *Kierkegaard's Philosophy: Self-deception and cowardice in the present age.* New York: A Mentor Book.

Eger, M. (1993) Hermeneutics as an Approach to Science. *Science and Education*. Vol 2, No 1. pp303–28.

Gadamer, H.-G. (1975) *Truth and Method*. New York: Continuum International Publishing Group.

Gellner, E. (1964) *Thought and Change*. London: Weidenfeld and Nicolson.

Heidegger, M. (1985) *Being and Time*. Oxford: Basil Blackwell.

Hill, L.A. (2003) *Becoming a Manager: How new managers master the challenges of leadership.* Boston: Harvard Business School Press.

Holt, R. and Cornelissen, J. (2013) Sensemaking Revisited. *Management Learning*. Vol. 45, No. 5, pp525–39.

Hooks, B. (1994) *Teaching to Transgress: Education as the practice of freedom.* New York: Routledge.

Keller, H. (1903) *The Story of My Life*. New York: Doubleday, Page & Co.

Kuhn, T. (1970) *The Structure of Scientific Revolutions.* Chicago: The University of Chicago Press.

Sandberg, J. and Dall'Alba, G. (2009) Returning to Practice Anew: A life-world perspective. *Organization Studies*. Vol 30, No 12. pp1349–68.

Sandberg, J. and Tsoukas, H. (2011) Grasping the Logic of Practice: Theorizing through practical rationality. *Academy of Management Review*. Vol 36, No 2. pp338–60.

Segal, S (2010) A Heideggerian Approach to Practice-based Reflexivity. *Management Learning*, Vol. 41, No. 4, pp379–89.

Stolorow, R. (2011) *Heidegger and Post Cartesian Psychoanalysis*. New York: Routledge.

Taylor, C. (1993) Engaged Agency and Background in Heidegger. In: Guignon, C. (ed.) *The Cambridge Companion to Heidegger*. Cambridge: Cambridge University Press.

Todres, L. (2007) *Embodied Enquiry: Phenomenological touchstones for research, psychotherapy and spirituality*. New York: Palgrave Macmillan.

Tsoukas, H. and Knudsen, C. (2003) Introduction: The need for meta-theoretical reflection in organization theory. In: Tsoukas, H. and Knudsen, C. (eds) *The Oxford Handbook of Organisational Theory*. Oxford: Oxford University Press.

Weick, K. (2003) Theory and Practice in the Real World. In: Tsoukas, H. and Knusden, T. (eds) *The Oxford Handbook of Organisational Theory*. New York: Oxford University Press.

PART V
The Hermeneutic Circle of Becoming a Manager

Chapter 12

The Hermeneutic Circle of Professional Development

Professional Development and Existentialism

It is not only research, management and leadership that are inhabited through the hermeneutic circle of existence. A number of writers on Heidegger allow us to see that professional practices are lived experiences of becoming and that in general they are established through the hermeneutic circle of existence. As Dall'Alba says (2009, p39), whether it is the "archaeologist, journalist or dentist," they all become as such through the hermeneutic circle of existence. The same point can be made of lawyers, doctors, engineers, carpenters, plumbers and artists: they inhabit their practice and develop their identity through the way in which they live forward and emerge backward. She further emphasizes her point by maintaining that "Heidegger points out that we 'grow into' a familiar way of interpreting ourselves that is reflected from our world" (2009, p40).

Dall'Alba (2009) maintains that learning to become a professional involves not only what we know and can do, but also who we are (becoming). She maintains that when professional development courses focus only on techniques or skills detached from everyday being, they do not bring out authentic dimensions of the professional. The latter is not given the opportunity to integrate the technique into their way of being and so it does not become their own. Rather they practice their profession in an average everyday way; one which does not allow for bringing out mastery in practice. She maintains that it is the development of the authentic way of being rather than only the theoretical dimension of a profession that is required for excellence in practice. Heidegger, she maintains, "regarded modes of knowing, such as architecture, biology, history and so on, as ways of being human" (2009, p35).

Becoming is central to being a professional; yet it is largely omitted from educational and training programs. As Dall'Alba says, "processes of becoming often go unacknowledged in theorizing and practice relating to higher education programs" (2009, p34).

This is seen in so many professions when students who have been awarded their degrees now turn to practice. Here it is worth quoting Herman Widlack again. He writes of what he calls the "real-life shock" experienced by teachers in the transition from university-based training to the contingent reality of the classroom. He claims that newly qualified teachers often respond to the trauma of transition "by a change in attitude from one which is university based, progressive and liberal to one which is conservative." He also notes that this shock manifests itself in experiences of teacher helplessness, insecurity and a general loss of proportion and perspective, which expresses itself in skepticism towards theory in which newly qualified teachers are advised to "Just forget what you have learnt" (Widlack 1980, p23).

This is because educational and training programs do not prepare the being of the student but their "minds" and thus fill them with knowledge that is abstracted from practice. This process applies across the board in professions. Dall'Alba (2009) summarizes her position by saying: "The purpose of professional education programs can then be conceptualized in terms of developing ways of being the professionals in question, rather than simply as a source of knowledge and skills acquisition" (2009, p13).

There are two particular groups of writers who allow us to understand this: on the one hand Hubert Dreyfus allows us to understand professional development as a movement from practical coping to practical wisdom via a comparison between Heidegger and Aristotle. Dall'Alba and Sandberg enable us to understand professional development as the lived experience of becoming x or y or whatever the profession may be. However, neither position goes as far as demonstrating that it is the hermeneutic circle of existence that is at the center of professional development. This chapter prepares the grounds for the hermeneutic circle of professional practice. It will set out Dreyfus and Dall'Alba's views, build on them and demonstrate their Heideggerian limitations and, in this context, bring out the hermeneutic circle of professional development.

Dreyfus's Concept of the Stages of Becoming

It is in the context of a paper called "Could Anything be more Intelligible than Everyday Intelligibility? Reinterpreting Division I of *Being and Time* in the Light of Division II" (2004) that Hubert Dreyfus allows for a Heideggerian understanding of professional development as a movement from practical coping to practical wisdom. In this paper, he acknowledges the limitations of his own reading of Heidegger as set out in his book *Being-in-the-World: A Commentary on Heidegger's Being and Time, Division 1* (1993). Here he confesses that in his initial reading he missed the fact that in Division II of *Being and Time* Heidegger offers a more "primordial" reading of practical coping than Heidegger does in Division I. For the sake of convenience I shall translate primordial reading as "existential reading." Furthermore, Dreyfus claims that he did not see this more existential or primordial reading of practical coping in his major reading of Heidegger, limiting himself to practical coping. He acknowledges that he did not see that this more existential reading of practical coping in Division II is actually a Heideggerian perspective of Aristotle's notion of practical wisdom (Dreyfus 2004).

The distinction between practical coping and practical wisdom is that the former allows for inhabiting of the "average everyday" ways of doing things of a domain of practice, whereas practical wisdom allows for mastery, the creation of new possibilities, the disclosure of new possibilities that go beyond but include the average everyday way of practical coping. Practical wisdom involves going beyond the way in which things get done and, through risking oneself in the unknown, establishing new ways of even idiosyncratic ways of doing things.

As some of his four stages will be used in the final outline of the hermeneutics of existence, I will briefly go through each of the stages. The first three are situated within the realm of practical coping and only the last one is identified as practical wisdom (Dreyfus 2004).

The first stage is that of a novice. This is the stage of the "beginner." A beginner is someone who does not have experience in a field. However, the first stage is a pre-experiential stage. It involves learning independently or outside of situation. The example he gives is driving. He says that before even beginning to drive the driver learns the rules of driving. He or she does this by "decomposing the task environment into context-free features" which become the basis for articulating and then following rules.

The second stage is that of the "advanced beginner." This stage involves coping with what he calls "actual real situations." This stage involves in-situation recognition and the development of a situational awareness through which the advanced beginner is able to relate and coordinate different parts of a situation. For example, the sound of a car going up a hill and the need to accelerate before the car stalls.

The third stage is called competence. Competence is based on mastering the challenge of increasing complexity. This stage is initially experienced as overwhelming and nerve-wracking because there is so much to do but the learner does not yet have a perspective through which to coordinate the parts into a whole. As the learner develops perspective, they are able to prioritize, thus being able to coordinate the relationship between the multiple parts or activities involved. Perspective at this stage is given through obeying rules and regulations. These are the competent driver's guide to driving. However, rules do not cover all situations and thus a driver becomes competent through deciding "for themselves in each situation which sort of situation they are in as well as what to do, without being sure that their understanding of the situation will be appropriate" (Dreyfus 2004).

Because of the risks involved in this form of situational deciding, some drivers may become defensive or avoidant of certain kinds of driving situations, for example, crossing bridges or going through tunnels.

But most importantly the driver learns to take ownership of driving and feel their way around the situation.

The fourth stage is called "expertise," practical wisdom or virtuosity. This is a stage in which a driver is able to coordinate the whole and parts without needing to think about what they are doing:

> The expert driver, generally without paying attention, not only feels in the seat of his pants when speed is the issue; he knows how to perform the appropriate action without calculating and comparing alternatives. On the off-ramp his foot just lifts off the accelerator or steps on the brake. What must be done, simply is done (Dreyfus 2004).

It is in this stage that we become more than an "average" in driving. We become ourselves as drivers and are more available for risk-taking, spotting opportunities, having the world of driving being disclosed to us. This is the world of the master driver or the virtuoso driver: "As a result of accepting risks and a commitment to being better than average, the virtuoso in living, develops the capacity to respond appropriately even in situations in which there are conflicting concerns and in which there seems to those looking on to be no appropriate way to act" (Dreyfus 2004).

This is a primordial stage because in it we are situated squarely within the existential dimensions of experience. This is because there are no rules to guide the driver in advance. The driver needs to decide without the comfort of the guidance of rules. They are situations that occur suddenly and we need to respond to them in what Heidegger understands as a "blink of the eye." The driver needs to be what Heidegger calls resolved; leaping into the uncertainty of a situation for which there is no advanced guide. It is this activity of risk-taking that allows for the possibility of new, unexpected and excellence to emerge. For the way we respond in the face of the uncertainty of the unknown allows for new possibilities to emerge.

Critique of Dreyfus's Stages of Becoming

Dreyfus's reading of Heidegger's sequence of skill acquisition has been critiqued on a number of grounds. For example, Hargreaves and Lane (2001) and Dall'Alba (2009) have argued that because it is sequential, Dreyfus's reading of skill acquisition is linear. It has also been argued that because professional development is situated in the context of lived experience, it does not begin, as Dreyfus and Dreyfus (2005) maintain, from a context-free perspective but from being always and already situated within experience. This view is shared by Adolfa Peña, who in his critique of Dreyfus and Dreyfus, argues that: "Learning cannot be detached from context" (2010). Furthermore, Peña argues that professional development, emotion and cognition cannot be separated from each other. Adding to this, Alan Sieler includes the body and embodied understanding (Sieler 2005) and maintains that a professional habit cannot be learned by following a set of rules but is developed through inhabiting a practice. This involves developing a felt sense of a practice. No amount of rule describing or following can express the felt sense of a habit or practice.

Dall'Alba (2009) has argued that it is not only the final stage of skill development that involves the lived experience of becoming, but the whole process. Indeed, that professional development is a process of becoming rather than a matter of learning only skills is something that has not been highlighted by many authors. In the context of education, Dall'Alba (2009) has argued this: "Learning to become a professional involves not only what we know and can do, but also who we are (becoming)" (2009, p1469). Dall'Alba (2009) maintains that skill development is only a part of the becoming of a professional. Learning techniques of a profession does not nurture and enable a professional attunement. Even learning the art of diagnosis in medicine is not enough to stimulate the care or concern or attunement of the doctor to the illness and well-being of a patient. Dall'Alba (2009) maintains that "processes of becoming often go unacknowledged in theorizing and practice relating to higher education programs."

Furthermore, Dreyfus does not touch on the Heideggerian notion of pre-conceptual or pre-thematic knowledge in skill development. A person learning to drive always and already has some sense of driving before they begin to drive. The role of this always and already is not brought out by Dreyfus at all. Even though an aspirant or novice in a particular profession may not have had any experience, they already have some kind of understanding of the field such that they are entering it. As Dall'Alba says:

> *Even aspiring professionals who may have no prior experience of being an archaeologist, journalist or dentist bring with them some notion of what these professions entail that, initially at least, underpins their becoming. However, when these aspiring professionals gain entry to their chosen profession, they have undergone substantial change, not least in their ways of being professionals (2009, p39).*

In the same way a driver brings with them some notion of driving before they begin driving. No one would do research if they did not have some sense of what research is before doing it.

Adding my own points of critique of Dreyfus's reading of skill development in Heidegger: Dreyfus's notion of rule following is not a Heideggerian notion of rule following. For Heidegger "average everyday" "rule following" is not a matter of being instructed in *obeying* a set of explicit rules. Rather, without even noticing it, we find ourselves always and already following rules—and we cannot, for the most part, even state what these rules are.

Contra the Dreyfus brothers' risk-taking is an experience that accompanies many, if not all, of the dimensions of developing a professional practice and that it is not only the domain of the virtuoso—even a novice involves risk-taking. This point is exemplified by Linda Hill in her description of the lived experience of becoming a manager. She maintains that managers needed to make decisions without having been instructed in the context-free rules of managerial decision-making: "They [managers in her study] were responsible for the lives of others, yet they had to make decisions and act before they understood what they were supposed to do" (Hill 2003, p67).

This quote demonstrates that it is not through following rules in advance that novice managers emerge, but it is only through making decisions that the rules, regulations and way of being of a novice are inhabited. This is consistent with Heidegger's understanding of rules in which, without even knowing it, we are, through our involvements and choices-in-action, conforming to rules from a very early age. It is also consistent with Lyotard's notion of an artist who will only know the rules of the work of art after the work has been completed.

Hill makes the point that new managers have to act without having the prior knowledge of how to act. Indeed, it is only through acting that they will inhabit this knowledge. Furthermore, as Hill suggests in the above quotation, it is only by making the decisions and acting before they understood what to do that the managers' *felt* sense of *becoming* a manager develops.

Risk-taking is central to professional development from the very beginning and not only from the stage of competency, as Dreyfus believes. Mastery also does not eliminate risk-taking but a particular attunement to risk-taking: it is the skill of risk-taking (or what Heidegger calls "resolve") in the context of a particular professional practice. While novices may be overwhelmed by taking risks, a master builds risk-taking into his or her professional practice. Mastery involves developing not only a balance within what I shall call the hermeneutic circle of professional practice, but a flowing felt sense and an aesthetic style within the hermeneutic circle of professional practice. Virtuosity is the mastery of the practice of balance in the ebb and flow of the hermeneutic circle of existence.

Dall'Alba: No Context-free Learning

In contrast to Dreyfus, Dall'Alba (2009) uses Heidegger's ontology to develop a theory of becoming. She undercuts Dreyfus's position by maintaining that we are always and already in a familiar world: "Heidegger points out that we 'grow into' a familiar way of interpreting ourselves that is reflected from our world. He argues that we understand ourselves in terms of this interpretation, which opens possibilities for being as well as constraining those possibilities" (2009, p40).

Before we even begin to think about it, as soon as we are in a situation we are developing a sense of and being transformed by the situation. The sense and transformation are prior to cognition. This is at work, at play, overseas, at home—and even in driving a car. Furthermore, Dall'Alba maintains that none of this learning occurs in a linear way: "Contrary to what prevalent models of professional development would have us believe, this process is unlikely to occur in a predetermined or linear sequence" (2009, p43). This is the point that I have made with regard to driving, writing a thesis and management.

Entwinement Versus Referential Whole to Describe Being-in-the-World

However, she articulates the basis of Heidegger's ontology of learning, his notion of being-in-the-world, in terms of a metaphor of "entwinement." She is correct in that Heidegger wants to break down the subject/object distinction but, as I have argued, professional development from a Heideggerian perspective is to be understood in terms of the notion of a hermeneutic circle rather than in terms of a metaphor of entwinement—which Heidegger never uses to characterize being-in-the-world. He uses the hermeneutic circle and the notions of "referential wholes" and equiprimordiality. However, I shall leave the latter out of this book but refer the reader to my 1988 paper on the ontological difference in Heidegger's *Being and Time*.

Just as a hermeneutic circle is a referential whole, so I will argue that a professional habit is a referential whole in which the parts become the parts they are in relation to the whole and the whole situates the parts in relationship to each other. This includes the identity of the professional. It itself only emerges in the context of the referential whole of the hermeneutic circle.

Even learning the skills and techniques of research is part of a practice of becoming. And it is Heidegger who enables us to situate skill development in the lived experience of becoming. But, in contrast to Dall'Alba (2014) and Sandberg and Dall'Alba (2009), it is not Heidegger's theory of being-in-the-world as entwinement but what I shall in the next chapter call the hermeneutics of habit that is at the core of professional development. The hermeneutics of habit allow us to include so many more dimensions of being-in-the-world than are included in Sandberg and Dall'Alba's (2009) understanding of Heidegger's notion of being-in-the-world. For example, it allows us to understand the lived experience of being-in-question, the fact that life is lived forward and understood backward, leaping into a way of life, being-in-time, being-towards-death and the resolve to embrace the uncertainty of the unknown. It allows us to unpack the existential and *existentiell* dimensions of inhabiting a way of doing things.

Practice is Only One Dimension of Existence

As already stated, Heidegger is much more than a philosopher of practice. He is a philosopher of existence and practice is one dimension of existence. We miss out on the challenges posed by existence if we reduce his ontology to that of a practice. An appreciation of existence includes a range of dimensions that are not typically brought out in theories of practice: for example, breakdowns in sense-making, leaping into the hermeneutic circle, the anxiety of becoming, the felt sense of becoming, resolve in facing or refusing the anxiety of becoming and so on. This is not to say that Heidegger does not have a place for practice, but it is understood as an "average everyday" context rather than as an existential dimension of being. It is one dimension of becoming.

References

Dall'Alba, G. (2009) Learning Professional Ways of Being: Ambiguities of becoming. *Educational Philosophy and Theory*. Vol 41, No 1. pp34–45.

Dreyfus, H. (1993) *Being-in-the-World: A Commentary on Heidegger's Being and Time, Division 1.* Boston: The MIT Press.

Dreyfus, H. (2004) Could Anything be more Intelligible than Everyday Intelligibility? Reinterpreting Division I of *Being and Time* in the Light of Division II. *Bulletin of Science Technology Society*. Vol 24, No 3. pp265–74.

Dreyfus, H. and Dreyfus, S. (2005) Expertise in Real World Contexts. *Organization Studies*. Vol 26, No 5. pp779–92.

Hargreaves, J. and Lane, D. (2001) From Expert to Novice: A critique of Benner's concept of context in the development of expert nursing practice. *International Journal of Nursing Studies*. Vol 38. pp389–94.

Hill, L.A. (2003) *Becoming a Manager: How new managers master the challenges of leadership.* Boston: Harvard Business School Press.

Peña, A. (2010) The Dreyfus Model of Clinical Problem-solving Skills Acquisition: A critical perspective. *Medical Education Online*. June. Vol 15.

Sandberg, J. and Dall'Alba, G. (2009) Returning to Practice Anew: A life-world perspective. *Organization Studies*. Vol 30, No 12. pp1349–68.

Segal, S. (1988) Ontological Difference in *Being and Time*. *South African Journal of Philosophy*. Vol 7. pp234–6.

Sieler, A. (2005) *Coaching to the Human Soul; Ontological coaching and deep change, Volume 1.* Sydney: Newfield Australia.

Widlack, H. (1980) Real-Life Shock: The inapplicability of theoretical knowledge to classroom practice. *Education.* Vol 34, No 1.

Chapter 13
Hermeneutics of Habits

Driving a Car

It is not only inquiry or research that can be conducted existentially. The way in which the human being develops its habits of practical coping are inhabited in the form of an existential hermeneutic circle. Indeed, there is a certain form of learning that is inhabited in the form of an existential hermeneutic circle. In this chapter I would like to proceed by example. I will start off with the example of inhabiting the hermeneutic circle of driving a car. And in the second part will look at Heidegger's description of becoming an artist. In the third part I shall outline the lived experience of inhabiting the ways of practical coping of research in terms of the hermeneutic circle of existence.

The first time that I took my daughter for a driving lesson I realized that learning to drive is not a linear sequence of activities but occurs in a complex circular process, in a "hermeneutic circle." Attaining the *balance* of driving a car is not something that a novice can learn through exercising one function at a time but requires being able to coordinate different activities simultaneously from the word "go"—from the activity of "leaping" into the hermeneutic circle of driving. It is not that a novice or new learner can learn the *balance* of driving by first pushing the brake ten times so as to practice it and subsequently the accelerator another ten practice turns, clutch and steering wheel, while then practicing a sense of making sure that one is centerd in one's lane and after that looking ahead. Balance is not the sum of the parts. Learning the *felt sense* of balance of driving a car is being able to do all of these activities simultaneously while on the move. There is a simultaneous going forward and backward until what I shall, following Heidegger, call a "familiar sense" or "felt sense" of the whole develops and a familiar sense of the whole allows each of the parts to stand in relationship to one another.

Gallagher describes the workings of hermeneutic circle:

> *The meaning [and exercising] of the part is only understood within the context of the whole; but the whole is never given unless through an understanding of the parts. Understanding [and practical coping] therefore requires a circular movement from parts to whole and from whole to parts. … The hermeneutical circle, therefore is not a vicious circle, the more movement in this circle, the larger the circle grows, embracing the expanding contexts that throw more and more light upon the parts (1992, p59).*

Initially there are multiple breakdowns in coordinating the relationship between the whole and parts which form the phenomenon or lived experience. In terms of my earlier example, the familiar sense of driving does not occur automatically but presupposes breakdowns in felt sense. These breakdowns are not breakdowns in the parts of the car or the items of equipment. It is a breakdown in the felt sense of coordinating the parts and whole. An accomplished driver does not need to think about driving while driving. Indeed, such thinking will get in his or her way. Because a novice driver has not yet inhabited the practice of driving, they are caught in between thinking about what they are doing while they are trying to do it. And so instead of being able to focus on the road ahead, they are focusing on their way of driving, on the clutch, brake, speed and so on. However, the more they think about the clutch or the other parts, the more they lose sight of the greater whole and the more paralyzed they get.

So too there is a hermeneutic circle within which a person becomes a driving teacher. I only inhabit the identity of a driving teacher through teaching my daughter to drive. She does not have a familiar sense for driving before driving and I do not have a familiar sense for teaching before actually teaching. In other words, the world of driving opens up to her through driving and the world of teaching opens up to me through teaching.

As my daughter learns to drive and I learn to teach, we begin to inhabit the world of "driving." In Heidegger's sense the notion of a "world" refers to a network of relationship of parts that are bound together in such a way that they form what he calls a "referential whole" (1985) in which the parts imply or refer to each other in such a way that each is the condition of the other. Together they constitute a referential whole. And this referential whole is the basis upon which they are defined as a practice, a workshop or a "world."

The referential whole for Heidegger is inhabited not through thinking about driving but by driving, by being within the referential whole of driving.

No matter how much we watch other people driving, we will not inhabit the felt sense required of driving. Furthermore, we will not inhabit the felt sense of driving by looking at and thinking about the individual parts or even reflecting on the relationship between the individual parts. For Heidegger the habit of driving is acquired through being involved in the activity of driving. Through the activity of driving, we develop a sense of familiarity with the relationship between the parts.

In a hermeneutic circle the whole and parts are not added one to another in a linear way but occur only in relationship to each other. One cannot learn one after another but only in relationship to the other parts. It is a circular activity where the novice develops a sense of the whole from the relationship between the parts and the whole which allows the parts to be situated in relationship to each other. In the hermeneutic activity, there is the dizziness of being confronted by all of the parts simultaneously; simultaneously going backward and forward from the one to the other until the balance of the whole is achieved.

Just as Heidegger argues that I do not inhabit a room bit by bit, taking in one aspect after the other, so my daughter did not learn to drive a car in a context-free way of taking in one element one after the other.

Learning to drive presupposes a leap into the unfamiliarity of a circular activity—both on the part of the driver and indeed of a father who is not accustomed to teaching his daughter how to drive.

After several lessons, I again looked at the driving manual which is given to all learner drivers. What I now noticed is that it represented learning to drive as a sequence of discrete activities divided into individual parts. For example, before driving ensure that the mirrors are positioned appropriately, check the indicators and so on. For the most part, it continued to represent the act of driving and the achievement of balance while driving as a sequence of linear activities.

I began to realize that the dissonance between the practice of driving and the way in which it is represented on paper reflects a "mindset," or way of thinking, about the activity of learning. Three things stood out for me: firstly, the attitude of "read the manual" as a precondition for learning to drive. Secondly, an analytical thinking practice which assumes that learning takes place by breaking things down into their smallest parts and then almost magically hoping that they will come together. And thirdly, the assumption that learning is a sequence of linear activities. These three assumptions have shaped our attitude towards learning and education, both at school and at university.

Habits of Professional Practice

All habits of practice and all professional practices or ways of what he calls (and we shall later explain as) being-in-the-world form existential hermeneutic circles. Heidegger's clearest and most articulate expression of the hermeneutic process of inhabiting a habit is given in his understanding of art. Art involves three terms: artwork, artist and art. Each of these are necessary conditions for each other but none are reducible to each other. It is only through drawing or painting on the canvas that the artist becomes an artist. The artist is not an artist in advance or prior to engaging in drawing or painting. Similarly, the artwork comes into being through this painting or drawing. "Art" defines the relationship between art and artwork but is not reducible to either of the terms. It is neither separate from the two terms nor is it identical with either one or both of the two terms. Together they form a hermeneutic whole, in which the parts (artist and artwork) give rise to the whole (art) and the whole situates the parts in relationship to each other. "Not only is the main step from work to art a circle like the step from art to work, but every separate step that we attempt circles this circle" (1975, p3).

To understand the becoming of an artist we need to understand the relationship between art, the artist and the work of art. Understanding of this relationship involves the understanding of a relationship between parts and whole: the parts are the "artist" and the "artwork" and the whole is "art." Heidegger continues by saying that the circular nature of hermeneutic inquiry is, unlike a vicious circle, the condition for thinking: "To enter upon the path is the strength of thought, to continue on it is the feast of thought, assuming thinking is a craft" (1975, p4).

An interesting illumination of this is given on the cover of this book. The self-portrait of Alex Alemany depicts a painter painting himself. This is not unusual. There are many examples of paintings within paintings (itself a hermeneutic circle). However, what is unusual about this painting is that it is not only a painter painting himself but that as he is painting himself he is simultaneously being painted by his painting. The hand extending from the painting within the painting demonstrates how he is being painted by his painting while painting it. His identity and way of being are formed from within the relationship to his work. This extended hand that is painting himself is usually hidden in our everyday activities. Thus when painting, we do not see that our identity or way of being a painter is being formed by the painting. Yet as we are painting, we are developing the attunement, the style, the habit of practice of a painter. The extended hand is the hermeneutic worm at the heart of painting. Furthermore, art comes into being only through this hermeneutic worm between the painter and the paint work.

Research as a Habit

The habits of conducting research are inhabited in terms of the hermeneutic circle of existence.

Let me give a concrete example. I would like to proceed anecdotally by describing a series of occasions while I was Director of Higher Degrees Research, administering a Doctor of Business Education which was structured in terms of a three-year program.

The first year of the program was centered on coursework. The coursework consisted of four units, including units on research design, development of a literature review, and a course on quantitative research methods followed by a unit on qualitative research methods. Successful completion of the four coursework units was seen as the condition for preparing doctoral students for the research part of their doctoral program in which they were expected to complete a thesis within a two-year period.

While many students performed well in the first-year research-theory coursework, in the subsequent research years many found themselves lost and confused. They found themselves without the structure of the "hidden curriculum" of the classroom. In the first year the curriculum was structured for them. It was divided into four courses on different aspects of research. Each course or unit had specific aims, objectives, means of evaluation and deadlines for handing in tasks. It was teacher-centric and so the lecturer took responsibility for preparing content, for structuring classroom time, for defining the questions to be asked.

However, once the first year was completed, the predefined structure of the classroom was no longer there as an implicit guide to research, that is, without the presence of a teacher, without a teacher to structure the unit, to define and break up content into a coherent and time-manageable whole, to highlight significant topics, to set deadlines, to set questions, mark and evaluate topics.

No matter how well the first year prepared them theoretically for the journey of research, the lived experience of doing research was one in which many students found themselves thrown into the deep end of research where, rather than assuming the existence of order, structure and balance, they were challenged by needing to build these for themselves.

Many a student requested us to structure their research work for them: "if only we could make it more like a classroom with deadlines and guidelines" was a regular comment made by our research students. Yet no matter how well we educated them in the rules or the conventions of the research game outside of or in advance of the research game, this was not enough to give them an embodied and felt sense of the practice of research. For in practice a researcher is responsible for constructing their pathway. Only as they do research does both the structure of the research project evolve and so too does structuring as a competency or habit of practice develop.

Re-emphasizing this, we came to see that the very hidden curriculum of a traditional classroom, that which is handed to pupils and students pre-thematically from the first year of school, is a set of skills or competencies that students need to inhabit in the context of research: ordering, structuring, balancing, developing the parts, forming a whole through the parts, allowing the parts to be placed in relationship to each other through the whole—these are skills or habits of practice that are only learned in the context of being immersed in research.

School and university education does students a disservice by simply providing these in advance; for it means the students do not need to develop these skills for themselves but just imitate them when they become managers and leaders. Yet in a world of creative disruption, these are precisely the skills that are needed to cope effectively when a career, a way of life, an organization and an industry are constantly being creatively destroyed. It is through learning the skills of working from disorder to order that are central to practical coping in the context of creative disruption.

Furthermore, none of the first-year course units focused on the students' own lived experience of research; or the way in which they experienced research or made sense of research. Rather than developing a reflexive sensitivity to their own taken-for-granted way of making sense of research, they focused on authors whom the lecturers considered to be experts in the field. In this sense, they developed what Heidegger would call an "average everyday" understanding of research, an understanding of research based on what "they," the experts, think research is. And at best they were asked to follow what "they" thought research was. In other words, at best they were taught to mimic historically traditional and legitimate forms of research. In this sense research was reduced to a "method" which they were expected to follow—what we have seen Eger (1993) call a "learn it and use it" approach to research.

In the second and third years of the DBA, the research students did not have a predefined and structured curriculum in terms of which to conduct research. While, as is the case with all research, they did have a supervisor whose role was not always too clear and differed from supervisor to supervisor, the supervisor did not, and in many ways could not, predefine the structure of the student's research. For it is part of the lived experience of research that a researcher does not know where they are going in advance.

As Einstein once said, it would not be called research if it did not involve a continuous process of re-searching, a process of going forward and backward until the whole and parts fitted together. But students did not always have a pre-conceptual understanding of Einstein's point, expecting a structure to be "there" or to be provided for them.

Indeed, this going backward and forward pertains to all aspects of research, including the reading for the literature review, the writing-up of a literature review, the very idea of doing a literature review. The same points hold for methodology, data collection and analysis and researching a conclusion. Furthermore, it also pertains to the research question. It is more often than not the case that the research question with which the student begins is not the one with which they end. Indeed, prominent researchers have often said that it is only at the end of the research that they come up with the question for the beginning of the research.

Foucault (1982), for example, in reflecting on his own practice of writing, is quite clear on this point when he says that it is only once he has been immersed in the writing of a text that he becomes aware of the ends of the text or the text as a whole such that the parts begin to fit together: "If you knew when you began a book what you would say at the end, do you think that you would have the courage to write it?" It is more frequently at the end of a text that the introduction becomes clearer and clearer.

Lyotard brings this point out well when he says that a researcher:

> *is in the position of a philosopher: the text he writes, the work he produces*
> *are not in principle governed by pre-established rules, and they cannot*
> *be judged according to a determining judgement, by applying familiar*
> *categories to the text or to the work. Those rules and those categories*
> *are what the work of art itself is looking for. The artist and the writer,*
> *then, are working without rules in order to formulate the rules of what*
> *will have been done (1984).*

Thus the rules for conducting research develop only in the context of doing research. This is precisely the principle of development of practical wisdom in research from an Aristotelian perspective and the notion of a hermeneutic circle from a Heideggerian perspective: in both cases, it is only through performing or being engaged in the activity that we develop both the habits of practice and the coherence of the research, the writing and the thesis.

While it might not be the case that the research of our research students is not governed by pre-established rules (that is, that they are not simply or actually reinventing the rules for themselves), the point is that they need to learn and discover these rules for themselves. No one can teach them the felt sense of the research parts and its relation to the whole. They need to inhabit them for themselves. No amount of teaching the conventions in the safety of a classroom or a theoretical form is a sufficient condition for inhabiting them. It is only as they (we), through doing research, acquire the habits of research, that we can inhabit these practices such that they become part of our way of being, such that we can see out of, respond out of and develop the know-how of not only doing research but dwelling in, developing a felt sense of and being at home in the research process. Furthermore, it is only when we inhabit research as a practice that we can move from novice to mastery in research. Of course we are not alone in these beliefs about acquiring the habits of practice of research. As we have already seen, Emily Borda has made the point that it is only from a positivistic perspective that scientific education leads teachers to present science as a body of "settled facts" and scientific research as a settled way of doing things (2007, p1027). Elaborating, she says:

> *many science courses, especially large introductory courses at the*
> *undergraduate level, are content-driven, leading instructors to present*
> *science as a body of "settled" facts. Such instruction is likely an*
> *artefact of positivistic notions of science as objective, static and able to*
> *uncover "truths". Because of such instruction, but perhaps also due*
> *to developmental restrictions students by and large come to science*
> *classrooms with positivistic images of science (2007, p1100).*

Eger has written, in the context of a Heideggerian existential approach to positivist science, of the way in which scientific work has been "decontextualized" and characterized by an "overdependence on formal methods" (1993, p7). He maintains that it is learned and taught "unreflectively yet authoritatively, in the manner of naive realism." It has what he calls a "'learn-it-and-use-it' tool kit approach" (1993, p4). This he argues takes the very mystery and questioning out of the practice of science (1993, p5). Yet it is the mood of curiosity and wonder that has underpinned research and philosophy ever since Plato.

The experience of being thrown into the unstructured experience of research was never part of the explicit theme of study in the first year of the DBA. The impact of structure and lack of structure on performance was not discussed and conversely preparing students to create their own structure was not discussed. It did not come up as a theme for discussion. Even when, at the beginning of the second year, I would, in my introductory address to the students, suggest that they would come up against the challenge of needing to structure their own research and that this would be a huge existential challenge, I was not taken seriously by many of the students who had not experienced doing research before. Because they did not have a felt sense of the challenges of research, they could not relate to the warnings about these challenges.

It was only in the second year, when students were left on their own to develop a structure, that they come across the dizziness of the challenges of developing a structure—their own personal responses to developing a structure, their own sense of projecting a timeline in terms of which to complete a thesis. And in many ways this was a matter of guesswork, for not having completed a thesis before, they did not have a well-developed but very broad and general sense of how to think about timing for completion.

This pertained to even those who had formal project management experience. Initially many thought they would turn a thesis into another project to be managed—only to find that the question was not as clear as they thought it was and was not given to them by the company or the organization, that is, that they had to keep discovering and rediscovering the question that they were asking, often because, to their disappointment, they had found that others had already asked the question they were asking and so needed to refine their question—and often because they had not actually asked the question in a clear and precise way. Thus the experience of a thesis was just as unfamiliar to these project managers and thus just as difficult to project a timeline.

In desperation, many asked the university to provide them with a structure, but I said a thesis and research by its nature is a messy business. You need to get your hands dirty. There is no "paint by numbers" approach to research. It requires a courageous qualitative jump or leap into the unknown. "Disruptions," and being constantly in question, combined with a productive "anxiety" are dynamic factors in the journey of "being in research."

This is where attitude is important. Victor Frankl, the Heideggerian-based existential logotherapist, once said: "Between stimulus and response, there is a space. In that space lays our freedom and power to choose our response. In our response lies our growth and freedom" (1967).

It is in this sense that doing a thesis becomes an existential test: are we prepared to embrace the freedom of being in the space of what Kierkegaard called the "dizziness of freedom" (1980), where there is no predefined structure and it is only as we respond that structure is going to form, or is the challenge of the dizziness of freedom too much and overwhelming? The choice is ours. But we can be supported in this through what we have come to call the holding space of a hermeneutic circle.

We achieve our self-efficacy as researchers by being challenged in the research process itself. Through the tensions inherent in the "disruptions" and revelations we begin to change our perceptions of threat, discomfort, anxiety and self-doubt and start to find those "cracks where the light shines through" (to paraphrase Leonard Cohen). Slowly, amongst many "rabbit holes," mazes and misdirections, confusions as well as moments of sharpened insight, we achieve the beginnings of a "felt sense" of what research is and the space that we occupy within its constructs. It is only as we engage in research that we develop the habits of research practice and, in a more general sense, a research compass. We do not as novices begin the research experience with such a compass that gives us an overall sense of what we are doing when we are doing research.

No amount of theorizing in advance of immersing oneself in the experience of research can make the felt sense of research available to a potential researcher. It is like learning to ride a bicycle: it is only in the act of riding a bicycle where one learns to develop balance while riding—guided by some support. And of course it is the right kind of support that is needed here. It is a mistake to think that research balance can be gained by reading, teaching or talking about research.

Thus what we begin to see is a difference between an explicit and a hidden curriculum. The explicit curriculum refers to the explicit ways in which a curriculum is structured. The hidden curriculum refers to the often unintended lessons, the unofficial and unwritten conventions that students inhabit by simplifying being in a classroom or program. Handed down from an early age of being at school, students inhabit a way of doing things without beginning to know that they are acquiring them.

Thus one of the dimensions that many students inhabit at school is the belief that a curriculum is highly structured, ordered, planned and led by the teacher. This was the hidden curriculum of their whole educational experience: from their first year at school to the last year of university, they were passive recipients of an already established order of things, one created by the teachers, lecturers and system and then imposed on them.

In their whole educational experience, they had not needed to confront the experience of conducting academic or scholarly activity without a curriculum. Without knowing it, they had been deeply socialized into a structure being put in place for them.

Many students could not get beyond this deeply entrenched belief when confronted with the need to construct their own structure in doing a thesis.

What interested me is that these students were all managers with at least five years' experience, most with much more. Many of them had MBAs. I assumed that they had not only an intellectual but deeply embedded understanding of structure, order, leading and planning. Management is so often defined as the art of organizing, planning, leading, ordering and controlling. Surely they would know about ordering and structuring a thesis based on their experience of ordering and structuring an office, a team, a project or even an organization. Surely they had learned how to create order where no order had existed before.

What began to dawn on me is that, as managers rather than, say, entrepreneurs, they had worked in an already established order of things, rather than worked towards creating an order; in general, they had not worked from "raw material" to order; or they had not worked from no material to an ordering of things. Their task was to maintain rather than create an order of things. And indeed, this is often how management has been defined.

In this they had been well disciplined by the conventions of school and university, where order is imposed and to be a good student one needs to internalize and obey the discipline of order.

The unofficial curriculum of learning to do research is very much like the artist, entrepreneur or the philosopher who moves from a "blooming buzzing confusion" to developing an order and structure out of this confusion. The poet, the painter, the writer may have an intuition in advance of what they want to do but it is only as they do it that the order and structure begins to emerge. The reflections of writers on their paths demonstrates this. The artist Vincent van Gogh expresses this well in the context of art when he says:

> But you will ask: What is your definite aim? That aim becomes more definite, will stand out slowly and surely, just as the rough draft becomes a sketch, and the sketch becomes a picture, little by little, by working seriously on it, by pondering over the idea, vague at first, over the thought that was fleeting and passing, till it gets fixed (1997).

Here we see circles within circles: the rough draft, the sketch, the picture. In writing terms, we could describe the same kind of process.

Learning to Create Order from Disorder as a Research Competency

Thus the issue of developing a structure is important on two levels: one is on the level of the actual level of the thesis. The second is on the level of a skillset or set of competencies for turning something that has no structure into a structure and order.

This is a very important skillset for managers and leaders in the context of a world of creative destruction; for creative destruction presupposes a set of skills from working from chaos to order. It is encapsulated in a quotation from Andy Grove (1996), who claims that in times of creative disruption a leader needs to allow chaos to reign in order to reign chaos in." Taking this further, Flores and Gray (2000) say that in a time period where careers are not given for life, we all need to become entrepreneurial in developing our ways of life. Unlike in the early days of the corporation, we are no longer promised a pathway for life.

This is the kind of skill that is being nurtured and inhabited in the context of research. Ironically research is preparing researchers with the competency set for living in the uncertainties of the twenty-first century.

Although I could not provide an order or structure for their research in advance, I did say to them that I could help them with the process of moving from the "raw material" of a thesis towards the establishment of a structure or ordering of a thesis, from a state of unfamiliarity to inhabiting the research experience.

Research Coach

In this context, I began to see myself as a "research coach," as someone who enabled people new to the field of research to develop their own sense of balance in the research process. My role would be to provide what psychologists call a "holding environment" for them to think through the often very painful experience of moving from not knowing where you are headed in research to developing a sense of how to work with not knowing where you are headed; from experiencing this as an obstacle to experiencing it as a central part of research; from having no balance to establishing a sense of landmarks through which to read the territory that you are in. In this sense I said that it was not good enough for me or anyone else to provide them with a map, but help them develop the art of mapping. Like a coach, this could only occur as we worked with their taken-for-granted assumptions and experience of mapping.

Instead of seeing the practice of inhabiting the lived experience of research as a byproduct of research, I saw it as the center of the lived experience of research and also saw that research preparation did not embrace the lived experience of research.

It was a hermeneutically based process of coaching. For hermeneutics allows for the consideration of our pre-conceptual and pre-reflective sense-making and understanding that occurs from very early involvements in learning and education. Indeed, hermeneutics allows for making explicit the pre-conceptual sense and understanding that students have acquired through involvement in education in general.

Unknowingly, we are guided by this pre-conceptual understanding. It shapes the way in which education is disclosed to us. It shapes our expectations, perceptions and experience of education. Rather than simply building new theories onto this pre-conceptual understanding, we need to deconstruct the preconception in order for students to be available for these new theories—rather than interpreting them in terms of already established pre-conceptual practices of understanding.

Furthermore, in order to open up the space of research which does not contain a predefined and hidden curriculum of structure, a deconstruction of structure, the way in which different research students respond to the unstructured early stages of research and how to create the competencies to work in the space of not having a predefined structure to work with is an important part of research practice.

However, both Heidegger and Aristotle point out how difficult it is to change ingrained habits. As Aristotle says: "It is impossible, or not easy, to alter by argument what has long been absorbed by habit." Heidegger would agree with this and argue that it is through acts of destruction or disruption that habits are changed. For habits are more than skills. They are ways of being familiar with the world. Unlike in unfamiliar situations where we may need to rely on others, the familiar is a place in which we are enabled and thus empowered. To lose the familiar is thus to lose the horizon which allows us to be powerful. And to lose power is to be helpless.

Only Through Being in the Uncertainty of the Questions of Research do the Questions of Research Content and Habits of Practice Emerge

The deconstruction of habits can only take place in the context of research. For it is only when research students bump up against the frustrations, perplexity and even feelings of low self-worth which are often but not always felt in the research experience that they are ready to raise the question of structure. Thus it is by working from within research that the questioning of research arises. And it arises in such a way that the research students' own assumptions about research become explicit for questioning. Furthermore, it is only when their own assumptions or pre-understanding of research are questioned that the possibility of opening them up in an effective way to new ways of doing research arises.

Instead of simply internalizing traditional teacher-centered understandings of research, hermeneutic coaching allows for a dialogical relationship between teacher, text and research student. Thus it is only when students bump against their pre-conceptual understanding of structure, order, managing, balance and so on in the research process that we can begin to unpack and reframe them for a research context.

Thus what we see is that a hermeneutic approach to research was now made possible. All the parts were discussed (research methods, literature review, research question) and as they emerged so too did the whole, and as the whole emerged so the relationship between the parts stood out clearly in relationship to each other. From an existential hermeneutic perspective, it is only in the context of doing a thesis that the structure and the ability to balance the relationship between the parts and the whole are developed. In addition this is, more often than not, not a linear process of moving incrementally from one part to the other but a backward and forward movement between the parts. Indeed, even each of the parts involves a backward and forward movement. We do not know in advance of doing a literature review how to do a literature review—no matter how much theoretical knowledge we have of it. It is only by confronting the dizziness of the infinite mass of papers and books on the subject that we are engaged in that we begin to develop a sense of the literature review. Furthermore, how we respond to the dizzy mass of papers is equally important: how do we deal with the way in which it overwhelms us? Are we able to embrace the experience of being overwhelmed or do we zone out? What is our sense of self that begins to emerge as we experience this? Do we have the existential resolve to work through?

This same point applies to writing a literature review. It is only by writing the parts that a sense of the whole begins to emerge which then shapes the relationship between the parts. Again, we cannot know the whole in advance; cannot know the end in advance. Only by working through does the whole begin to emerge. We thus need to be able to stay with not knowing where we are going in order to write the literature review.

Even the particular research method cannot be known in advance; for it is only as we are developing the method that we gain an understanding of research methods. Thus again we need to be able to embrace the uncertainty of moving forward without the skills of moving forward already honed and developed into habits. Indeed, they only become habits through performing them.

Putting the whole and parts of the whole thesis together involves the same process. Again, as Einstein says, it would not be called research if it did not involve re-search, the forward and backward movement of a hermeneutic circle.

Because the dizziness of the forward and backward movement and the uncertainty of going into the unknown is so central to the thesis, doing a thesis often involves very painful and challenging experiences.

Thinking through or deconstructing the taken-for-granted but deeply ingrained belief in having a structure defined was a challenging task for many of the students. It meant moving away from a traditional preach and teach process to a much more coaching style of bringing out and then subjecting to questioning the "hidden curriculum" of both the classroom and the lecture theater in which the expectation of structure was formed and sedimented without both the students and lecturers realizing this.

The same point applies to any habit of practice. Management is a relationship between the parts and the whole—between the manager and the managed—and so too is leadership. Interestingly enough, when one of my MBA students conducted a series of interviews with managers on the question of a contrast between a liner and hermeneutic view of being a manager, the manager used the image of learning how to drive a car as a way in which to describe what it means to become a manager. He described the process:

> *You sort of learn over time and you realize that it's kind of like driving a car. When you are driving for the first time, you are worried about the right acceleration, and the gear shift, and the signs on the road, and the horn, and the instructor, you know, it's too confusing! But when you have driven the car for a few years, you realize that it's automatic and you're also learning to text (on the) phone while driving.*

Perhaps it is not so much a matter of being able to text while driving but it is a matter of attempting to coordinate several roles, functions or even tasks simultaneously. At first you can hold only two or three parts of the role of manager together, but as you progress you learn to coordinate and balance many more parts—as a juggler does. The point is that managing is made up of a relationship between the parts and a whole and these come together in the act of balancing.

References

Borda, E.J. (2007) Applying Gadamer's Concept of Disposition to Science and Science Education. *Science and Education*. Vol 16, No 9–10. pp1027–41.

Eger, M. (1993) Hermeneutics as an Approach to Science. *Science and Education*. Vol 2, No 1. pp303–28.

Flores, F. and Gray, J. (2000) The Last Days of the Career? In: Flores, F. and Gray, J. (eds) *Entrepreneurship and the Wired Life: Work in the Wake of Careers*. London: Demos.

Foucault, M. (1982) Truth, Power, Self: An Interview with Michel Foucault (25 October 1982).

Frankl, V. (1967) *Psychotherapy and existentialism: selected papers on logotherapy.* London: Penguin Books.

Gallagher, S. (1992) *Hermeneutics and Education.* Albany, NY: State University of New York Press.

Grove, A. (1996) *Only the Paranoid Survive.* London: Harper Collins Publishers.

Heidegger, M. (1985) *Being and Time.* Oxford: Basil Blackwell.

Heidegger, M. (1975) *Poetry, Language, Thought* (translation by Albert Hofstadter). New York: Harper & Row Publishers.

Kierkegaard, S. (1980) *The Concept of Anxiety.* Princeton: Princeton University Press.

Lyotard, J.F. (1984) *The Postmodern Condition: A report on knowledge.* Minneapolis: University of Minnesota Press.

Van Gogh, V. (1997) *The Letters of Vincent Van Gogh* (selected and edited by Ronald de Leeuw). London: Penguin Books.

Chapter 14

From the Hermeneutics of Practical Coping to the Hermeneutics of Practical Wisdom

Summarizing Heidegger

In this chapter I would like to reframe Dreyfus's model of skill development or professional practice in terms of the hermeneutic circle of existence. However, before detailing a reframed Heideggerian theory of professional development, let me summarize some of the points already made and which will serve as a basis for making the claim that professional development is an existential hermeneutic activity of inhabiting existence.

We have already seen how a workshop is a referential whole for Heidegger. A nail is seen as such only in relation to a hammer, which is seen as such in relation to a table, which is seen as such in relation to a purpose of the human being, which is acquired through its "average everyday intelligibility." A hammer is not first an object to be stared at but an item of use, and no matter how much we just stare at the hammer, we do not develop a felt sense of its use. It is only by using it that we develop a felt sense of its use. This kind of knowledge, knowledge of use, cannot be reduced to cognitive or propositional knowledge. Furthermore, we emerge as the beings that we are through the way in which we use equipment. Just as we transform the world through equipment, so equipment transforms us and is the basis of our inhabiting or dwelling in the world. Thus our sense of home is formed by the referential whole of equipment of which we are a part.

This referential whole is a hermeneutic phenomenon in that the parts are constituted as parts only in relationship or reference to each other. They are not parts independently of each other. The relationship between the parts forms the whole and the whole situates the parts in relationship to each other. The whole is the workshop and the workshop is not primarily a physical space but the way in which the parts form a referential whole.

The referential whole is never inhabited by simply gazing at it. As we have already seen Heidegger say, we do not inhabit a room by looking at one item at a time and then adding them up to form a whole. It is only through being-in the room that we develop a sense of knowing our way about the room. It is by being-in the referential whole that the specific world of the referential whole discloses itself to us.

Our habits of practice are developed hermeneutically. Thus the way of being of an artist, a driver, a manager and a professional in general are developed through the hermeneutic involvement in existence. We also become who we are through participating in the circle of existence and we never get out of the circle of existence. Our identity is formed through being part of the circle of existence.

The idea of a hermeneutic circle also refers to the fact that as the human being ventures out into the world, it also returns to its pre-conceptual context. For Heidegger, questioning our pre-conceptual awareness or questioning our assumptions is not an "armchair" activity but is something that is done in the context of the involvements of existence, in particular in the disruptive moments of involvement.

The hermeneutic circle in this sense is like a boomerang: we discover or uncover our pre-thematic or pre-reflective assumptions only as we go out and are involved in the challenges of existing. Or to use a Heideggerian phrase, existence gets sorted out through existing. And only as we are challenged in this way do these pre-conceptual understandings become explicit such that we can challenge, affirm or transform them. Again, questioning of our pre-conceptual assumptions is not just an intellectual activity but occurs in the context of the disruptions and breakdowns of sense-making as we are immersed in the challenges of everyday living.

For Heidegger questioning occurs in the disruption of everyday activities. There are disruptions within practical coping and disruptions of practical coping itself. This work is concerned mainly with disruptions of practical coping and not disruptions within practical coping. It is as our ways of making sense are ruptured, so we cannot take practical coping for granted. The breakdown of sense-making and of practical coping as such is the basis for questioning our pre-conceptual understanding. We saw this especially, but not only, in the case of inhabiting the order, structure and way of doing research, but it applies equally to developing any professional practice. It is important to note that the kind of disruptions in practical coping here are not in items of equipment ready-to-hand but in the fact that we have not yet embodied or inhabited a way of existing.

As we question our pre-conceptual understanding through disruptive moments of sense-making or ways of practical coping as such, we begin to open up new possibilities for ourselves or affirm the ways of practical coping that we have inherited but of which we have had nothing more than a pre-thematic attunement. The disclosure of new possibilities or the affirmation of existing ways of doing things is the beginning of mastery or virtuosity.

Now let me go into some of the range of moments in the hermeneutic circle of existence through which mastery of a professional practice emerges. I say some because I do not claim to have defined the dimensions of the hermeneutic circle of existence but am alluding to some of the dimensions involved in it. Although following this applies to all forms of professional practice, I will work with the two anecdotal examples that I have used: teaching my daughter to drive and running a DBA research program.

Pre-reflective and Pre-conceptual Sense of Research

Before even beginning research, research participants already have a pre-reflective sense of research such that they wish to or think about conducting research. If they did not already have the idea of research, they would not even have the notion of research as a possibility in which they engage. It is this pre-reflective sense of research that allows them to entertain the possibility of research. If they were thrown into an average everyday context in which "research" was not a way of doing things, research would not have popped up as a possibility.

However, as we saw in the example, their pre-reflective sense of research is in the background rather than the foreground of their attention. It is pre-reflective. It shapes the way they approach issues of structuring without knowing that they are doing so, that is, they expect the research to be structured for them—just as their classroom learning was structured.

Thus in this pre-conceptual phase they have historically inhabited assumptions based on notions of structure and balance in which they are handed the structure and order; not one in which they need to develop their own structure, develop their own research voice and habits of practice as researchers. Rather they want to rely on existing habits of practice, methodologies or routines for doing things. They want to be handed the way in which things are done: the formulae of research.

Novice

Whereas Dreyfus and Dreyfus (2005) see the defining feature of a novice as being "context-free" instruction, a Heideggerian account would see the novice as unfamiliar with the referential whole of the habit or profession which he or she is about to enter. This point has been made countless times in this work. Hubert Dreyfus himself makes this point when he quotes Heidegger as saying that when we enter a room we do not take in one context-free thing after another but establish familiarity with the referential whole called the "room." It is against the background of the referential whole that individual activities within the room may stand out.

The "room" can be called the workshop. It can be called habit and it can be called a profession. In *Being and Time*, as Dreyfus well knows, context-free activity happens only when there is a breakdown in items of equipment "ready-to-hand." This is not the case with regard to the novice. It is not the case that any item of equipment has broken down. Rather the novice is unfamiliar with an appreciation of their way around the referential whole. Thus the novice driver is unfamiliar with their way around the referential whole; the researcher, the teacher, the doctor, the lawyer, the novice baker are all unfamiliar with their way around the referential whole. There is no breakdown within practical coping; there is as yet no inhabited pattern of practical coping.

The Heideggerian question for the novice is: how does the novice transition from a state of unfamiliarity to a state of familiarity? In the opinion of this author, Heidegger spent so much time in *Being and Time* arguing against the position that the first step in inhabiting a practice is to think about it in a context-free way. Rather it is by being involved and immersing themselves in the referential whole that the novice starts to inhabit it. Thinking through the habit happens in the context of involvement. Thus the novice driver, researcher, leader and manager begin by immersing themselves in the lived experience of the practice. Only then do they begin to gain a sense of familiarity with it. And it is in the context of this familiarity that thinking emerges as a possibility. Heideggerian thinking and questioning is a questioning from within a referential whole and not from outside of it. It is only under certain conditions of disruption that items of equipment are freed from the referential whole such that they become context-free.

This is as true for Kierkegaard as it is for Heidegger. I use the comparison between Kierkegaard and Heidegger because it is one that Dreyfus (2004) uses very often. In his understanding of life's "stages," Kierkegaard (1980) is quite clear that movement between the aesthetic, the ethical and religious is not dependent on context-free, representational and rule-bound thinking. Indeed, it is only as a person takes a leap into the unfamiliar that the rules, conventions and ways of attunement of the new stage begin to open up. This is because the difference between different stages is qualitative and not quantitative. In his work *The Concept of Anxiety* (1980), Kierkegaard is at pains to stress that a qualitative shift cannot be made quantitatively and that a qualitative shift involves leaping across a chasm between two ways of life. It is a passage of transition in which the old no longer sustains us but the new has not yet come into being.

By definition, the novice does not have an embodied sense of the rules of the game. The felt sense of the rules only develop during the playing of the game. The crucial point is that the novice needs to leap into the game. No matter how well the rules of the game may be described, the felt sense of inhabiting the rules only occurs through the leap into the unfamiliar.

There is a great unsteadiness in the novice. Thus the novice driver does not have a felt sense of speed and so may press the accelerator too hard, responds by being alarmed and pulls back in a jerking way. Similarly, the novice researcher, by definition, will not have an inhabited sense of how to go about conducting research into a question or reading for a literature review. More often than not, they will read too much or too little at the beginning. Only as they read and write do they develop an inhabited sense of the rules of the game or of practical coping.

Adding more complexity to this is that the novice researcher or driver does not have a felt sense of the relationship between the parts and the whole. The novice driver does not have a felt sense of coordinating the parts and the whole of the practice of driving a car. The novice researcher does not yet have an embodied sense of how to go about putting the parts and the whole of a thesis together.

Only in the context of putting the whole and the parts together will the novice develop an inhabited sense of the way of doing things. Instruction may be important but only inside of the practice of research or driving. As has been indicated in the anecdote, instruction in the theory of research in a decontextualized way is neither necessary nor sufficient for developing a felt sense. Or to use the language of Gilbert Ryle (1978), knowing the rules of cricket cognitively is neither a necessary nor sufficient condition to play cricket. One can have a knowledge of the rules of cricket without being able to "apply" them or play cricket. And one can play cricket without having an explicit knowledge of the rules of cricket.

Because the novice has not developed a felt sense of practical coping, they are attuned not only to the context or the outcomes but to the know-how or "how to do" itself. Thus the novice driver is attuned to the act of driving itself and not only to the journey. Similarly, the researcher is attuned not only to the research content or outcomes but to the "know-how" of research itself. The novice is attuned to what they are doing while they are doing it. There is a heightened awareness of the lived experience of the practice itself in inhabiting a practice.

The lack of familiarity ought not to be interpreted as a breakdown in any item of equipment ready-to-hand but as an unfamiliarity with the know-how of practical coping. In the case of the novice driver, for example, it is not that a part of the car (the clutch or the brakes, for example) are not working, but that the novice does not have a familiar sense of how to go about driving. The same applies to the researcher as well.

Embracing being a novice also involves a faith in leaping into the unknown. For the novice needs to embrace the risk of leaping into the unfamiliar in order to develop a felt sense of their activity. Linda Hill (2003) has made this point with novice managers who need to make decisions before they have knowledge: the knowledge will emerge out of the decisions—and it applies equally to researchers and drivers.

Existentialists have referred to this leap into the unfamiliar "existential anxiety." It is a kind of uncertainty that is experienced where we are called upon to take a qualitative leap, a leap into that for which a blueprint cannot be given in advance.

Furthermore, it is arguable that it is more a coach, guide or mentor rather than an instructor that the novice needs. For a coach brings out the background pre-thematic or pre-conceptual understanding of an activity that the novice already has. For to drive presupposes an "always already" understanding of driving and, as we have already seen, research presupposes "an always already" understanding itself. It may be one that enables or is an obstacle to driving or research, but it defines the horizon within which the novice is attuned to the lived experience to be performed. As Dall'Alba (2009) argues, it is in the context of involvement that this pre-thematic understanding begins to emerge. And it begins to emerge only if there is someone there to bring it out, that is, a coach. Dall'Alba quotes Thompson, who says the purpose of professional development is "to bring us full circle back to ourselves, first by turning us away from the world in which we are most immediately immersed, then by turning us back to this world in a more reflexive way" (2009, p37). Continuing her point, she says: "Becoming a teacher, physiotherapist or lawyer, then, involves 'turning around' or transforming the self." I would like to call this the boomerang effect. As we throw ourselves out into the world, we are returned to the pre-conceptual horizon out of which our way of existing emerges. As we become attuned to this so we can examine, transform or embrace our pre-conceptual understanding.

It has also been demonstrated that it is not possible to break the whole down into qualitatively distinct parts. As already maintained, each item in the referential whole implies the being of all other items: in a car, the clutch, the brake, the steering, the accelerator are all co-constituted in such a way that we cannot perform the one without the other. Only when one item of equipment breaks down can we take a context-free perspective.

The novice is thus needing to coordinate the relationship between whole and parts simultaneously. A sense of what Kierkegaard calls the "dizziness" (1980) of not yet having an embodied sense of balance or relationship between whole and parts in the referential whole expresses the state of the novice. The researcher finds themselves going down many "rabbit holes" of ideas: doing too much reading, too little writing, wanting to define the beginning at the beginning and not at the end when they are ready to put the parts and whole in perspective; wanting to move in a linear way forward rather than the backward and forward movement of a hermeneutic circle.

The novice may bump up against some of their own pre-conceptual assumptions or expectations. This was seen in the case of Linda Hill's (2003) new managers, who were often surprised at the unexpected ways of doing things in management; so too with the DBA students, who expected structure to be provided for them and were surprised that no structure was pre-given for a thesis.

How a novice works with the surprise of disruption of expectations or pre-conceptual understanding is the basis of existential questioning, that is, questioning that occurs in the context of attempting to cope with the lived experience of the activity.

Thus the inability or lack of skill of the novice to cope practically are not so much breakdowns of the tools of research, but not having yet developed a sense of familiarity with the lived experience of bringing the whole and parts together. It is a lack of familiarity with the being able to dwell in the uncertainty of not knowing in advance where we are going. This is where students often panic and get freaked out. And this panic and freak-out is not abnormal but an integral part of the research experience. For it is about dealing with the unknown in the lack of a sense of embodied familiarity that is crucial.

Practical Coping

The second moment in developing a professional practice from a Heideggerian perspective is called technically "circumspective concern," but Dreyfus (1993) has popularized the phrase "practical coping." The latter refers to the way in which a person has developed a familiar sense of the workshop world. They know their way around the world of the workshop without having to think in a detached and explicit way about the workshop. There is a flow to the way in which they get around the workshop world.

In the context of this reading of Heidegger, to be able to cope practically is to know one's way about the hermeneutic circle of a habit or way of doing things. Thus one can move backward and forward from the parts to each other, the parts to the whole and the whole to the parts in a seamless flow. Someone who can cope practically has gone beyond the "dizziness" of the novice who is caught and jammed in the movement between the parts and a whole.

In driving a car, for example, practical coping expresses itself in the felt sense of the coordination of the parts and the whole. In research there is a playfulness in the movement between the parts and the whole. Furthermore, there is a movement beyond thinking about the lived experience of the activity in which one is involved to the subject matter of focus. Thus neither the driver nor the researcher needs to focus on either the act of driving or research itself but on the destination or responding to the research question.

However, practical coping has its limitations. It does not go beyond enabling a person to have what Heidegger calls an "average everyday" appreciation of an activity. Or, in non-Heideggerian terms, it culminates in the development of a conventional sense of doing things. It is doing things in the expected or common-sense way of doing things. It is the publicly acceptable way of doing things; the way in which "they" do things; or the way in which things get done around here.

As such, practical coping does not allow for innovation or for the opening up of new possibilities. While it is not to be confused with standardization and thus does allow for flexibility within a given way of doing things, it is limited to what can be seen and done out of the horizon of the latter.

Practical Wisdom

This occurs where a person is able to go beyond the publicly acceptable ways of doing things. It is the existential loneliness of, say, the leader or the maverick who sees that the institutionalized ways of doing things are no limiting factors in coping with everyday lived experience. In his third thesis on Feuerbach, Karl Marx said that circumstances change and the educator must themselves be educated. In this situation the educator can no longer rely on conventions for education or doing things but needs to be able to respond to the uniqueness of the situation—a uniqueness for which there are as yet no established rules. Dreyfus quotes Heidegger to bring out and justify this point:

> Dasein (or the being of the human being), as acting in each case now, is determined by its situation in the largest sense. This situation is in every case different. The circumstances, the givens, the times and the people vary. The meaning of the action itself, i.e. precisely what I want to do, varies as well. ... It is precisely the achievement of phronesis (practical wisdom) to disclose the respective Dasein as acting now in the full situation within which it acts and in which it is in each case different (1993).

The master is able to respond to situations as they arise; can respond to the specificity of the situation and can respond to contingencies in the situation; can embrace the unexpected and works with style and grace in this space. They have built disruption into their practice. Because they are no longer governed by the conventional way of doing things, this is a moment of what Heidegger calls individualization; a moment in which a person's own way of doing things begins to emerge. This is not say that the master's way of doing things is not built on the work of authorities in the field. It goes beyond them. It builds on the work of experts in the field but is not dependent on the work of experts.

Heidegger uses a range of language to describe practical wisdom. It is the world of tension between actuality and possibility. Whereas someone who copes practically is locked into the world of actuality, the person of practical wisdom can see beyond the present horizon—for example, Andrew Grove, in his work *Only the Paranoid Survive* (1996), writes about not being stuck in one perspective but, like a neurotic, anticipating possibilities beyond the present way of doing things. Indeed, Kierkegaard's master blends the world of the hypochondriac with the world of actuality—having a foot in both worlds and not only in one world. It is because of the dialectic between actuality and possibility that the virtuoso is not the grand visionary who is not grounded in everyday reality.

The phrase "disclosing new worlds" was one developed by Spinosa et al. (1997) to describe what they call the phenomenon of "history making." The latter occurs when someone disrupts existing paradigms and opens up the possibility of seeing the world in new ways. Einstein, Heisenberg, Bohr, Jobs, artists and philosophers who open up new ways of being in the world are world-disclosers and history-makers. They are people who destroy existing conventions and open up new possibilities. Spinosa et al. (1997) point to entrepreneurs in this category. They are people who are willing to dwell in the unknown without certainty and guarantee, work through it until they open up new ways. Flores and Gray (2000) sees Henry Ford as an exemplar of this category: "Henry Ford was not only designing cars. He was designing cities. He was designing economies. He was building a way of life."

Adding to this, Farson has said: "Henry Ford's automobile 'has created not just cities but also their opposite, suburbs. ... The existence of automobiles has changed our courtship patterns, our sexual practices, and especially our environment. It has also changed our identities" (Farson 1996, p47).

Flores and Gray go on to maintain that in the twenty-first century, the skill of world disclosure and history-making is a sensitivity that needs to be cultivated amongst citizens. For nothing is built to last. Careers, organizations, industries and ways of life are constantly being creatively destroyed: "We are like Henry Fords in the past. ... We are doing this on a much bigger scale today. My plea to you is let us take more seriously that human beings are like narratives."

The Existential Dimensions of the Hermeneutic Circle of Research

It is important to remind the reader that for Heidegger it is not only in the context of experience that the movement from novice to virtuoso takes place. It is in the context of the existential dimensions of experience. The existential dimensions of experience are focused on the theme of existence and that existence means that the human being is in question in all of its experiences. Life is lived forward and understood backward—the dots are joined only afterwards, the uncertainty of the unfamiliar, a leap into the unknown, the resolve to embrace anxiety, irregularity, surprise, disruption, breakdown, being-in-question and questioning our way of being from within the breakdown of the hermeneutic circle of existence.

Conclusion

The relationship between all these parts is not linear, but that of a hermeneutic circle. Furthermore, they are a circle of existence. For it is our way of being in the world that is at stake and in question in this circle. We do not know who we are in advance of living; it is only through living that we can turn back to see how we have become and project ourselves into the future. One dimension of what it means to become today is that of a professional. Being a professional is a way of being. This means that it is more than a technique, set of competencies or skills. It is a way in which we are attuned to and care for and in the world in which we exist.

Being a professional is also itself a part in a greater whole. As Heidegger says, we are circles within circles. To understand ourselves as professionals is to understand the world within which we exist. We are part of the hermeneutic circle of existence, and thus to understand ourselves is to understand the relationship between the whole and parts which make up the hermeneutic circle of existence and how we emerge from it. Just as in the painting by Alemany, we are being painted by existence while we paint existence. To understand the relationship between the two is the key to understanding.

In a truly hermeneutic circular fashion, as I now come to the end of the book, I realize what the book is about such that I can go back to the beginning to rewrite the introduction—and hopefully not rewrite the book. For in a fashion true to the hermeneutics of practical wisdom, the "truth" of this book has emerged only towards the end of the book ... and it never ends! As I wrote the book, I began to become aware of my own narrative in the book and that this narrative was one of working through disorder. I then situated my own narrative of being disrupted by disorder at the beginning of the book and now at the end of the book working through the disruption of disorder becomes an essential skill for living in the twenty-first century.

I hope this is the same for the reader: that the parts form a whole and, having read the whole, the relationship between the parts is now made clear. Or is this just my prejudice? Have I just been unpacking my prejudices? I look forward to conversations with the reader in working through this question.

References

Dall'Alba, G. (2009) Learning Professional Ways of Being: Ambiguities of becoming. *Educational Philosophy and Theory.* Vol 41, No 1. pp34–45.

Dreyfus, H. (1993) *Being-in-the-World: A Commentary on Heidegger's Being and Time, Division 1.* Boston: The MIT Press.

Dreyfus, H. (2004) Could Anything be more Intelligible than Everyday Intelligibility? Reinterpreting Division I of *Being and Time* in the Light of Division II. *Bulletin of Science Technology Society.* Vol 24, No 3. pp265–74.

Dreyfus, H. and Dreyfus, S. (2005) Expertise in Real World Contexts. *Organization Studies.* Vol 26, No 5. pp779–92.

Farson, R. (1996) *Management of the Absurd.* New York: Touchstone.

Flores, F. and Gray, J. (2000) The Last Days of the Career? In: Flores, F. and Gray, J. (eds) *Entrepreneurship and the Wired Life: Work in the Wake of Careers.* London: Demos.

Grove, A. (1996) *Only the Paranoid Survive.* London: Harper Collins Publishers.

Hill, L.A. (2003) *Becoming a Manager: How new managers master the challenges of leadership.* Boston: Harvard Business School Press.

Kierkegaard, S. (1980) *The Concept of Anxiety.* Princeton: Princeton University Press.

Ryle, G. (1978) *The Concept of Mind.* London: Penguin Books.

Spinosa, C., Flores, F. and Dreyfus, H. (1997) *Disclosing New Worlds: Entrepreneurship, democratic action, and the cultivation of solidarity.* Cambridge, MA: MIT Press.

Chapter 15
The Hermeneutic Circle of Becoming a Manager

Professional Development in the Form of a Hermeneutic Circle

It is not only research that can be understood as a hermeneutic circle of existence; so too can management and leadership. Indeed, any being or becoming a professional can be understood in terms of the hermeneutic circle of existence.

In this chapter, the way in which leadership and management can be understood in terms of the hermeneutic circle of existence will be developed. I shall focus on the work of a specific writer in management: Linda Hill (2003). I shall also make brief reference to Henry Mintzberg (2004), as his work is heading in an existential direction but does not quite develop an existential and being underpinning.

On Becoming a Manager

There is a powerful qualitative but almost imperceptible shift that occurs in Linda Hill's book *On Becoming a Manager* (2003). This is a shift from a scientifically technique-based view of management to an existential hermeneutic being based view of management. For what Hill is concerned with is the experience of *becoming* a manager. *Becoming* is a being and existential lived experience. Her book is grounded in the way in which people become managers by the way in which they respond to the rich uncertainty of experience. Such responding involves more than an intellectual or cognitive process but the whole being or a fully embodied experience of learning in the context of living through the unknown and unfamiliar transitions of the lived experience of managing.

While Hill does write copiously about overcoming the uncertainties and challenges posed by the unfamiliarity of the transitions of lived experience in the *being* and *becoming* of a manager, she offers neither a theory of becoming a manager nor that management involves a practice of becoming a manager.

In fact, the word becoming was omitted from the index of her book, suggesting that Hill may have overlooked the significance of the term she had raised although she did state in the preface of the book that she is focused on "a rich and textured understanding of the challenges involved in becoming a manager" (Hill 2003, pxvii).

In her 2004 *Academy of Management Executive* article, Hill does state that "becoming a manager required a profound psychological adjustment—a *transformation of professional identity*" (2004, p121). Hill also adds that this involves the anxiety of unlearning "deeply held attitudes and habits they had developed when they were responsible simply for their own performance" (2004, p121).

Hermeneutics of Becoming

In this chapter, we will offer a theoretical framework to understand the turn towards *being* and *becoming* a manager by using a range of data drawn from Hill's empirical work to support this turn towards a being and becoming based view of management. The theoretical underpinning that will bring out the significance of the turn towards a being and becoming based view of management will be drawn from the writing of Aristotle, Martin Heidegger and a range of existential philosophers.

Aristotle allows us to talk about management as inhabiting the world in a certain way. Management habits, as any other habit of practice, cannot be learned from a scientific and objective distance or by reading texts on leadership and management. It is only through the existential and crucible moments of immersing oneself in the lived experience or practice of management that one develops the felt sense or the existential familiarity of habits of management practice and of leadership.

The existential hermeneutic philosophy of Martin Heidegger and others allows us to understand the lived experience of becoming a leader or manager in terms of the process of a hermeneutic circle. It allows us to understand how becoming a manager emerges out of the way in which managers cope with the challenges, surprises and shocks that Hill sees as central to becoming a manager. It allows us to make coherent sense of the circular proposition that it is only through leaping into management or leadership that one learns to become a leader or manager.

However, becoming a leader or manager is a hermeneutic practice. As has been seen, in reflecting on his career as an entrepreneur, Steve Jobs once mentioned that he did not know in advance of becoming an entrepreneur that he was going to become an entrepreneur. It was only as he engaged in entrepreneurial activity that he became an entrepreneur and was only upon looking back that he could see that he had become an entrepreneur. Steve Jobs maintained that he could not join the dots of his career going forward but only by going backward (Jobs 2005). As has been stated, Kierkegaard says that "life is lived forwards and understood backwards." This process of joining the dots backwards rather than forwards is a hermeneutic process. For the arrangement of the relationship between the parts and the whole occurs as we reflect on what we are becoming. In terms of Heidegger's existential hermeneutics, we do not know who we are in advance of engaging in existence. Only as we exist do we become.

The process of joining the dots to form the whole is a hermeneutic process. And thus, the *being* and *becoming* of a manager and leader is, as we will show in this chapter, a hermeneutic and existential process.

Linear and Sequential versus Hermeneutic Practices of Becoming

We shall contrast a hermeneutic process with a linear process, which is a sequential process in which we move logically from A–Z. A hermeneutic process, however, is more like a jigsaw puzzle in which we need to be able to roam all over the puzzle to fit the parts and whole together. In this process, we go forward and backward to advance forward again. Previously, management and leadership have been mainly understood as a linear process. The dominant metaphor of "climbing the corporate ladder" suggests very strongly the linear assumptions implicit in *becoming* a manager or leader, for a ladder involves a direct step-by-step process, one in which the top can be seen from the bottom.

The hermeneutic process, however, suggests that a leader and manager may need to go backward, forward, sideways, slip and slide before they become a manager or leader. The whole *leader* only comes together as the parts of the puzzle are put in place. Furthermore, the hermeneutic process suggests that the transitions between the layers of management and leadership are qualitative rather than quantitative. This process, again, is unlike taking a step up a ladder but rather like a rite of passage in which one needs to leap into the lived experience of the new position or the new way of being.

Hill's position may be summarized by quoting her directly:

> They [the new managers] remind us that you become a manager mainly by on-the-job learning. By grappling with real problems and facing real consequences, they learned when they had to; that is, when confronted with circumstances they did not understand or did not know how to handle. By trial and error, observation and interpretation, and introspection they made sense of and learned from their experiences (2003, p193).

In this quotation, Hill has explicitly stated that management is a practice of becoming, that becoming (a manager) involves the way in which "managers" respond to challenges in the context of real-life experience, that this real experience involves "observation and interpretation," and trial and error—not from a scientific distance but by being within the situation, with one's way of doing things (2003).

Becoming through Choice-in-Action

The theme of choice-in-action is a theme that underpins the work of existential thinkers from Kierkegaard to Sartre. Jean Paul Sartre tells us that no one is born a hero or a coward. It is only as we act that we become. Sartre says "that the coward makes himself cowardly, the hero makes himself heroic" (1948). Furthermore, he goes on to say that being a hero once or even twice does not ensure that we have a heroic "self" or "personality"—just as being a coward once or twice does not stamp its mark on us permanently: "there is always a possibility for the coward to give up cowardice and for the hero to stop being a hero" (1948).

Sartre (1948) rejects the idea that there is a self or personality that develops from birth to death. Rather he maintains that the human being is a series of "undertakings" that is always in context and under construction: "What we mean to say is that a man is no other than a series of undertakings, that he is the sum, the organization, the set of relations that constitute these undertakings" (1948).

It is important to understand that in existentialism deliberation does not precede choice. As Sartre says, "by the time the die is cast, the choice has already been made". It is choice that influences deliberation. This can be witnessed in the way in which leaders develop their outlook: it is not first by sitting at a desk and thinking about it but in the context of the choices-in-action that their thinking is developed. An interesting example of this is to be found in Lou Gerstner's (2002) autobiography, where it is only towards the end of his experience at IBM that he tries to abstract a set of principles for practice and not in advance of practice.

Only through Managing Do We Become Managers

Kierkegaard (1980) has a circular way of explaining the activity of becoming. He claims that sin emerges in the world through the act of sinning. Prior to the act of sinning Adam and Eve have no sense of what a sin is; only by sinning do they understand the distinction between life and death, the phenomenon of time and the distinction between good and evil. While they may have been able to mouth these words before sin, they had no felt sense of it. The act of sinning transforms their way of being attuned to the world.

This situation is not so different from that of a little child who one warns not to go out to play. This warning carries a threat of punishment. The prohibition evokes both fear and excitement; the excitement of being able to do (go out to play) and the fear of punishment. However, the little child understands neither the notion of going out to play nor the experience of punishment. For it is only through being punished that they will understand punishment and it is only by going out to play that they will understand "going out to play." They are caught between the dizziness of the known and the unknown, standing between a sense of and no sense of play or punishment. Without even knowing it they have been thrown into a choice but they have no grounds upon which to choose. The choice cannot be made rationally for they know neither play nor punishment. They need to take what Kierkegaard calls a qualitative leap through the unknown into play and punish.

The same set of points can be made in terms of becoming a manager: only by managing is the meaning of the world of management opened up to one. While one may be able to mouth the concepts in advance of the experience, it is only through being immersed in experience that the world of management and leadership—and for that matter research—is disclosed to one.

Sartre and Kierkegaard's circular reasoning goes back to Aristotle, who maintains that "neither by nature, then, nor contrary to nature do the virtues arise in us; rather we are adapted by nature to receive them, and are made perfect by habit. We become just by doing just acts, temperate by doing temperate acts, brave by doing brave acts" (Aristotle 1962, p33).

Furthermore, in the quotation above, the act of becoming a manager is, as Hill states, a state of interpreting or a "sense-making" experience. *Sense-making* is at the heart of the practice of interpretation, which is a hermeneutic activity. It is also part of what the existential philosopher Martin Heidegger understands as the essence of the being of the human.

Hill (2003) also allows us to infer that the central challenge is the experience of *becoming* in the face of the unknown and unfamiliar. This is by dealing with circumstances that the managers do not understand or do not have the "habits of practice" through which they can "handle" being managers. Broadly speaking, from an existential perspective, *becoming* involves experience of overcoming experience of the unfamiliar and unknown. It is through such experiences that we learn to dwell in or inhabit the world and, thus, develop effective habits of managerial practice. We do not inhabit the world or develop habits of practice without immersing ourselves in experience.

These themes of becoming a manager and inhabiting the practice of being a manager through responding to the unknown are repeated throughout Hill's work. From as early as the opening page of the introduction, Hill quotes a manager who compares the experience of becoming a manager with that of becoming a parent and in which both "become" by working through the unknown:

> *Do you know how hard it is to be the boss when you are so out of control? It's hard to verbalize. It's the feeling you get when you have a child. On day X minus 1, you still don't have a child. On day X, all of a sudden you're a mother or a father and you're supposed to know everything there is to know about taking care of a kid.*

A close look at the language involved in this statement refers to the notions of being and becoming a boss and a parent: "be the boss" and "are a mother or father" are both *being* and *becoming* phrases—so too is the idea of "feeling you get" (2003, p3).

Furthermore, the relationship between "day X minus 1 and day X" is not a quantitative, gradual and sequential step but rather a qualitative and sudden shift in a way of being. Becoming a parent is a sudden, qualitative transition in a way of being. It is only as one gives birth to and raises children that one becomes a parent. So, too, is the transition from *not being* a manager to *being* a manager. It is not a gradual and linear process but rather a sudden and qualitative shift. This point is exemplified in the following quotation from Hill:

> *The day before, I was on the battlefield with them, on the floor day after day. ... Then review time came around. They changed their view of me. All of a sudden I became someone who threatened their survival. ... It was quite an exercise, it forced me out of the mode of friendship and made me look at how I perceived results. It caused me a great deal of soul-searching, and I really wondered if I could do it. You hold their job— their career—in your hands, so to speak. They have an inbred fear (Hill 2003, p65, emphasis added).*

I have italicized parts of this to emphasize the qualitative shift in the activity of becoming. It is, as stated in the quotation, "all of a sudden" and the way in which thinking needs to change in line with this sudden shift. Both the shift in way of being and thinking are not gradual. Managers are caught by surprise in this shift. The experience of becoming penetrated to the "essence" or existence—as exemplified in the phrase "soul-searching"—parts of this manager. Furthermore, the notion of inbred fear is itself a "mood" word, indicating *being* and *becoming*.

Hill writes of what can be called an existential responsibility in becoming a manager, a responsibility that is part of the essence of who one is: "Like individuals who must suddenly face the transition to parenthood, the managers had to learn on the job. ... They were responsible for the lives of others. And like new parents, the managers were transformed by the experience" (Hill 2003, p8).

This sense of responsibility is not just a concept but is lived out existentially in the way in which managers develop their way of being or habits of practice as they respond or choose as they are thrown into circumstances of managing. This is a central point in the philosophy of Sartre: the way we respond to the context, or what he calls the co-efficient of adversity, into which we are thrown (that is, the context of managing) shapes who we become as managers.

As Martin Buber points out through his notion of the existential test, it also shapes a manager's sense of self-worth. And as Sartre points out, how we choose to respond in situations can also be a condition of bad faith rather than authenticity, that is, instead of being ourselves, we can lose ourselves and "play the game" of managing rather than embracing the challenges of managing.

Many famous leaders, such as Jack Welch, Andrew Grove, and others, have written about the way in which the anxiety of the unfamiliarity of becoming a leader led them into moments of bad faith rather than into the development of their authentic way of being as a manager.

What begins to emerge is a theme central to the notion of becoming. Becoming occurs only as we choose in the context of action. And there are particular kinds of contexts of action that are more crucial. This is the experience of the unknown, the unfamiliar, surprise and shock that shake people to the core of their being: "As the managers learned about the realities of managerial work, they were plagued by a particular kind of *surprise* that arises when tacit job expectations are not met or features of the job are not anticipated" (Hill 2003, p23).

Qualitative Dimensions of Management Transition Stages

There is, according to Hill, an existential sense of bewilderment in becoming a manager when their taken-for-granted expectations are not met. Writing about a professional who has recently undergone a transition from a technical expert to a manager, she quotes:

> *Suddenly, I found myself saying, "boy, I can't be responsible for getting all the revenue. I don't have the time." Suddenly, you've got to go from yourself and say "now I'm the manager, and what does a manager do?" It takes a while thinking about it for it to really hit you—a manager gets things done through others. That's a very hard transition to make (Hill 2003, p90).*

Here, we get a strong sense of being overwhelmed by the experience only to find insight and make new ways of being possible for this manager—or to develop a felt sense for, and inhabit the way of, being of a manager.

Here we see how it is not abstract thought but concrete experience that throws the novice manager's expectations into question—a theme central to Heidegger, as we have seen. Furthermore, what brings this closer into line with an existential notion of becoming is the required role played by having the faith of leaping into the unknown during the qualitative shift of becoming a manager. Hill makes the point that new managers have to act without having the prior knowledge of how to act. Indeed, it is only through acting that they will inhabit this knowledge: "They [managers in her study] were responsible for the lives of others, yet they had to make decisions and act before they understood what they were supposed to do" (Hill 2003, p67).

Furthermore, as Hill suggests in the above quotation, it is only by making the decisions and acting before they understood what to do that the managers' *felt* sense of *becoming* a manager develops. They develop the habits of management through the practice of management—just as for Aristotle virtue emerges through virtue and for Sartre a hero emerges through the acts performed.

Hill is also suggesting that the world of management was not disclosed to them before leaping into the unknown but only as they committed themselves without prior objective knowledge to the lived experience of managing. Thus no matter how many texts they may or may not have read prior to being thrown into choosing in the context of action, these texts would not have disclosed the world of managing—just as the world of a new city is not disclosed through reading texts or looking at maps but by walking up and down the city in a hermeneutic way, linking the parts and whole together.

Hill also believes that leadership and management is a journey of becoming a leader and that this is a transitional process where the leader has to unlearn in the context of the contingencies of lived experience that were previously learned in order to make space for the new learnings (Markowitz 2010). She also stated when interviewed that she advises her Harvard Business School students at the start of her class that they will learn to lead through experiences rather than through what is taught in her class (Markowitz 2010). This "practical learning" process is the hermeneutic learning model that this research sets out to test. For hermeneutics is the act of learning to lead through addressing the questions that are raised concretely through the disruptions and surprises involved in actually leading. Hermeneutics is the lived experience of inhabiting a practice through the decisions and actions made in advance of understanding and through which understanding as *know-how* or *felt sense* or *habit* emerges.

In addition, the process of "learning and unlearning" that Hill mentions is reminiscent of the hermeneutic learning process where preconceived assumptions are experientially surfaced and challenged before leaders can travel through a transition phase. As such, Hill also suggests that leadership learning is a change in mindset and adopting a different set of values.

These theories are not unique to Hill. We can find the emphasis on learning through experience and even the notion of becoming a manager or leader in the work of Henry Mintzberg and many others. Mintzberg always emphasizes the role of what he calls "firsthand experience" (2004, p56) rather than representations of experience in case studies or texts in learning about management. He emphasizes that firsthand experience is the basis for "discovering for themselves what does and does not work." Although he does not call this existential, it is, in so far as it is only by leaping into the unknown that managers are going to find out what works and does not. It cannot be given in advance.

However, Mintzberg does not discuss either the role of existence or the phenomenon of becoming in the development of managers. Indeed, neither term is thematized or mentioned in the index to his book. What I have sought to highlight is the role of existential dimensions of experiences in the role of becoming a manager.

Summing up the *being* and *becoming* notions involved in management and leadership, an entrepreneur leader states:

> So the reason I'm a valuable CEO now is because of what I've been through. ... I've got my resilience because I've seen what can happen, good and bad. ... The fact is I lived through that and I saw a set of reasons why a company goes under and now I'm much more prepared to handle whatever the market sends me (Cope 2011, p616).

Several aspects of the hermeneutic learning process resonate with the leader's words. Firstly, he did not believe that he became a valuable leader through a "class room environment." It was through the existential experiences that he had seen and lived through. They were existential because he did not have a knowledge of them in advance of going through the unknown or unfamiliar events. The second hermeneutic aspect touched on by this leader's response is that he had gone through at least one process of transition, where he was challenged and saw how the company that he led failed and that he gained learning insights from this transition. Another entrepreneur confirms his learning through failures, "I'm not afraid of starting another company ... in fact, I'm stronger from the experience" (Cope 2011, p616). In hermeneutic terminology, by experiencing and overcoming the challenges in this leader's transition phase, he emerged with added resilience. More precisely, this leader speaks about himself and his *being* as stronger. Thus, this manager is *becoming* by the way in which he responds to experience. His resilience develops in the act of being resilient.

Leaders on International Assignments

It is now a cliché to say that we live in a global world. Living in such a world means that managers are sent to unfamiliar countries in order to lead. No matter how much they learn about the theories of other cultures in advance, it is only by being in the culture that a felt sense for the unfamiliar culture develops. This requires leaping into the unknown. As Carlos Ghosn of Nissan and Renault said: "I did not try to learn too much about Japan before coming, because I didn't want to have too many preconceived ideas. I wanted to discover Japan by being in Japan with Japanese people" (2002).

A core principle of global mindset learning is that we learn by being immersed, engaged and involved in a situation. We do not learn experientially by being a disengaged observer—the model of a scientist. Furthermore, as Ghosn himself acknowledges, it is crucial to allow oneself to make mistakes while one leads and learns in unfamiliar situations. It is by making mistakes that we are able to question our own assumptions so that we can be open to learning new ways of seeing and doing things in the world. "Well, I think I am a practical person. I know I may fail at any moment. In my opinion, it was extremely helpful to be practical [at Nissan], not to be arrogant, and to realize that I could fail at any moment" (2002).

He goes on to say that it was by being placed in strange and unfamiliar situations while growing up that he learned to change himself in such a way that the initial anxiety experienced in unfamiliar places was transformed into a sense of curiosity in the unfamiliar. Indeed, he says that although it is often uncomfortable for them, he raises his children by encouraging them to be immersed and educated in the unfamiliarity of difference: "When my kids change schools, they don't like it. But at the same time, I understand that this will make them stronger" (2002).

Through being able to respond to the anxiety of the unfamiliar in a proactive way, he learned to embrace the uncertainty of difference and the unknown. The challenge that managers face in a global situation is to turn the anxiety of otherness into experiences of curiosity. Yet as Ghosn himself says, managers and leaders are too often afraid of the unfamiliarity of difference: "It's interesting to see how human beings handle difference. People have always had problems about what is different from them. Different religion, different race, different colour, different sex, different age, different training—human beings have always had a challenge confronting what is different" (2002).

He traces the source of the fear of difference to the need for security. Those that can embrace uncertainty are able and willing to turn difference into curiosity and thus an opportunity for learning, while those who are defensive in the face of difference cling to the security of the familiar: "Now, we come to the basic acknowledgement that you feel more secure with somebody who is like you. You feel more comfortable, you feel more secure. You feel insecure with someone who is different from you" (Ghosn 2002).

Yet, paradoxically, if we are not able to learn from people who are other and different from ourselves, we miss out on the opportunity to learn about ourselves and to open up new possibilities for ourselves: "But I recognize that even if someone is different, I'm going to learn a lot. We have a tendency to reject what is different. And at the same time, we need what is different. Because what is different is the only way we can grow by confronting ourselves" (Ghosn 2002).

Thus through being immersed in others' ways of doing things, we learn about our own way of doing things. It is as our taken-for-granted habitual ways of doing things are disturbed by the others' ways of doing things that we come face to face with both the others' and our own ways of doing things.

This point is made by, amongst others, Bauman, who says that in meeting people who are unlike us, "our unconscious customs and habits have been shown to us in a mirror of sorts. We have been forced to look at them, ... to stand at a critical distance from our own lives" (1995, p60).

Thus, as Bauman and many others have pointed out, when we are in the mindset of the conventions of our own culture, we neither see the mindset nor the conventions that we are in. We need to bump up against the limits of our mindset to see our own mindset.

As Adler (2002) has observed: "Although we think that the major obstacle in international business is in understanding the foreigner, the greater difficulty involves becoming aware of our own cultural conditioning." As anthropologist Edward Hall has explained, "What is known least well, and is therefore in the poorest position to be studied, is what is closest to oneself" (quoted in Adler 2002, p45). We are generally least aware of our own cultural characteristics and are quite surprised when we hear foreigners' descriptions of us.

Again, what is crucial is how a leader or manager deals with the anxiety of the unknown. For it can lead to inhabiting the scripts of the culture but it can also lead to an alienation from the culture. As Gundling and Zanchettin (2006) say, they:

> *saw people who were prominent leaders at home who crumbled in global roles. Those who failed were inflexible, simply followed rules, and did what they were told to drive an existing process. The couldn't get the job done and couldn't understand why; they would raise their volume 5 times louder but the others still did not understand no matter how loudly these executives yelled or stamped their feet.*

There is the circular paradox involved in leading in an unfamiliar cultural context. In order to lead, we need to understand the cultural context of the employees, but it is only by leaping into leading that we will develop a felt sense of the way of doing things of the unfamiliar context. Paraphrasing Jamshed Bharucha, it can be said that "before you [lead people within] another culture, master it to the point at which its proponents or members recognize that you get it" (2008). Furthermore, what "you" need to get, as we will explain in the context of participant observation, is not primarily the symbols, rituals or even behaviors of people of the unfamiliar culture, but the way in which their way of making sense of the world is a response to the conditions under which they live. As Nehru put it: "If we seek to understand a people, we have to try to put ourselves, as far as we can, in that particular historical and cultural background" (quoted in Adler 2002, p63).

The hermeneutic circle is that it is only through the lived experience of leading that we become leaders.

References

Adler, N.J. (2002) *International Dimensions of Organizational Behavior* (4th edition). Cincinnati: South-Western Thomson Learning.

Aristotle (1962) *Nichomechian Ethics*. Indianapolis, IN: Bobbs-Merrill.

Bauman, Z. (1995) Modernity and Ambivalence. In: Featherstone, M. (ed.) *Global Culture: Nationalism, globalization and modernity*. London: Sage Publications.

Bharucha, J. (2008) Cognitive Dilemmas in Higher Education. In: Devlin, M.E. (ed.) *Futures Forum 2008*. Cambridge, MA: Forum for the Future of Higher Education and NACUBO.

Cope, J. (2011) Entrepreneurial Learning from Failure: An interpretive phenomenological analysis. *Journal of Business Venturing*. Vol 26, No 6. pp604–23.

Gerstner, L. (2002) *Who Says Elephants Can't Dance? Inside IBM's Historic Turnaround* Australia: Harper Business.

Ghosn, C. (2002) Standing at the Global Crossing. *Trends in Japan*. 5 April.

Gundling, E. and Zanchettin, A. (eds) (2006) *Global Diversity: Winning customers and engaging employees within world markets*. Boston: Nicholas Brealey International.

Hill, L.A. (2003) *Becoming a Manager: How new managers master the challenges of leadership*. Boston: Harvard Business School Press.

Hill, L.A. (2004) New Manager Development for the 21st Century. *Academy of Management Executive*. Vol 18, No 3. pp121–6.

Jobs, S. (2005) *You've Got to Find What You Love*. Available at: http://news.stanford.edu/news/2005/june15/jobs-061505.html.

Kierkegaard, S. (1980) *The Concept of Anxiety*. Princeton: Princeton University Press.

Markowitz E. (2010) Becoming a Better Leader: Interview with Linda A. Hill. *Inc*. 17 December.

Mintzberg, H. (2004) *Managers not MBAs: A hard look at the soft practice of managing*. San Francisco: Berrett-Koehler.

Sartre, J.P. (1948) *Existentialism and Humanism*. London: Methuen.

Conclusion

In the context of the uncertainty of creative destruction and thus of industries, institutions, businesses and careers, existential philosophical reflexivity is not a luxury but a necessary competency for everyday living. It is the basis for absorbing the pain of the destruction of the old and the excitement of developing new possibilities. It allows us to change our ways of thinking, being, doing and "mindsets" or ways of being attuned with the way in which circumstances are changing. For existential philosophical reflexivity provides the basis for questioning, making explicit, examining and transforming the assumptions that are embodied in our everyday ways of existing as people and professionals.

Existential forms of questioning are those forms of questioning in which our way of being a manager, leader, professional, mother or father are in question. It is about working with, rather than against, the uncertainty of being-in-question. It is thus about seeing the uncertainty of being-in-question as an opportunity to disclose new ways of being.

It is crucial to leaders and managers who not only command change but are themselves in change. It is central to managers on international assignments who cannot assume their own mindsets but need to learn to see through the lens and ways of doing things of the other. It is central to practices of innovation in which new possibilities need to be opened up. Strategic thinking that does not want to be wedded to taken-for-granted past patterns of doing things but wants to create an unknown future has much to benefit from existential philosophical reflexivity. The vision of leaders is bound up with the insight, hindsight and foresight that comes from living forward and understanding backward. Career transformation requires existential philosophical reflexivity.

Existential philosophical reflexivity comes in many shapes and forms. It occurs on a daily basis in the workplace. In the many surprises, disturbances and perplexities of felt sense that occur almost imperceptibly on a daily basis at work and at home, the seeds of existential philosophical reflexivity are there. A role of the educator is to take these seeds and turn them into disciplined ways of questioning. For the researcher, they offer the opportunity into the lived experience of reflexivity at work.

It occurs on more fundamental levels in job retrenchments, the collapse of business and industries. Again, the crucial point is to turn these moments of pain into opportunities for disclosing the world in new ways. This is central to existential philosophical reflexivity. Borrowing a line from Holderlin, Heidegger says that only where the danger is, so the saving power grows.

Existential philosophical reflexivity is central to rethinking the concepts and common-sense frameworks through which we make sense of everyday work and public reality. It is in this sense that a difference between it and psychological forms of reflexivity need to be made. For historically psychology is concerned with the self and not so much with what Heidegger calls the "average everyday" context in which the self is situated. The latter is the focus of existential reflexivity: destroying and disclosing new possibilities in the context of action.

Existential philosophical reflexivity is central to research in management, especially research in the context of the professional development of managers and leaders. For it offers a real-life basis upon which to explore the real-time conditions within which management and leadership occur. It provides the basis for asking questions that emerge out of the practices of managers and leaders and it allows them to explore their practices from within rather than from without—the paradigm of positivist science.

How existential philosophical research occurs will be the theme of the next book. In the next book, *Existentialism and Management Inquiry*, a number of completed PhD candidates will explore the way in which they used an existential hermeneutic approach to explore their own managerial and leadership practices. Some of them will explore the way in which their lived experience of conducting research was itself an existential hermeneutic process, a process in which they did not know in advance where they were headed, but through having the hermeneutic patience and resilience to stay in the unknown, were able to allow their thesis to emerge, form, morph and transform.

We will also explore what we have come to call the hermeneutic circle for the development of research practitioners. This is a space in which a number of researchers in management and related fields explore the research experience in monthly conversations with each other. The main focus is not the technology of research but the lived experience of research. It is based on the principle that we only inhabit the practice of research by conducting and reflecting on the way in which we conduct research. Learning the theories of experts is not enough to become an effective research practitioner. We need to be able to highlight, examine, affirm or destroy our own taken-for-granted assumptions about research. We can only do this in those existential moments in which our ways of doing research are thrown into question. The existential hermeneutic circle is a way of doing this.

But enough for now: practices of existential hermeneutic and philosophical research in the context of management will be explored in a forthcoming book.

Index